A.R. GURNEY

Nine Early Plays 1961-1973

A.R. GURNEY

Nine Early Plays 1961-1973

Contemporary Playwrights Series

SK
A Smith and Kraus Book

A Smith and Kraus Book
Published by Smith and Kraus, Inc.

Copyright © 1995 by A.R. Gurney.
All rights reserved

Manufactured in the United States of America

Cover and Text Design by Julia Hill
Cover Photo ©1994 by Susan Johann

First Edition: July 1995
9 8 7 6 5 4 3 2 1

Library of Congress Cataloguing-in-Publication Data

Gurney, A.R. (Albert Ramsdell), 1930-
      A.R. Gurney early plays / A.R. Gurney. --1st ed.
      p. cm. --Contemporary Playwrights series)
      ISBN 1-880399-88-1 (alk. paper)
      I. Title. II. Series.
      PS3557.U82A6   1995
      812'.54--dc20
                      95-19638
                           CIP

To my family.

CONTENTS

FOREWORD

A.R. Gurney's comedies first attracted attention because they enact the ordeals of characters who live by values and rules that once defined the American way of life. But they retain the interest of theater lovers, on stage and in the house, because the words his characters speak and the moves they make spring from Gurney's deep understanding of the community of the play.

In other words, A.R Gurney is an artist, and as an artist, he merits sustained study which he rewards with the pleasures that theater, at its best, abundantly provides: incandescent immediacy, engagement, energy, and beauty.

As members of an audience, we may see a play only once in a lifetime—a few cherished plays more than once. Under such a condition, naturally, we want to know, first, What will happen? Who will suffer—and how? Aristotle rightly listed plot and character as the primary points of concentration in dramatic storytelling. The conditions under which plays are written, however, impose more complicated responsibilities. The actual writing of dialogue may not even begin until after a playwright settles in his mind most of the questions about plot and character. Meeting these responsibilities—to the art of the drama, to actors, directors, producers, designers, financial backers, as well as audiences—means that playwrights live intensely with a play for months prior to its première, and it is common to live intimately with a play for years before.

The best evidence of a playwright's skill in meeting these responsibilities may be found not in any single feature but in the form of the play. Form is the playwright's answer to the question, How can I tell my story so that I fulfill the promises that theater makes to all those who participate in the performance?

Gurney's glory as an artist is that play after play, for forty years, he has kept the promise of the theater.

This is not easy to do, even if a playwright is lucky enough to live in a time and place that supportes theater lavishly and enthusiastcally, such as Athens in the fifth century BCE, or London from the sixteenth to the eighteenth centuries. During the first sixty years of this century, Broadway, with all its faults, shined a bright, hot light on new plays, bringing international fame to playwrights and prestige to the art of playwriting. In the last forty years of the twentieth century in the United States, however, the lot of playwrights has been harder than usual, considered from the historian's perspective. In the 1950s, the time when Gurney began to write professionally, the cumulative effects of the faults inherent in commercial theatrical production combined with changes in the education of all theater artists to produce a new form of organization—non-profit theater.

The shape of Gurney's career and the forms of his plays matured in the precincts of this new type of theater. These early plays developed from principles that Gurney experimented with in theater workshops at Yale, MIT, and the Tanglewood Festival. They led to Gurney's long and continuing relationships with the Hartford Stage Company, the Old Globe Theater in San Diego, and Playwrights Horizons in New York City. Nikos Psacharopoulos, Harold Clurman, Eliot Norton, and Edith Oliver inspired and supported Gurney's struggle during the years he wrote the plays in this volume. Some aspects of their forms deserve attention.

The reader will notice the extreme simplicity of scenic requirements. Gurney wrote these plays for theater groups with little money to spend on scenery. What money they have they are well advised to spend on actors. Consequently, the reader may also notice language of unusual rhythmic vitality, with vivid detail and imagery, and polished subtlety. This is so not only because Gurney is interested in the predicaments of articulate and literate people, but also because skillful and creative actors like to speak lines with these qualities, and because theater requires more of language than do television and movies. Furthermore, Gurney brings to the community of his plays high admiration for, among others, William Congreve and Oscar Wilde. These playwrights knew how to turn lines that called on the best of an actor's intelligence and powers of expression, as well as an actor's ability to probe the depths of character.

Nor have those depths been fully appreciated. Gurney writes about people who restrain their emotions. John Tillinger, who has directed a half-dozen of Gurney's plays, has said, "The point is that [his characters] have the same feelings as everybody else, they just express them in a different way...They try to keep their manners...They tend to be non-confrontational...but that saves people's feelings and keeps the boat from turning upside down." Tillinger's image may have been inspired by a scene from *Scenes from American Life* in which a father and son confront each other violently while sailing and do, indeed, almost upset their boat.

The reader will also notice Gurney's characteristically expressive and seamless use of time and space. It is fashionable nowadays to refer to Gurney's practices as "cinematic", as if playwrights had to wait for the invention of motion pictures to learn the secrets of rapid cutting between scenes and the depiction of simultaneous action. In fact, playwrights perfected these techniques centuries ago, but lost the use of them during the nineteenth century and the early twentieth century as the realistic tastes of urban audiences required greater expenditures by producers on scenic effects. Writing for non-profit theaters led to the recovery of these techniques and our theater is more vital because of it. *The Old One Two* and *Scenes From American Life* illustrate Gurney's skill in applying them to contemporary characters and ideas.

One other characteristic deserves mention. In *The Comeback, The Golden Fleece,* and *The David Show,* Gurney subverts the pretensions and anxieties of modern life by infusing the plots with the power of ancient myth or scripture. In the comedy that results, Gurney holds a double mirror up to our natures, and the incongruities of this reflexive vision produces a sweet agony of recognition which is only partly assuaged by hospitable laughter.

It is one sign of the low state of criticism in our era that only a few reviewers have accurately evaluated Gurney's achievement. On the whole, the visions of Gurney's plays manifested in the reviews are unreliable and do not penetrate beneath the social content. The reader of this volume, and its companions, is more fortunate. The plays printed here offer an excellent opportunity to observe the development of a superb artist who entertains us in a style that attains the highest theatrical standards.

—*Arvid Sponberg*

INTRODUCTION

These early works by A. R. Gurney show that, even at the beginning of his career, he was already displaying the dazzling combination of comic inventiveness, biting satire, and theatrical originality which are the trademarks of his dramatic oeuvre.

It is not surprising, given the fact that when Gurney wrote these plays he was a teacher of the classics at M. I. T., that a number of them juxtapose the classical and the modern. Nor is it unexpected that several take place in university settings. What is remarkable, however, is the amount of risky experimentation present so early in his career.

From the beginning, Gurney seems to have been fascinated by what he after described as "a theatricality which undercuts the conventions of realistic drama and the complacencies of the upper-middle-class which I tend to write about." Whether it is presenting Odysseus' return to Penelope as a news story covered by a skeptical modern reporter in his first play, *The Comeback*, or setting the crowning of King David within the format of a TV show in *The David Show*, or having the Jason and Medea story relayed to us by a squabbling suburban couple in *The Golden Fleece*, he has found a technique which enables him simultaneously to make quite often caustic commentary on modern society in the guise of benign social or absurdist comedy. Similarly, in his plays about academia—principally among these early works, *The Love Course* and *The Old One-Two*—the frequently uproariously paralleling of the classical material taught in the classroom with the actions of the modern characters who teach it enables Gurney very cleverly to avoid making his evident distress about the changes being wrought in late twentieth-century American life too ponderously grave or his humor so frivolously lightweight that we cannot see through to its serious core.

Undoubtedly drawing on his knowledge of classical drama, Gurney also seems in his early plays to have been attracted to the use of offstage characters and scenes which, he has explained, give "a kind of pressure and resonance to what is shown on-stage." The offstage parties in *The*

Comeback and *The Rape of Bunny Stuntz*, the mysterious man "in a red Impala" in the latter play; Jason and Medea, who never appear in *The Golden Fleece*, and Dick in *The Open Meeting* dominate these plays much as the offstage Gods dominate Greek drama.

But in a technical echo of Gurney's thematic juxtaposition of the classical and the modern, these first plays also depart radically from the classics in what Gurney describes as their "continuing need to involve an audience more immediately in an action." His presentational approach, in which we become the class attending *The Love Course* or the studio audience watching the taping of *The David Show* or the members attending *The Open Meeting*, constantly draws attention to the fact that we are watching a play. This technique reminds us of Brecht, Wilder, and others of the post-Ibsen period who have attempted to break through the fourth wall of theatrical realism.

These themes and techniques are masterfully drawn together and fully developed in *Scenes from American Life*, Gurney's first full-length play, which closes this volume. There, the frequently presentational style, the omnipresent offstage character of Snoozer, and the blending of the comic and the serious are seamlessly woven together in an apparently random montage which daringly abandons all unities of time and space and place for an ingenious cinematic structure. A relentless satire of WASP culture from the 1930s to the present, *Scenes from American Life* foreshadows the themes, attitudes, and style of Gurney's later work. Displaying the "double vision" of such great satirists of WASP culture as Edith Wharton and F. Scott Fitzgerald, Gurney's portraits are as affectionate as they are uncompromising, as witty as they are devastating.

"In everything I write," he has observed, "I always persuade myself that I'm dealing with complex characters in a profound way, but sometimes I guess it looks as if I'm just kidding." In fact, even in these earliest plays, there is already abundant evidence of what is never lost on Gurney's audience—that he is both "kidding" and "profound."

—*Jackson R. Bryer*

A.R. GURNEY

Nine Early Plays 1961-1973

The Comeback

A Play in One Act

Here is my first public attempt to play with a Classical myth on stage. I was very impressed by the French playwrights Anouilh and Giraudoux at the time, and I'm afraid it shows.

Original Production

THE COMEBACK was first presented by the Club 47, Inc. in Cambridge, Massachusetts, on January 6, 1965. The production was by the Image Theater Workshop, and the director was Paul John Austin. The cast, in order of appearance, was as follows:

The Reporter	Paul John Austin
Euryclea	Jean Comstock
Telemachus	Edmond Genest
Antinuous	François-Regis
Penelope	Susan Dorlen
Odysseus	Armand Asselin

The Characters
in the order in which they speak

A REPORTER
EURYCLEA, an old nurse
TELEMACHUS, son of Odysseus
ANTINUOUS, a suitor for Penelope
PENELOPE, wife of Odysseus
ODYSSEUS, king of Ithaca

Setting

The events take place on the steps of the palace of Odysseus during the evening of a Labor Day.

The Passage from the Odyssey *is from Robert Fitzgerald's translation.*

THE COMEBACK

Euryclea, an old maid in a black maid's outfit, comes out of the house, carrying a load of empty liquor bottles. The Reporter calls out from the audience.

REPORTER: Euryclea!
    (She stops, squints out. The Reporter comes up onto the stage.)
    It's me, old thing. Remember me?
EURYCLEA: *(Looking him over.)* Oh yes. Now I remember. Every Labor Day you come around, don't you?
REPORTER: I'm still looking for my story, old girl.
EURYCLEA: You won't find it here, mister. You never have, and you never will.
REPORTER: I dunno. *(Indicates audience.)* There's quite a group gathered this year. All waiting. Maybe something's in the air.
EURYCLEA: Nothing's in the air except the smell of burning leaves.
REPORTER: Telemachus thinks different. He's been spreading the word all over town. Today's the day, he says. This is it.
EURYCLEA: Oh well, Telemachus. Every fall he thinks his father is coming home. Last year he thought it would be in disguise. He went through a big recognition scene with the plumber. Now me. I've given up the whole business. I'm content to dream about the old days, before the war, before Odysseus went away, when everyone was happy, and these bottles were full to the brim.

REPORTER: The old days were never like that, Euryclea, and you know it.

EURYCLEA: Ah, if they weren't, I'd never admit it. They've carried me through these last twenty years and I'm counting on them again this winter.

REPORTER: So you think we're wasting our time, huh?

EURYCLEA: Oh, we all waste time. I waste mine looking back, Telemachus wastes his looking forward, and all of you might as well waste yours looking on...

(She starts out, as Telemachus comes out of the house. He jostles Euryclea in his eagerness. "Watch it, you," she may mutter, as she goes out.)

TELEMACHUS: *(The sounds of the party become louder.)* Hear it? Hear it? That terrible noise! Put that in your paper, Reporter. Lead off by describing that debauch in there.

REPORTER: Telemachus, I like to think I've graduated beyond the society page.

TELEMACHUS: No. See it for what it is. Give it, for once, the right slant. Open by saying you have heard the sound of hell!

REPORTER: Hell? Why, Telemachus, that's just a bunch of people having a party.

TELEMACHUS: Exactly! Just a bunch of people! Oh my friend, if hell has any sound at all, it is the sound of just a bunch of people at a party!

REPORTER: *(Indicating audience.)* We're people, too, boy. We're used to it.

TELEMACHUS: I'll never be used to it! Never! For twenty years, I've heard that sound. When I was a child, that was supposed to by my lullaby. I couldn't sleep. I'd wander downstairs, rubbing my eyes, and the suitors would hoist me up on the piano and serenade me in hoarse, boozy harmony... "Sleep, Kentucky Babe!"...Finally my mother...*(To audience.)* Your queen, friends! Your Penelope!...Would spike my milk bottle with gin, and have old Euryclea lug me back to bed.

REPORTER: Kid, you got personal problems, we all know that, but I don't see how I can open them up for the general reading public.

TELEMACHUS: Listen, the public knows that noise too! It has spilled out of the house into the town. During the day, the shouts from the tennis, the groans from the golf, the booms of the starting guns for the sailing races. And at night the roar of sports cars as they race to the beach to go skinny-swimming! Oh yes. *(To audience.)* We're all in this together, you people and I. And that's why we're all here now, on the steps of the palace, waiting for my father to come home! *(He leaps onto a bench.)* And the time is ripe! The summer's over—this summer of twenty years. He's coming home, home, in an autumn blaze of glory to give us a world which will last all winter long.

REPORTER: All I want is a story which will hold for a couple of days on the front page.

(Enter Antinuous from the house.)

ANTINUOUS: *(To the Reporter and the audience.)* Goodbye, goodbye. All of you, please, goodbye. Out, out. No reporter, no crowds. This is a private party.

REPORTER: Which one of the suitors are you? I can't keep your names straight.

ANTINUOUS: No comment. No names. We don't want our names in the paper.

TELEMACHUS: You see? Even the suitors feel guilty. They hate publicity.

ANTINUOUS: Guilty? Guilty? Why guilty? No, we simply don't want to have a lot of crank calls from outsiders. *(To Reporter.)* Don't quote me on that. Goodbye.

REPORTER: *(To Telemachus.)* I'll give you half an hour more, Telemachus, to come up with something I can use. Right now, this is simply a back page column on how to wait for the doctor when you know he won't show up. *(He exits into the audience.)*

ANTINUOUS: *(To Telemachus, low.)* Why's he here? *(Glancing out at audience.)* And why are all these townies here? Is there no privacy left in the world? Are we living in a fishbowl? Is this the price we pay for courting royalty?

TELEMACHUS: We're waiting for something to happen, Antinuous.

ANTINUOUS: Happen? Everything's already happened. *(To audience, nervously.)* Did you see the tournament? Wasn't Penelope splendid? Did you notice her backhand? Pow! There are very few women, people, there are very few women in this world who can hit a backhand like that. Lovely legs, too. Lovely legs. Now go home and think about your queen's backhand. *(To Telemachus, after a pause.)* What do you want? A little speech. A little talk, commemorating the end of summer?

TELEMACHUS: We're waiting for Odysseus to come home.

ANTINUOUS: You're waiting for who to do what?

TELEMACHUS: My father, and their king, to—

ANTINUOUS: Never mind! I said, never mind!...That remark irritates me. That remark irritates me very much. *(To audience.)* People, what in heaven's name is the matter? Why is it—I ask you—why is it, that in autumn we have these peculiar flurries of discontent? Is it something you eat? Is it a question of too much corn on the cob? Or is it this boy here, this disgruntled boy, who stirs you up? Now it's a lovely evening. In all my years here, I have never seen a lovelier Labor Day. So go home, my friends, and cook steak over charcoal. Toss a football around with your nice children. Cut your good, green grass one last time. Turn on your televisions and watch pleasant summer reruns. Why just...hang around here?

TELEMACHUS: Because we're tired of being oppressed by you suitors! We're tired of seeing our land, this fair land, wasted away! What have I got after these twenty years? A bank account totally overdrawn! A deep freeze totally depleted! The orchards riddled with Dutch elm disease! The sheep teeming with foot-in-mouth! Tennis balls in the plumbing, darts in the woodwork, beanbags in the chandelier!

ANTINUOUS: That is not true, boy! The ecomony is teeming. We spend more money on martinis and beanbags and tennis balls than any other country in the world!

ANTINUOUS: Pah! You're dreaming again. Why impose your nightmares on these simple people? *(To audience.)* My friends, listen to me. Apparently you have forgotten how things were before we suitors came. Think back. Why twenty years ago, none of you—not one—would have had the *leisure* to come up here, to sit here comfortably side by side, and indulge yourselves in the idleness of watching and waiting. No sir. The reason you're all here is because *we're* all here, we, the suitors of your queen. One hundred men have, over the years, invested their time, their energies, and their private incomes into making this little island a prosperous and happy place for all of you to live! *(Picks out a man in the audience.)* You, sir! Where would your shop be today if it were not for our backing and patronage? Or you?... Your bank. Whose money do you think is earning you interest?... Or you, dear lady, in that attractive gown. Twenty years ago at this hour, you were in your apron, doing diapers on a washboard! *(To Telemachus.)* And last but not least, you, young man! Why do you think you've been able to sit around all summer, reading Kafka, and Dostoyevsky? I'll tell you why: because one hundred hard-working, hard-playing men have come to Ithaca to court your pretty mother!

TELEMACHUS: *(Sarcastically.)* Welcome to the Fun House, people! Welcome to this Disneyland of diversion!

ANTINUOUS: *(Striding to the house, opening the door so that the party can be heard.)* Listen to that! All of you! Listen! That is the sound of civilization in there! One hundred men are getting along extremely well with one pretty woman, and that's pretty civilized, it seems to me! We've had very few fights, very few injuries! Empires have struggled for centuries to establish what we've all hammered out here in two brief decades. And you are all reaping the rewards. And so if anyone waltzed in here and tried to change all this, why I think I'd have to kill him. For your sake as well as mine. And I speak for all the suitors! We would have to kill your O-what's-his-name!

TELEMACHUS: Not if he killed you first.

ANTINUOUS: Ah, my young friend, the odds are one hundred to one against that.

TELEMACHUS: *(Looking towards the door.)* Penelope knows different.

(Penelope appears at the door, carrying the glass.)

PENELOPE: Penelope knows nothing, darling, except that we're running out of gin.

ANTINUOUS: *(Bussing her on the cheek.)* And that's the most serious crisis of the evening. *(He exists into the house.)*

TELEMACHUS: *(To audience.)* See? Typical. She waits—she waits inside—until the proper moment to make a superficial entrance.

PENELOPE: *(Surveying audience.)* Oh my God! The gang's all here! Hail, hail, hello, everybody! Hello, my people! It's your old boozed up queen! *(Singing.)* "In the Good Old Summertime..."

TELEMACHUS: *(Bitterly, to audience.)* Meet my mother. Clear-eyed Penelope.

PENELOPE: I can't help it, sweetheart. *(To audience.)* I can't help it. I'm in a party mood. We've been at it ever since we finished the tennis tournament, and I don't care who knows it. *(To Telemachus.)* Now, baby, here's what I want you to do. I want you to dash inside, and go down in the cellar, and lug up one of those big barrels of wine, and some paper cups, and we're going to have a party, right out here...Aren't we? Certainly we are. I'm your queen, and that's an order. Here we all are, and what the hell? I can't promise you dinner. I've got a huge chicken casserole, but not *that* huge. Well, maybe. Let's play it by ear. *(To Telemachus.)* Go on, dear. Get the wine. Meanwhile...*(To audience.)* Follow the bouncing ball, people. "In the Good Old Summertime!"

SOMEONE FROM THE AUDIENCE: "In the Good Old Summertime!"

PENELOPE: Exactly! A community sing!

(She continues to sing, Telemachus shouts her down.)

TELEMACHUS: We're not here to sing songs, Mother! And you know it!

The reason we're here is the same reason you've been belting gin since four P.M. *(Pause.)*

PENELOPE: *(Quietly.)* We're in public, darling.

TELEMACHUS: Yes, and this is a public issue.

PENELOPE: *(Taking a sip of her drink.)* He's not coming. Why would he? He's had plenty of time to come. *(To audience.)* I mean, how long does it *take* to cross the eastern Mediterranean? *(Pause.)* All right. If he does come home, he'll walk into one hell of a good party.

TELEMACHUS: He doesn't like parties, Mother.

PENELOPE: How do *you* know, kid? You never even knew him. You were a mere babe in swaddling clothes when he left. You waved bye-bye to him from the ducky chair. *(To audience.)* Of course he likes parties. He always did. You older people, you remember. He loved a good party. Why, we gave him a going-away party the day he left and the damn thing has just sort of gone on, for twenty years. *(To Telemachus.)* Listen, if he does come home, this is how it will be: we'll all be in the living room, see, after dinner. Telemachus, you can be off in the corner reading *Lord of the Flies.* And then suddenly, in he'll walk, in a new madras dinner jacket, sporting a glorious tan, and carrying a huge stack of Kodachrome slides to show us of his trip. That's the way he'll come home. That's the way husbands *should* come home after twenty years. He can step into the party without skipping a beat. Now go get that wine, sweetie.

TELEMACHUS: I'll get no more wine, Mother! Never again! I'm through playing the cup-bearer. For you, or for anyone else.

PENELOPE: And if your poor father wants some little pick-me-up after his long day's journey...

TELEMACHUS: He won't.

PENELOPE: How do you know?

TELEMACHUS: I've had another dream.

PENELOPE: *(To audience.)* Another dream! He puts all his faith in dreams. Dream after dream is gone into in the most loo-goo-bree-ous detail! Normally at breakfast. *(To Telemachus.)* You dream because you're not active enough. You've been sitting around all summer. Of course you're going to have peculiar dreams, because you don't keep busy. I told you I'd give you ten dollars if you beat me in tennis, and you haven't even tried. *(To audience.)* Now I don't dream. I'm dead to the world at night. Because I stay busy.

TELEMACHUS: I'm going to tell you my dream, Mother.

PENELOPE: I'm not interested. This is still daylight. I'm not going to be dragged into the psychological life of someone else.

TELEMACHUS: I'm serious.

PENELOPE: Oh I know you're serious. That's just the trouble. You always have been. *(To audience.)* When he was a child, he wanted nothing but educational toys. And the only sport he showed any real interest in was weight-lifting. *(To Telemachus.)* Now cut it out. You're making all of us feel uncomfortable and uneasy. You're a skunk at a garden party, to put it bluntly. *(To audience.)* I'm sorry we have to air our family squabbles in front of all of you. But I'm worried about this boy and you should be, too. He's the Crown Prince. You'll have to live with him long after I'm gone. What do I do with him? What do you do with someone who refuses to have any fun out of life? I'm asking you. I suppose what he needs is a good...

TELEMACHUS: I need a good father.

PENELOPE: You do *not* need a good father! You have one hundred good fathers right in that house! No, frankly, what you need is a good, sweet, attractive, pretty girl. *(To audience.)* Am I right, or am I right?

TELEMACHUS: I dreamt he came home tonight, Mother. Resplendent in armor, steeped in the wisdom of the world. And we embraced, he and I, and I told him what had gone on here since he was away. And then we calmly, without malice, killed the suitors, one by one, and established a kingdom here of justice and truth and equal opportunity under law. *(Pause.)*

PENELOPE: And then?

TELEMACHUS: Isn't that enough?

PENELOPE: What happened to me? Did you and your father kill me, too?

TELEMACHUS: Mother, you weren't even *in* the dream. You're too trivial to be in my dreams.

PENELOPE: Thanks a bunch. *(To audience.)* You see? You see what I'm up against, twenty-four hours of the goddamn day? *(To Telemachus.)* Let me tell you this, dear boy. There are one hundred men in that house who love me very much and who for twenty years haven't thought me trivial at all. *(To audience.)* I've done everything for him. You know that. I've tried to be both a mother and a father to him. From the time he could walk, I'd be up at the crack of dawn, trying to get him down on the courts, or play catch, or sail his sailfish which I bought specially from F.A.O. Schwarz. But not him. Oh no. All he wanted to do was read stories from the *Bible*. *(A sip of the drink, a tear or two.)* So now I'm trivial. I'm a nonentity. I'm sorry. But it hurts a mother to hear that.

TELEMACHUS: *(A little tenderness.)* Get married, Mother.

(Penelope looks at him.)

Marry one of your suitors. Tonight. Now. Then leave. Leave Odysseus and me to put this house in order. *(To audience.)* Shouldn't she? Isn't that the logical thing for her?

PENELOPE: I'll get married when I finish my knitting. That was the deal.

TELEMACHUS: Your knitting? Where's your knitting?

PENELOPE: I don't know where my knitting is at this particular moment.

TELEMACHUS: I know. It's in the hall closet, hidden behind the Bongo Board, where it's been for the past five years. I'll get it. *(Starts for door, then turns.)* Mother, here's a chance for you to get out while the getting's good. I'm thinking of you. With all your faults, it is still your womb from which I issued forth. *(He exists into the house.)*

PENELOPE: *(To audience.)* See? He can even make motherhood sound vaguely unpleasant!

(Telemachus comes back out of the house carrying a mothy, half-knitted, ratty sock on knitting needles. He holds it out to the audience.)

TELEMACHUS: Look! Look at the famous handiwork of Penelope! See what she has been up to for the past twenty years!

PENELOPE: *(To audience.)* Well it always seemed like occupational therapy!

TELEMACHUS: *(Forcing it on her.)* Finish it. Right now. For your own sake. Knit one, purl two, Mother.

(Penelope looks at him, looks at the audience, then takes the knitting. She fiddles with it, horses around, takes the extra needle and pretends to duel with him.)

Come on, Mother.

(She uses the needle as a baton, attempts to lead the audience in "I Want a Girl Just Like the Girl That Married Dear Old Dad.")

Mother, that was the deal, a long time ago.

(She sighs, is about to knit, when Euryclea appears at the door, carrying a trayful of empty glasses.)

EURYCLEA: Madam, the suitors want you to join them for a round of charades.

PENELOPE: Thank you, Euryclea. *(To audience.)* Saved by the bell.

EURYCLEA: And madam, dinner will be a little late tonight.

PENELOPE: Why is that, Euryclea?

EURYCLEA: Because I can't serve drinks, and make hot hors d'oeuvres, and fix dinner for one hundred men, when there's someone bothering me in my kitchen.

TELEMACHUS: Someone...bothering you?

EURYCLEA: Yes sir. Talking my ear off. Asking me questions about you and the madam.

PENELOPE: *(Quietly.)* Who is it, Euryclea? Do you know?

EURYCLEA: Well he looked like a beggarman. And here's a funny thing: I made him wash his feet before he muddied my clean floor. And while he was washing his feet, I saw a scar...on his ankle...which made me think that my old master Odysseus had come home to roost.

TELEMACHUS: He's here! He's here! *(He rushes into the house.)*

EURYCLEA: He's wrong. It wasn't Odysseus. Oh no. Because when I whispered his name, he looked at me funny, and ran outside. Just...ran away. The old master wouldn't have done that, ma'am. Oh no. He would have kissed me. He would have wept with me for all the times gone by. So it wasn't the old master, was it, ma'am?

PENELOPE: No...Euryclea...it wasn't...

(Euryclea starts in.)

Oh Euryclea, would you bring me another drink?

EURYCLEA: Yes madam. *(Euryclea goes into the house.)*

PENELOPE: *(To audience.)* So...This is it, eh?...Home is the sailor. In a tramp costume, yet. Appearing furtively in the kitchen, interrogating the maid, and then suh-linking off into the night. Oh boy. How to humor your wife. I've had it, haven't I? Penelope, your sweet hour is at hand. Telemachus was right. The man's become complicated now. He's become deeeeep. And tricky. *(Pause.)* He wasn't always that way, was he? You older people out there: you remember. Before the war. How things were. You know what I remember most? I remember that first Labor Day tournament. We had a grass court, then. Not hard surface. The dew was still on it, and it was freshly rolled, and there were clean, white, bright lines which everyone could see. We had ball boys then, too, remember, and a nice old man with good eyes who sat up on a stepladder and was referee. And we both wore white, then, Odysseus and I, and when we walked on, everyone clapped. I swear they did. Without our hitting a shot, everyone clapped for us. And then we played. Oh, I admit he was sort of cagey, even then. He cut too much, we all knew that, and he'd argue with the referee, and he'd razz the opponents. But he stayed within the lines. We all knew where we were. And I remember one point, oh it only lasted two or three minutes, but we were on top of it, he and I. It was beautiful. And as we both went to the net and he smashed it deep to their backhand, I remember thinking...there! That's it! That's the game!...That's the set!...That's the match! So we took the cup, hands down, and our names are still on it, and I don't think any doubles team in the history of the world could have taken it away from us. *(Pause.)* And now he's back. And changed. And I have no idea what the score is. But I have the feeling that poor Penelope is going to be the victim of some awful squeeze play so that he can steal home.

(Euryclea comes in with a drink on a tray.)

What is it, sweetheart? Poison? Has he sent me poison?

EURYCLEA: How should I know? I only work here.

(Euryclea exits. Penelope takes a big slug of her drink, waits a beat.)

PENELOPE: No. It's not poison...that would be too simple for...old foxy, I'm afraid. So. What to do? What to do, what to do? I'd welcome suggestions, gang. Your ku-ween is open to suggestion. Shall I kill myself? Or shall I get the boys to kill him? Or shall I... *(She stops, thinks, then squares her shoulders.)* ...Shall I call my own shots? Shall I take him on? Shall I play the ace I have held up my sleeve these last twenty years? He's changed, has he? Well, I've changed too! And one hundred men in there are in love with the result!

(She goes to the door, opens it: the sounds of the party can now be heard from within, she faces the audience.)

So if you see that tramp, people, you can tell him I don't recognize him. No sir. I haven't the faintest idea who the hell he is!

(Penelope exits into the house, as Telemachus enters from offstage.)

TELEMACHUS: I've looked everywhere for him. I called his name. Nothing. Silence. Why?

(The Reporter comes up from the audience.)

REPORTER: Kid, I gotta shove off.

TELEMACHUS: What do you mean? He's here. Everything points to it.

REPORTER: He may be here, he may not be here, all I know is there's no story here, kid. It's light, frankly. It's frivolous. Next time get someone from *The New Yorker.*

TELEMACHUS: Light? Frivolous? You're talking about them, in there! Not me! I'm your story. Concentrate on me! And my father!

REPORTER: You're not big enough. I'm interested in something big. I covered the war, boy. I saw men die.

TELEMACHUS: Oh listen, I'm big. Believe me. Do you know how hard I've worked to be ready for him? Do you know how hard I've studied so that I'd have something profound to say? Do you know how I've exercised so I'd be strong and pleasing in his eyes? Do you know of my charity to the poor? Of my frugality with myself? Of how I'm loved by my friends and feared by my enemies? Of how I've avoided harlots and hypocrites and humbugs all the days of my life?

REPORTER: I dunno, kid. You just don't seem to gel... I've got a nose for these things. I want to say something postwar, something about men at peace. I've got all sorts of words, all sorts of ideas in my mind, and I've been waiting for years to find the right situation to hang them on. That's why I came here in the first place. I thought the Homecoming of Odysseus might be it. But it isn't. I sense it. Things are slipping away.

TELEMACHUS: No, look. Stay. I know what's wrong. I haven't done enough. He's disappointed in me, and he's hanging back. He's inquired about me, and he's waiting...he's waiting for me to do something tremendously spectacular before he acknowledges me as his son. I'll do it. I'm going to do it. Wait. Give me a half an hour more. Everything will click into place. Stay. Please.

REPORTER: *(Shrugging.)* O.K., boy. But make it good. Because what we got now will never go beyond Ithaca.

(Exits into the audience.)

TELEMACHUS: *(Stretching out his arms.)* Odysseus, if you're here, hear me. What should I do that I haven't done? What have I done that I shouldn't do? Why is he right, this reporter? Why do I feel—why have I always felt—this lack, this worthlessness, this...this fundamental awkwardness, as if I were trying to play some game by some terribly difficult rulebook, held all the time in my hand? Forgive me, father. Forgive me, and tell me how to make it up. Give me a word, or a sign, at least. I'm waiting now. I'm listening.

(Silence for a moment. Then Antinous runs out of the house.)

ANTINOUS: Great news, people! Great news! Your queen has decided to marry!

TELEMACHUS: When? What do you mean?

ANTINOUS: Just now! She came in and announced to us all that she would at last make up her mind. You should have heard the cheers and whistles and applause. When things calmed down, we followed her into the rumpus room. She went to the wall, and took down an old bow which was used in archery contests before the war.

TELEMACHUS: My father's bow!

ANTINUOUS: We cheered again, and formed a circle around her: then she announced in her delightful voice that whoever could hit the center of the target, shooting across the room, from behind the billiard table, would win her. Then came the loudest cheer of all! There it was, at long, long last! Everyone threw off his coat, and because there was quite a line, I thought I'd dash out here to tell all of you.

TELEMACHUS: My father's bow! *(He runs into the house.)*

ANTINUOUS: *(Lighting a cigarette.)* I can only stay a minute, people. Don't want to miss my turn. Can hardly wait. Can hardly wait. What a woman! Lucky the man who wins her! After all these years! Twenty years! Twenty! And now: wedding bells. Oh golly, this is something. It really is. Charming, sweet, good disposition, lovely shoulders and legs. So. I'd better hurry right in there and take my chances. Right? Can't keep the bride waiting, can I? *(But he stays.)* But shouldn't we toast the bride? Join me, good friends, in a toast to a lovely woman— no, in a toast to a pretty girl. Let us now praise pretty girls. Nobody says much about them these days. Everything we read, everything we see on the stage is written by angries, and beatniks, and homosexuals. And the critics who tell us to like the stuff are a bunch of screwballs, too. It's a closed circuit, it's an in-group, and they've forgotten all about the importance of pretty girls. Yet aren't they the heart of the matter? Aren't they what makes us tick? Look at the war. What caused it? A pretty girl. Look at all of us here. What keeps us going? A pretty girl. Look at your old king, O-what's-his-name. What keeps him away? You're heard those rumors: a pretty girl! Oh there are things which make us weep for their perfection. A Rolls Royce engine, idling, makes me weep. Head skis, settling into new powder snow, make me weep. The Columbia, sailing downwind under her spinnaker, makes me weep. And Penelope, this girl, this pretty girl in all her glory, makes me weep most of all. And so to be able to win her...to marry her...to say forever after that this pretty girl is mine! Why— *(He raises his glass, pauses, then lets his arm fall.)* Why then it will all be over, won't it? It will all be gone...

(Penelope and Telemachus come out of the house, Penelope carries a large, unstrung bow, with arrows.)

PENELOPE: Your turn, your turn, Antinuous! Ninety-nine men in there have tried for my hand, but they haven't even been able to *string* this damn thing! String it, and I'm yours.

TELEMACHUS: No one can string it. It's my father's bow. *(To audience.)* Only my father can string it. *(To Penelope.)* Why did you suddenly turn to an archery contest, Mother? You're stalling. It's that knitting business all over again.

PENELOPE: It is not! Oh believe me, it's not. I'm in a big hurry... Here, Antinuous... *(To audience.)* I had to pick something for them to do. There had to be some sort of competition. So I thought of this... Here, Antinuous, sweetheart.

TELEMACHUS: Why didn't you have them draw lots? What differences does it make?

PENELOPE: Oh but I deserve a game of skill after all these years. At least give me that... This bow is so appropriate, somehow... My second husband taking my first husband's place... Whoever strings this, strings me, so to speak... *(To audience.)* Because frankly, people, at the moment, your queen is a little unstrung... Antinuous, my love, the bow.

TELEMACHUS: You and your contests and silly rituals... *(He snatches the bow.)* This magnificent implement—to become the center of a party game, pawed over by those parasites! What battles this has seen! What causes of justice has this served! Oh this should have been used to kill the suitors, not to select them!

PENELOPE: Give it to your stepfather, dear.

TELEMACHUS: *(Testing the spring of the bow.)* In one of my dreams, my father came home... *(He bends the bow a little.)* and gave me this bow, and taught me how to... *(He strings the bow, easily)*...string it. *(Long pause.)*

PENELOPE: You've...strung...your father's bow!

TELEMACHUS: *(Shocked.)* It was easy. Look.
(He unstrings it, strings it again.)

PENELOPE: *(Quietly.)* Let me try. *(She takes the bow, unstrings it, strings it again easily.)* Why it's a perfect cinch! *(To the audience.)* But I swear ninety-nine men in there couldn't string it!

ANTINUOUS: May I speak to this? May I say something?

TELEMACHUS: *(To audience.)* It's obviously not my father's bow. Obviously. My mother went and picked the wrong bow.

PENELOPE: *(To audience.)* Or else ninety-nine men in there weren't even trying...

ANTINUOUS: May I say a word here? May I interject a comment?

TELEMACHUS: *(To audience.)* Figure it out. Odysseus would have taken his best bow with him to Troy, obviously. This is a second-rate bow.

PENELOPE: *(To audience.)* Ninety-nine men in there weren't even trying! And there's no reason to suppose that Antinuous would try any harder. People, your queen has been found wanting by one hundred men.

ANTINUOUS: May I intrude here, please? May I have the floor?

TELEMACHUS: No! You've intruded here for twenty years! You've made this house the scene of a cruel hoax! You've lied and deceived and insulted my mother!

ANTINUOUS: We have glorified, we have defied, we have idolized your mother!

TELEMACHUS: All she is, is a good excuse for a party. When the chips are down, you don't take her seriously enough to marry her.

ANTINUOUS: When the chips are down, we take her far too seriously to marry her! Penelope, you're like...Steuben Glass. Always beautifully advertised, but not for the kitchen...you're the Queen Bee. And since we can't mate with you in the air, it's better not to mate with you at all.

TELEMACHUS: Yes! Drones, slugs, parasites! Consumers of all the honey in the hive!

ANTINUOUS: Besides, we couldn't marry her even if we wanted to.

PENELOPE: Why not, sweetheart? I'm available, Lord knows.

ANTINUOUS: Yes, but we're not. *(To audience.)* Here it comes. *(To Penelope.)* We all have wives.

PENELOPE: Wives?

ANTINUOUS: Yes. We see them on business trips. They meet us in motels, where we can get away from the children. You suspected it, didn't you? Our mysterious disappearances on Christmas and Thanksgiving?

PENELOPE: I knew there was a little hanky-panky going on, but I didn't think it had gone that far!

ANTINUOUS: Twenty years is a long, long time, Penelope.

TELEMACHUS: Too long a time! It's over now! The party's over!

PENELOPE: Yes, everything's over. So please leave me alone... Both of you. The queen wants to be alone with her people. So shoo! Shoo!

TELEMACHUS: You're going to pay, Antinuous! All of you! For every minute you spent in this house! Now I know what I must do!
(He grabs the bow and exits into the house.)

ANTINUOUS: I know people in Athens. I think I can get the kid drafted. *(He starts in after Telemachus, then turns and looks at Penelope.)* Forgive us, Penelope.

PENELOPE: There's nothing to forgive. It's my own damn fault. I'm getting just what I asked for. I set up the rules of the game at the start. I made myself the gilded trophy which everyone plays for, and no one's supposed to take home. So the least I can do is be a good sport when you put me back on the shelf.

ANTINUOUS: I suppose...I suppose this means that there won't be any more touch football this fall.

PENELOPE: I'm afraid not, sweetheart. I'm tired, I'm suddenly very tired of just...playing touch. I'm tired of being just a thing—just a mechanical rabbit which you dogs are not supposed to catch up to.

Antinuous. Yes. Well. It's been real, Penelope.

PENELOPE: No, it's been unreal. But it's been fun.

(Antinuous exits sadly into the house. Penelope speaks to the audience.)
Fun. That's the whole trouble, isn't it? There's no room for frivolity these days. Don't be frivolous, people. Listen to your queen. Commit yourselves. Make choices. *Decide* something. Otherwise you'll become an object of attention only. The world will dance circles around you. You'll end like me, a museum piece, on display, under glass. Odysseus will tell you this, I'm sure, if, as, and when he gets around to it. *(Pause.)* Odysseus. I keep forgetting him. At this moment, he's probably aiming an arrow right at my palpitating little heart. So what am I doing? I'm getting out, but quick. I'm too old to go to Mississippi, so I'm going the other way. I'm going to Athens, people. There's good theatre there. I'm going to watch plays for a change, instead of trying to be in them. I imagine Euryclea has already packed my bag for my ha-ha wedding trip.

(Euryclea appears at the door.)
EURYCLEA: No, Euryclea hasn't.

PENELOPE: And why not, Euryclea?

EURYCLEA: Because I couldn't get into your bedroom. The door was locked.

PENELOPE: Locked?

EURYCLEA: So I had to go down and get the key. And when I got the key, and opened the door, I still couldn't pack.

PENELOPE: Why not, Euryclea?

EURYCLEA: Because someone was in your bed.

PENELOPE: In my bed?

EURYCLEA: In your bed, madam. Asleep. In his birthday suit. I think it was that beggarman.

PENELOPE: So what did you do?

EURYCLEA: I said "Wake up, wake up, you!" but he didn't. He was sound asleep. So I came down here to tell you.

(Odysseus appears at the door, leaning against the jamb, a beard, dressed in beggar's clothes.)

ODYSSEUS: I wasn't asleep. I was just pretending.

EURYCLEA: You see? You see? He's not Odysseus. Odysseus would not have tried to fool his old nurse. Now I'll go pack. Madam.

(As Euryclea exits, Odysseus hands her a plumber's friend.)

ODYSSEUS: There's a tennis ball in the plumbing.

(Euryclea exits huffily. A long pause. Penelope and Odysseus look at each other. Then Penelope turns away from him and speaks to the audience.)

PENELOPE: What...what are we supposed to think of a man who comes home after twenty years, and all he does is go to bed?

ODYSSEUS: *(To audience.)* I was tired. And I think I was running a slight temperature.

PENELOPE: *(To audience.)* I must say that the tramp costume lives up to our wildest expectations.

ODYSSEUS: *(To audience.)* This is no costume. This is what I am. These rags, these wrinkles, this beard...they're all me. I'm a man who's been through hell and high water, and I look the part.

PENELOPE: *(To audience.)* We can understand why he's avoided seeing me, can't we? But not to meet his son? Not to reveal himself to his old nurse! Simply to go to bed!

ODYSSEUS: *(To audience.)* You can't squeeze all these lost years into a series of five minute recognition scenes. Everyone would break...There's a problem with re-entry here. How does a man who has been in outer space get back into the atmosphere of the commonplace?

PENELOPE: *(To audience.)* Commonplace! Now we're commonplace, people! Tell him, tell him what I've been up to!

ODYSSEUS: *(To audience.)* Don't bother. I know. Let's put it this way, then, to avoid offense. I've been in the sea for twenty years, and needed a decompression chamber to avoid the bends.

PENELOPE: *(To audience.)* Oh God! These analogies!

ODYSSEUS: *(To audience.)* See? Right now. How hard it is for my wife and I. All we do is hover on either side of this great gap of time, shouting through other people, peering at each other, before we wave goodbye.

PENELOPE: *(Turning to him quickly.)* Goodbye?...Oh. You heard I was leaving.

ODYSSEUS: No, I'm leaving.

PENELOPE: *You're* leaving? You mean, you just came home to take a nap?

ODYSSEUS: In a way, yes. Really. I came home because I wanted to sleep. I'm tired, Penelope. I want out. I've spent my best years in war and at sea. I'm tired of the world, tired of people, tired of myself. I want time out. I thought home would be the one place on earth where I wouldn't have to be tricky.

PENELOPE: And isn't it? Who's asking you to be tricky?

ODYSSEUS: Everyone. I've had my nose pressed to your picture window for quite a while. I've seen and heard what you all want of me, and I can't meet your terms. I've nothing more to give. I now know that coming home is the hardest adventure of all. I'm too old to take it on, and so I'm taking off.

PENELOPE: But where will you go? You've been everywhere.

ODYSSEUS: I'm going back...back to the Lotus Eaters. The island of forgetfulness. Where you sleep away your remaining years munching some drowsy flower. A couple of good, stiff lotuses and I'll forget all this hangover hankering to come home.

PENELOPE: Oh Odysseus, stay! We'll both stay! I'll keep everyone quiet. You can sleep ten, twelve hours a day.

ODYSSEUS: No, I'd have to get up eventually. And that would be the trouble. I'm like an old boxer trying to make a come-back in the wrestling ring...or an old Shakespearean actor making an attempt at musical comedy.

PENELOPE: All these words... All these Homeric comparisons...

ODYSSEUS: I know. That's just my trouble. I'm overtrained, over-rehearsed. I've spent too long in graduate school. Getting here was all the fun. I feel as if I'm looking over my shoulder, breathing down my own neck. Odysseus kibitzing on Odysseus. The Sunday morning quarterback, watching a rerun of his own game. My story's over, Penelope. I'm on tape. I've got twenty-twenty vision, hindsight. I'm a man caught between myths he no longer believes and games he no longer plays. *(To audience.)* Oh it's debilitating, my friends. And ultimately boring. To you, I'm sure, as it is to me. But boredom leads to sleep. *(He lies down on a bench.)* Sleep. Prone on a couch. With a lotus falling languorously from my hand. *(He closes his eyes.)*

PENELOPE: *(Shaking him.)* Wake up! Wake up! What about me? You know all the answers. What should I do?

ODYSSEUS: *(Eyes closed.)* Do what you've always done. The world can't get along without its Penelopes. Dye your hair a beautiful blue. Go to Stowe and Saint Thomas and Edgartown. Modulate gracefully from quarterback to umpire until you are last seen sitting straight as a ramrod in the bleachers, looking over the tops of your reading glasses, your bracelets rattling in the breeze, shouting in a strong, hoarse, alcoholic voice, "Play ball." *(He opens one eye, raises his hand lethargically to her.)* Oh I salute you, Penelope. We who are about to go to sleep salute you.

PENELOPE: *(Shaking him again.)* Oh stop! Wake up! What about Telemachus? What about your son? Haven't you something to say about him?

ODYSSEUS: I've got something to *say* about anything you want. Telemachus. Telemachus will stay here, where he belongs. He will pull Ithaca along like one of those donkeys who see a carrot on the end of a stick. I'm the carrot. If he ever caught up with me, everything would stop.

PENELOPE: It all sounds so...pat, so neat...

ODYSSEUS: We're Greeks, dear. We're supposed to be symmetrical.

PENELOPE: We're not statues. Can't you come to life?

ODYSSEUS: No. I've lost my momentum. I'm out of gas.

PENELOPE: And I suppose I've been arrested for speeding. Permanently arrested at the age of twenty... Oh but who's the villain here, then? Who do I get mad at? I feel like socking someone right in the nose. We can't blame it all simply on the war. What's the trouble? Why have you and I turned into such creeps? You'd think it would be so easy for two people who were once congenial to get together after a lapse of time. We had such a good thing going once.

ODYSSEUS: That's the trouble. Good things go. Time's your villain, if you have to have one. He's like a child put into our custody when we're too young for the responsibility. So you ignored him; and I asked too much of him. And now we're older, he's making us pay for it.

PENELOPE: Time! Don't tell me about time. When you first went away, I'd lie awake at night thinking of you and what you were going through. I could always hear the sea pounding beneath my window. You know the sea, I assume. It was the worst way of constantly reminding people of death, time, eternity, all that stuff. It drove me mad. It got so I'd hear it day and night. The sound of waves became the tick of a great clock hanging over my head. What could I do? Gardening, for one thing. Fingers in the good earth. Dirty hands, all right, but also broken fingernails. I gave up gardening. What else was there? Games. Any game. Anything with something to go for and rules to abide by. I started with solitaire. The sound of the sea became softer. I challenged Euryclea to ping pong. The sea only whispered a protest. The suitors showed up. They're better at ping pong than Euryclea. One thing led to another. And now the sea is simply something to swim in.

ODYSSEUS: Ah. You see? You tried to drown it out. I tried to immerse my-self in it. Take it all on. And I did. And the sea immersed itself in me. I must have swallowed half the Mediterranean. And now here I am, cast up on the land like an old sea turtle, flippers waving feebly in the air, waiting for the Lotus Eaters to come along and give me artificial respiration.

PENELOPE: Oh Odysseus, no! Stay here with me! Please! I'm...I'm in trou-ble. I'm...I'm getting too old for singles. I'm losing. Things are a lit-tle desperate. I need you.

ODYSSEUS: I'd drag you down. I'm a rusty anchor.

PENELOPE: No you're not. No. Stay here. Please. We'll ease into our golden years. I'll...I'll put a rope tow on the golf course, and you can spend the winter following me downhill in a series of easy, linked turns.

ODYSSEUS: I'd fall.

PENELOPE: No, no. Listen. I'll meet you half way. I'll try reading again. I'll cancel my subscription to *Sports Illustrated* and send for *Horizon.*

ODYSSEUS: It's too late, sweetheart.

PENELOPE: No it isn't, no it isn't. And when I'm not reading, I'm going to be thoroughly psychoanalyzed. And when I'm not doing that, I'm go-ing to be down in the town, working in hospitals, talking to Negro cleaning women, getting involved in the Republican party. I'm going to learn to be at home with time and myself and you!

ODYSSEUS: It's too late.

PENELOPE: Oh please, Odysseus. Let me try. I'm going in to start reading right now. We'll have all winter to simmer me down and spruce you up. We'll send Telemachus to Andover. We'll have wonderful things to say to each other by spring.

(She starts in, but Euryclea appears at the door.)

EURYCLEA: Madam, I still can't fix supper.

PENELOPE: Why not, Euryclea?

EURYCLEA: Because Telemachus has locked all the suitors in the rumpus room, and he wants me to stand by to clean up the blood.

(Exits, with a sniff at Odysseus.)

ODYSSEUS: *(To Penelope.)* I thought today's youth advocated nonviolence.

PENELOPE: Well *I* advocate your talking to him. Now you're got to stay.

ODYSSEUS: No I don't. You handle it.

PENELOPE: You're his father!

ODYSSEUS: Tell him I said not to. Tell him I said, "Thou shalt not kill."

PENELOPE: Tell him yourself. I'll send him right out before he does some-thing very, very silly. *(Exits into the house.)*

ODYSSEUS: *(Calling after her.)* Penelope, I can't! *(Pause. To audience.)* People, I can't. I'm too old to go through some agonized father and son scene. Let her tell him. You tell him. Somebody tell him. *(He looks at the house, starts offstage, then stops.)* What can I do? When he sees me, when he hears what little I have to say, it will puncture all the bright balloons. He has ideals. You'll admit that, I hope. It's important for a young man to have ideals. I never had them, when I was young. At his age, I was figuring out ways to dodge the draft for the Trojan War. They had to drag me kicking and screaming into the crusade for the glory of Greece. I missed something. Let the kid dream. Maybe he'll end up more awake than I am. Do I have to shake him? Do I have to tell him everything, so he'll believe in nothing? No. Goodbye.

(But he doesn't go. Telemachus appears at the door, carrying a machine gun. Odysseus talks on to the audience, not seeing him.)

And suppose I did tell him everything. What is everything? That nothing in the world is what you expect it to be and so the best thing to do is to expect very little. Shall I tell him that? Shall I tell him that Troy was a hick town, with poor plumbing, which held out for ten years only because of some savvy logistics officer who knew how to conserve supplies. That Helen was an aging doxy with fat ankles. That Circe was as tedious as all pornography? And is all that true? Sometimes I wonder. Sometimes, when the sun shines, and I have a glass of wine in my hand, it all comes back in soft focus, filtered through cheese cloth, lovely and technicolored. Troy's topless towers rise again. Helen's ankle tapers gloriously to her foot. Calypso whispers love songs, and the Cyclops throws huge boulders at me while I sleep in the sun...*(Pause.)* So which is right? Both, neither? Does the truth lie somewhere in between? Gray, hardly memorable. Like... Hades. The Greeks have the word for it. I'll tell him that. Life is Hades, son. Occasional flames, occasional green fields, but mostly a gray, rather undistinguished place, where people wander around, thinking up things to do with their time. Yes. I'll tell him that. And then I'll say, don't kill people if they haven't seen the same movie you have. It's all relative, I'll say. It's all right. And it's all wrong. And so then Telemachus will become like me, a man half-asleep, running a slight temperature, talking too much, doing too little. I pity him. And I pity you. I can go off, but you will have to live with him.

TELEMACHUS: *(Slowly.)* You're not my father.

ODYSSEUS: *(Turning, reaching for his foot.)* Oh look. I've got this scar...

TELEMACHUS: *(Coming toward audience.)* My father has no scars! No! Not one! There is nothing scarred or marred about my father. I've known him well for twenty years.

ODYSSEUS: But—

TELEMACHUS: No. "buts." No "ifs." No qualifications. My father taught me to make up my mind.

ODYSSEUS: Then he taught you to kill one hundred men.

TELEMACHUS: I overcompensated. But he taught me to make distinctions. He gave me a point of view. I won't let it go. I won't be content with a manic-depressive circling around a gray hell.

ODYSSEUS: Then you'll never be content here.

TELEMACHUS: Where do I go, then? You're the man who's been around.

ODYSSEUS: *(More enthusiastically.)* One place only. I passed through it once. Go to Judea, boy! You might be happy there.

TELEMACHUS: Tell me more. What's it like?

Odysseus. Ah, the women! Lovely, limpid, dark-eyed...

TELEMACHUS: Never mind the women! What do the men believe?

ODYSSEUS: Just what you do. The almighty father, the promised land, all that.

TELEMACHUS: Go on! Go on! I like the sound of it!

ODYSSEUS: They play a formidable game. Incredibly difficult rules!

TELEMACHUS: So the reward at the end must be sensational!

ODYSSEUS: I don't even know what it is.

TELEMACHUS: I do! I can imagine! Oh I'm going! I'm going to Judea!

ODYSSEUS: *(Clapping him on the shoulders.)* Good luck, boy! Stick with it!
(Penelope comes out of the house, carrying books, wearing horn-rimmed glasses.)

PENELOPE: *(A little gloomily.)* What's all the excitement, gang?

ODYSSEUS: *(Enthusiastically.)* He's off to Judea to find his father!

PENELOPE: Skip it. I want to talk about myself.

ODYSSEUS: Do, do!

PENELOPE: Well, I'm in a bind. I've been writhing around in a chair upstairs, trying to read Plato and James Baldwin in roughly that order. But no go. I don't get them, and I can't concentrate, because I keep hearing sounds of a party.

ODYSSEUS: Another party?

PENELOPE: I think so...And it almost sounds like more fun than James Baldwin and Plato.

(Antinuous comes out of the house. The sounds of a lively party within.)

ANTINUOUS: It is, Penelope! Much more fun!...We got bored, locked in the Rumpus Room. So we figured out a new game. It's called *Scram*. All we need is one pretty girl!

PENELOPE: *(Exultantly, handing her books to Telemachus, putting her glasses on Odysseus.)* Then ready or not, I'm coming! Iron out the rules! I'll be in in a minute!

ANTINUOUS: *(Enthusiastically.)* Ah Penelope! You're home free!

(He exits into the house.)

ODYSSEUS: Incredible Penelope! You amaze me!

PENELOPE: I'm afraid it's a little late for that!

ODYSSEUS: No, I'm amazed by you all!

PENELOPE: Why? Because we've all found something we want to do.

ODYSSEUS: *(With fire.)* Yes! Exactly! Knowing what you know, still going on to do what you do. And I have no doubt you'll do it well! Magnificently! Look at you! Telemachus turning pro without ever having played as an amateur! You and the suitors, Penelope, eagerly improvising an arbitrary diversion, late in the evening, late in the year! What fight! What energy! I'm catching fire from all of you! I'm waking up, at last! I'm swinging!

PENELOPE: Then swing *at* something, for God's sake. Come in and play *Scram*. We'll revise the rules for senior citizens.

TELEMACHUS: No, swing *for* something, Odysseus. Play for the big time. Come with me to Judea.

ODYSSEUS: No. Neither one. I have my own alternative. I remember now. I heard a prophecy when I was in hell. I am to spend my last days walking around with an oar on my shoulder. I laughed at it then; I accept it now.

TELEMACHUS: Why that's absurd. And fatalistic.

PENELOPE: We don't have any oars. And I won't let you go off with the outboard motor.

(Euryclea comes out of the house carrying a large, cumbersome oar.)

EURYCLEA: This oar just arrived by special delivery. It's for Odysseus, who's not here.

ODYSSEUS: Oh I'm here, all right! *(Takes the oar, holds it aloft.)* See? Here's my fate, and I submit to it! I've got to carry this on my shoulder, far,

far inland to where they've never seen one. And then I plant it. And then I die.

TELEMACHUS: Why that's the most ludicrous game of all!

PENELOPE: Don't get fresh with your father...He's going to do something symbolic.

ODYSSEUS: I'm going to bring the sea to the land. Then time will stop, and our games will be over. *(He scans the audience.)* Where's that reporter? Wasn't there a reporter here somewhere? We should have a record of the first and last time this strange family was all together.

(The Reporter comes up from the audience with his camera ready.)

REPORTER: I'll take a picture, but I can't see much here to go with it.

ODYSSEUS: *(Getting everyone into position.)* Come on, everyone. Look pretty. Smile. You too, Euryclea.

TELEMACHUS: *(To Penelope as he stands behind her.)* I'll think of you, Mother, playing in the dark, when the sun comes up over Judea.

PENELOPE: Yes, remember your mother, dear. Because I have the feeling I'm going to forget you.

ODYSSEUS: *(Joining them in the picture.)* No, we must all remember each other. That's important. We must always remember that at one time in history, this strange family met, and stood together, and smiled.

(They smile. The Reporter takes the picture.)

Hold onto that picture. Make plenty of copies. It's valuable.

(The group starts to break up.)

REPORTER: No! No, wait. I see things now! Stay there! Don't move! Stay together! There's a story here! I see it now!

PENELOPE: *(Standing up.)* We've got things to do, Reporter. You heard us before.

Odysseus. Yes. And we'll try to do them well. That's the point of your story, if you want to write it.

REPORTER: *(Attempting to keep them together.)* No! I can't write that! What can you really do without each other! Oh stick together, you guys! Don't leave it as just a flash in the night! What a family you'd be, what an island this would be, what a world we'd have, if you'd all stay side by side! There's your comeback! There's your homecoming! *(To audience.)* Isn't it, people? Isn't that what we've been waiting for? Oh together, you three would drive out the suitors forever!... If you split up, you'll just be trivial type-characters ending a foolish farce.

TELEMACHUS: *(Stepping out of the picture.)* I've waited too long. I'm off to Judea. So long, Dad. I'll be back to inherit the kingdom.

(Telemachus shakes hands with Odysseus, bounces off.)

REPORTER: *(Calling after him.)* Wait, kid! You'll get in trouble! *(To Odysseus and Penelope.)* At least you two. Stay. There's such a story here if you'll get together again.
(Penelope busses Odysseus and starts off.)

ODYSSEUS: Oh we'll get together again. We'll both crop up in Telemachus' children.

PENELOPE: *(As she exits.)* Yes. In probably all the wrong proportions. Heaven help the poor tormented little psyches of our grandchildren!
(Waves goodbye to Odysseus, and exits into the house.)

REPORTER: *(To Odysseus.)* Get her back, man. Go on. Show some fight. Give us some glory.

ODYSSEUS: *(Sadly.)* The glory that was Greece.

REPORTER: Sure. Listen. It's all coming now. I can feel it. I'll start at the beginning:

> Sing in me, Muse, and through me tell the story
> Of that man, skilled in all ways of contending...

(Odysseus looks at him, shrugs and walks off, hoisting his oar on his shoulder.)

> The wanderer, harried for years on end...

(The Reporter stops, seeing that Odysseus has gone.)

EURYCLEA: *(Her eyes still closed from the flash of the picture.)* That's him... That's Odysseus you're talking about...

REPORTER: Open your eyes, Euryclea. He's gone. They've all gone.

EURYCLEA: *(Eyes still closed.)* No, Homer. Close your eyes. And go on.
(The Reporter takes a deep breath, closes his eyes tight, and continues loud and clear.)

REPORTER:

> "The wanderer, harried for years on end,
> After he plundered the stronghold
> On the proud height of Troy..."

(Euryclea rocks and nods.)

BLACKOUT

END OF PLAY

The Rape of Bunny Stuntz

A Play in One Act

This play was first produced in a workshop situation at M.I.T., where I was teaching in the Department of Humanities. Full of experimental fervor, I was attempting to write a play and create an audience to go with it.

Original Production

The Rape of Bunny Stuntz was first professionally produced in 1964 by the Playwrights Unit, under the auspices of Edward Albee, Richard Barr and Clinton Wilder. It opened at the Cherry Lane Theatre in New York City with Helene Westcott playing Bunny and Charles Guys directing.

The Characters

Bunny Stuntz, a bright, efficient, and attractive woman, anywhere from twenty-five to forty-five. She wears a dress or suit.

Wilma Trumbo, should be cast in contrast to Bunny. Heavier or lighter, shorter or taller. Preferably younger. She should have a more rumpled appearance, and a more naive, wide-eyed stance.

Howie Hale, a hale fellow, well met. Anywhere from thirty to fifty. Wears a suit or a sports jacket.

Setting

The action takes place at an evening meeting in an indeterminate meeting hall—a school, a club, a theatre.

The Rape
of Bunny Stuntz

We see a small table, with a chair behind it, facing the audience. After a moment, Bunny Stuntz comes briskly up onto stage from the audience. A claque of Applause accompanies her. She carries a square metal box. Pinned on her chest is an unusually large round name-tag which reads "Hi! I'm Bunny Stuntz!" She clicks around behind the podium and places the box neatly in front of her, squaring it with the edge of the table. As the Applause dies down, she smiles at the audience.

BUNNY: Hi! I'm Bunny Stuntz! *(Looks around brightly.)* And I want to welcome all you newcomers to our meeting tonight. I'm sure that before the evening is over, we'll have the opportunity to know each other much, much better. *(More seriously.)* I also want to thank all of you—veterans, shall we say—for electing me chairman last week. I will try to do my best tonight, and in the months ahead. Now, to business—*(She smiles again, and briskly tries to open the box in front of her. It doesn't open. She struggles with the catch. No result. She smiles at the audience.)* I must have locked this—*(Pause. Then in a whisper.)* Purse—*(She snaps open her purse and fumbles in it. No result. Pause. Another whisper.)* Pin—*(She reaches into her hair and removes a bobby pin, tries it in the lock. No result. She bangs the box on the table, always sweetly, and then shakes it a couple of times. No result.)* Why, I could have sworn—*(She looks out over the audience, shading her eyes.)* Is Howard Hale out there? Howie, are you out there, please?
HOWIE: *(Who has been standing in the rear.)* Right here, Bunny!
BUNNY: Howie, would you come up here a moment? *(Howie comes up*

onto stage, bright and eager. On the lapel of his coat is also a name-tag: "Hi! I'm Howie Hale!" He smiles self-consciously at the audience, perhaps nods or waves to a couple of familiar faces.) Howie, I think I forgot the key to this thing. *(Howie looks at Bunny, looks at the box, and then putters with it, while Bunny speaks to the audience.)* This is Howie Hale. If you want to have anything done around here, ask Howie.

HOWIE: *(To Bunny.)* It's locked.

BUNNY: I think it is. Yes. I must have left the key home.

HOWIE: Let's go on, anyway. Let's go on without it.

BUNNY: With*out* it? *(Pause.)* No, we can't Howie. No, we really can't. *(Smiles at audience.)* If you'll bear with us, people. *(To Howie.)* No, Howie. Everything's in here. The minutes from last week, the agenda for this week, the mailing list, the money—everything. *(Howie looks at her, then reaches in his pocket, takes out his own key ring, examines a bunch of keys; he begins trying them on the box with great dedication.)* Oh, it won't open with just any old key, Howie. That I know…It requires a special key, I'm afraid. *(To audience.)* Oh darn it. This is an inauspicious beginning for my maiden voyage, isn't it? *(To Howie, who is having no success with his keys.)* Howie, I know where the key is. I left it home. Now it comes back. It's in a cubbyhole in my desk, actually.

HOWIE: In a cubbyhole?

BUNNY: Exactly. In my desk. Now look, Howie—*(She fumbles in her purse, takes out a piece of paper and a ballpoint pen.)* Call Bill…Here's the number—*(She writes down the number, then smiles at the audience.)* My husband Bill's sitting with our three kiddos—*(Back to her writing.)* And Howie, tell him to look in the third cubbyhole from the right—third from right—and get the key—which has a tag on it—tag—and then to bring it over…Tell him to get Debbie Bayliss from next door—here's her number—just say Debbie, he'll know—and Debbie can stay with the kiddos while Bill brings the key over here. *(She folds the paper neatly and hands it to Howie.)* Would you do that, Howie?

HOWIE: *(Saluting her.)* Yavohl, mein capitan! *(He exits into the audience and out.)*

BUNNY: *(Calling after him.)* You're a peach, Howie. *(To audience.)* He's a peach. I hope you all get to know Howie before we're through. He's a do-er. *(Pause. She straightens the box on the table.)* Well. It will be about ten minutes, people. I apologize. I'm terribly sorry. The best laid plans gang oft agley. I think I locked this thing because of the kiddos, and after supper, I was in such a hurry to get here that I must have forgotten the key. *(Pause. She taps her teeth with her pen.)* Why—while we're waiting—are we here? Is it fair to ask that? I think it is. I was thinking of tonight, as I left my family: why? Why have so many of us, from so many different walks of life, left our homes, our comfortable chairs, those easy—routines which we all have at the end of a busy day—why do we leave all that, to come here? It costs money to come here. I know that. The group has to charge its dues, of course, and when you add on the sitter's fees, and the gas and depreciation to *get* here, and perhaps even a dinner out—why, I can imagine that it has cost some of us a good ten dollars, in toto, to come here. And yet we are here, you and I, all in this thing together. Why? *(She smiles.)* Certainly you didn't come here just to see me. Just to see a lady forget her key... No, you expect things to happen here tonight, don't you? And they will! I can promise you that. We'll go somewhere, if I have anything to do with it. Because—*(A car is heard, faintly, she stops, listens.)* Do I hear someone tooting his horn out in the parking lot. *(She shades her eyes, looks out over the audience.)* Wilma Trumbo, do I see you by the door? Wilma, would you just run out to the parking lot and find out what's what? Thanks, Wilma. You're a peach. *(To audience.)* It sounded like a familiar horn. I suspect it was my husband Bill. With my key. He might have thought of it, all by himself. And dashed over with it. He's very thoughtful. Quiet, uncomplicated, thoughtful. He encourages me to be active. He'd be here himself, but he's terribly tired. He travels all the time, and so when he's home, naturally he wants to rest. But he gives me my head. That's the point. "Fulfill yourself," he says. "Go on. More power to you."...And so here I am, standing up here in front of all of you. *(Pause)* But why here? What is fulfilling about all of this for all of us? That's the question we should be chewing and digesting at the moment. I mean, we're not just here to be enter*tained*. We could get that, staying at home, watching our boob tubes. No. All of us here—no matter what our race, creed, or color—all of us are in some way unhappy people. Oh not un-*happy*-unhappy. Heaven forbid!... Just—discontented—concerned—and so: involved. Oh, we have rich full lives at home. Or in the marketplace. I don't mean that. I just mean—I just mean that what goes on there is not *enough*. Husband, children, home—they just don't—fill the gap, do they?

(*Wilma Trumbo calls softly from halfway up the aisle. She is younger than Bunny, with frillier clothes. She too wears a badge: "Hi! I'm Wilma Trumbo!"*)

WILMA: Bunny, may I speak to you for moment?

BUNNY: Of course, Wilma. (*Wilma joins Bunny On-stage, and whispers something in her ear. Bunny steps back.*) Why that's the silliest thing I ever heard, Wilma.

WILMA: That's how I understood it, Bunny.

BUNNY: (*Looks at Wilma, then laughs.*) I think we should share this news item with our friends, Wilma. (*Bunny, with her arm around Wilma, brings her Down-stage and speaks to the audience.*) People, Wilma says that there's a man out there in the parking lot in a red car—

WILMA: (*To Bunny.*) A red Impala—

BUNNY: A red Impala, who has been fuh-rantically tooting his horn because he claims—Oh, you tell them, Wilma—

WILMA: (*To audience.*) He says he's waiting for Bunny.

BUNNY: (*Laughing.*) Waiting for me!

WILMA: (*To audience.*) For Bunny Stuntz.

BUNNY: (*To audience.*) All right, now, who knows anything about this? Who's trying to be funny? Is this some—secret initiation for your new chairman?...Seriously, we've got a long way to go tonight. Who knows anyone belonging to a red—what is it, Wilma?

WILMA: Impala.

BUNNY: Impala. I've got a date, now, with an Impala yet...Describe him, Wilma. I'll figure out who it is. (*To audience.*) Or one of you can.

WILMA: (*Hesitatingly; to audience.*) I couldn't see him very well—it was dark out there, in the parking lot...He had a jacket on—a leather jacket, because it sort of glistened—and a sort of whispering voice—and he was chewing gum...I don't know. I never saw him before. (*A pause.*)

BUNNY: Oh, Wilma, you make him sound so *menacing.* (*To audience.*) Doesn't Wilma sound scary? (*More seriously.*) No. He sounds like some—teenager, trying to be funny. Some teenager. We ought to have a place where teenagers can go. I have a note on that, right in this box. (*Howie comes onto the stage.*) Yes, Howie?

HOWIE: Bill can't find the key, Bunny.

BUNNY: Oh, now Howie—

HOWIE: He looked everywhere while I stayed on the phone.

BUNNY: It was in the cubbyhole in my—

HOWIE: He looked there, Bunny.

WILMA: Maybe you lost it, Bunny.

BUNNY: I did not lose it, Wilma. I do not lose things! *(She remembers the audience; smiles.)* I don't lose keys.

HOWIE: Let's go on, anyway, Bunny. Let's play it by ear.

WILMA: Yes, Bunny—

BUNNY: *(Holding the box.)* I hate to do that. I really hate to do that. *(To audience.)* Everything—everything's in here. All the previous minutes, the money, all the proposals for tonight. I had everything all worked out. I had divided up the topics. I had divided up all of us. I had group captains—Howie, you were one, and Wilma, so were you. It's all here. In this box. The whole thing. *(To Howie, more softly.)* Did Bill look in the bedroom for the key?

HOWIE: He said he looked everywhere, Bunny.

BUNNY: *(A touch of bitterness.)* I'll bet he didn't look in the bedroom. Knowing Bill. *(Pause, Wilma and Howie look at her, waiting for a decision. She looks at them, at the box, at the audience, then comes to a decision.)* I'll whip home. It will take me fifteen minutes at the most. *(To audience.)* People, why don't you talk quietly among yourselves? Raise issues, ascertain facts, hammer out modes of action.

HOWIE AND WILMA: Aw, Bunny—come off it—

BUNNY: *(To audience.)* People, I really don't think I can be of much good to anyone without that key.

HOWIE: Can we break out the coffee, down in the cafeteria?

BUNNY: But we have so much to do!

HOWIE: We can do it over coffee.

WILMA: Yes. That's right. Coffee now. Instead of later.

BUNNY: *(Pondering.)* Will you *promise* me, all of you, that you'll stay within the general lines of our purpose? I mean, coffee breaks can get so—chatty. Will you promise me you'll try to get something done, albeit informally, over coffee?

HOWIE: Oh, sure Bunny.

BUNNY: *(Suddenly and determinedly.)* Howie, go down and start the coffee. *(To audience.)* But those of you who want to stay here in your seats for a more formal program can do so. Wilma can be discussion leader. *(Howie salutes her, and bustles off into audience.)*

HOWIE: C'mon, gang. Anyone for coffee? *(Exits.)* *(Wilma settles nervously into Bunny's seat behind the table.)*

BUNNY: All set, Wilma?

WILMA: *(Meekly.)* I guess so—

BUNNY: *(Appraising her.)* Beautiful! Meanwhile, back to the ranch! *(She picks up her box, and starts off left, then stops, clutching the box; to Wilma.)* Who's that out there?

WILMA: *(Looking off left.)* Where?

BUNNY: *(Low, to Wilma.)* There's somebody slouching out there in the shadows. *(To audience.)* There's somebody slouching out there in the wings.

WILMA: *(Looking.)* I think it's him.

BUNNY: You think it's who, Wilma?

WILMA: I think it's the man with the Impala. *(Pause. Bunny squints, looking off left.)*

BUNNY: All right, all right. Who's there? *(Pause.)* Who are you out there, please? *(Pause. She turns to audience.)* Whoever is out there is being very, very silly, indeed. Frankly. *(Back to left.)* Will you come in, please, and make yourself known?...Will you come in, please? *(Pause.)* Wilma, would you go ask him, please, to come in? *(Wilma nods and exits, a little warily. Bunny turns to the audience, still clutching the box.)* Why, this is the limit, isn't it? I mean, he's just slinking around out there, like a—snake. *(She turns back to the left, fascinated. Wilma comes back in.)*

WILMA: He wants you, Bunny.

BUNNY: Oh. He wants me, does he? *(She speaks to the left.)* Well, he's not going to get me till he comes into the light. *(To audience.)* Is he? *(To Wilma.)* If he wants to join the meeting, then he's welcome to come right in and join it. *(To audience.)* Isn't he? *(To left.)* Sir, if you want to join the meeting, then you're welcome to join us. It's an open meeting. I had it announced as such. There are plenty of new people here. From all walks of life. *(To audience.)* Aren't there? *(Back to left.)* You can come in and sit down, or you can go down in the cafeteria and have coffee. Either one. I'm Bunny Stuntz. I'm chairing this meeting, and I'll be glad to talk to you personally right after I whip home and get the key to this box. *(She starts off in the other direction, as if to exit through the audience. Then she stops.)* Wilma, give him a name-tag.

WILMA: I left them at the door, Bunny.

BUNNY: Then here—*(She takes off her own name-tag.)* He can turn this around. *(She takes her ballpoint pen out of her purse.)* Tell him he can write his name on the back of this. *(She hands Wilma the name-tag and the pen. Wilma exits, left. Bunny speaks to the audience.)* He should identify himself. As we all have. *(Pause.)* I feel so—naked without my—fig leaf. *(She smiles.)* But I think you all know me pretty well by now. *(She takes another step or two, as if to leave, but seems fascinated by what is happening off left.)* I know what this is all about. I've seen it happen, oh, many times. Some people are terribly, terribly shy. They want to join groups, and yet they find it terribly difficult. They go through all sorts of peculiar maneuvers. First they throw away our notices. Then they drive by the place, but don't come in. Then they *come* in and stand on the sidelines. *Fin* ally, especially if someone takes them in tow, they join, and they generally end up being one of the most active participants. You watch. *(Wilma comes in from the left, slowly.)* What happened, Wilma?

WILMA: *(Holding out two halves of the name-tag.)* He tore it up.

BUNNY: *(Taking the two halves.)* He tore it *up?* *(She tries to piece the two halves together, vaguely.)*

WILMA: I gave it to him with the pen, and I said "Please write your name on the back." And he snatched it away, and tore it up, and handed back the pieces. He put the pen in his pocket.

BUNNY: Oh, now, *honestly. (She looks off left, then turns to audience.)* He's just *standing* there.

WILMA: He's not a teenager, either. He's got five o'clock shadow.

BUNNY: Did he *say* anything? *(To audience, smiling nervously.)* Does it *speak?*

WILMA: Yes, he said one thing, when he handed back the mutilated name-tag.

BUNNY: And what was that, pray tell?

WILMA: He said he had the key. *(Pause.)*

BUNNY: *(Slowly, with great intensity.)* He has no key.

WILMA: All I know is what he said, Bunny. *(To audience.)* I'm just reporting what the man said.

BUNNY: *(More briskly again.)* He does not have my key. My key's at home. How could he possibly have the key? I'm going home right now to get the key. *(She starts again to exit into the audience, then stops, braces herself, and steps a little toward the left. She speaks very slowly to the left.)* How could you possibly have the key, sir? *(Pause, while she listens. She takes a step closer.)* What? *(Another pause, another step; then she turns to Wilma.)* He whispers. He hisses. I can't hear a word he says.

WILMA: I heard one word.

BUNNY: What word? What word?

WILMA: Hotel. *(Pause.)*

BUNNY: Ho—

WILMA: —tel.

BUNNY: Hotel? Ho-*tel?* What hotel? I don't know anything about hotels. I don't go to hotels. *(Calling out left.)* What do you mean, hotel? *(Pause, she turns to Wilma.)* I still can't hear a damn thing he's saying.

WILMA: Maybe he's saying you left the key in a hotel. *(Pause.)*

BUNNY: *(Slowly; to audience.)* That man is mad. The key is home.

WILMA: Shall we call the police, then?

BUNNY: *(To audience.)* The man is stark, raving mad.

WILMA: Should we get Howie and some of the men to throw him out?

BUNNY: *(To the audience.)* The only hotel I've been in in years was last May when I went down to New York with Rosie Rinehart to see the James Baldwin thing. *(To Wilma.)* That's the only hotel room I've been in in years, Wilma. *(To audience.)* When I go anywhere, I go with friends. Or with my family. And we stay with friends. We have friends all over the eastern seaboard. Friends from school, friends from college, friends from Bill's business. Why, I don't think we *ever* fall back on hotels or motels or things like that. Lonely, sleazy rooms. Never.

WILMA: Oh, I know it, Bunny. Oh, I know it. Knowing you, I can believe it. Knowing you.

BUNNY: *(She glances at Wilma peculiarly, and then looks off left.)* What's he doing out there? Is he twirling something on the end of a chain? What's he twirling? I can't see.

WILMA: *(Looking out.)* It's the key.

BUNNY: It is *not* the key!...It is not the key.

WILMA: Do you suppose he's trying to hypnotize you, Bunny?

BUNNY: *(Snapping out of it, looking away from left.)* Ignore him, Wilma— I said, ignore him, Wilma. *(Wilma snaps out of it; Bunny speaks to audience.)* Ignore him, everybody. Ignore him. I'm going to ignore him. He's an—exhibitionist, obviously. He wants a fuss, and when he doesn't get one, he'll go away. So just forget that there's anybody out there. Just—ignore him. *(She cradles the box in her arms. Howie comes onstage from the audience. His coat is off, and he hides a can of beer behind his back.)*

HOWIE: Hey, Bun! Get the key yet?

BUNNY: No, Howie. We were—delayed.

WILMA: Howie, there's a—

BUNNY: *(Quickly.)* Never mind, Wilma...We were delayed, Howie. Let's leave it at that. *(She notices he is hiding something.)* What's that, Howie?

HOWIE: *(A little defiantly, holding out the beer.)* That's beer.

BUNNY: Beer?

HOWIE: Yeah. Beer. Someone broke out some beer, down in the cafeteria. And there's a piano there. Doc Feldstein's playing sing-along songs from our college days.

WILMA: *(Clapping her hands.)* Oh, what fun!

BUNNY: *(After a glance at Wilma.)* Howie, I don't understand this. I don't think we are here to have a party.

HOWIE: Yeah, well what the hell?

BUNNY: *(Indicating audience.)* I don't think all these people are here, Howie, simply to drink beer and sing outmoded songs.

HOWIE: *(With feeling.)* Yeah, well maybe we better skip the key. *(Then, guiltily.)* We had nothing to do down there, Bun. I dunno. We got nervous. Sort of uneasy...So we're having a party. *(Pause. Bunny looks from Howie to the audience to the box to off left.)*

BUNNY: I have decided—not to bother with the key....I'll try to remember the agenda. *(Takes another pen and notebook out of her purse.)* Howie, you and I and Wilma can quickly jot down a few notes so that we'll have something to go on. I mean, there's no point in being completely random.

HOWIE: *(Leaving the stage.)* Um—give me a yell when you're ready to roll, Bun.

BUNNY: Howie—

HOWIE: *(Singing, imitation operetta singer.)* "Tell me, pretty maiden, are there any more at home like you?" *(He exits.)*

WILMA: (Continuing, softly, longingly.) "There are a few, kind sir..." *(She peters out.)*

BUNNY: *(She looks at Wilma, glances off left, then speaks half to Wilma, half to audience.)* Anyone who wants to go down to the cafeteria *can,* you know. I mean if that's what you want. If that's what you came for. Musical comedy. I myself am just going to jot down a few quick topics for those who are just interested enough to stick it out. *(She goes to the chair.)*

WILMA: *(A little wistfully; looking out at the audience.)* Lots of people are going down, Bunny.

BUNNY: *(Beginning to write on a piece of paper.)* Would you like to go, Wilma? Tell me the truth. *(To audience, smiling nervously.)* I mean, what *am* I? A slavedriver? A dictator? *(To Wilma.)* If you want to go down there, you should go, Wilma. *(With a glance off left.)* I can handle things by myself.

WILMA: No, I'll stay. I'll help you. *(She stands behind Bunny's chair.)*

BUNNY: *(Writing.)* Now. Well. Let's see. I had broken the thing down into goals. Immediate goals, A and far-reaching goals, B. *(From off left, the sound of music, cool jazz, insinuating, without a vocal. Both women look up and off.)*

WILMA: He's got a transistor radio.

BUNNY: *(Setting her jaw.)* I had set up three major committees, Wilma. A fact-finding committee, a ways-and-means committee *and*—*(The music becomes louder. Bunny has to shout to be heard.)* and an ultimate objectives committee. I thought that Howie could be chairman of—*(She stops, closes her eyes, puts down her pen, then stands up and strides toward the left.)* Would you turn that off, please? *(The music continues.)* I said, would you turn that off, please! We are having a meeting here. *(The music plays a little longer, then cuts out.)* Thank you so much. *(Pause. The music starts again, loud. Bunny shouts it down.)* All Right! *(The music stops.)* We will talk, you and I. *(To audience, a little sarcastically.)* He and I will commu-*u*-nicate.

WILMA: Oh, Bunny—

BUNNY: *(Dryly.)* It's all right, Wilma. I think it's trying to tell us something. *(To off left.)* *Ser*-iously, sir, you think you know me, but you have made a mistake. We have never met. We have never crossed paths or swords or anything else. Period. *(Pause.)* Never. Never, never, never. I'm sorry. No. It's not true.

WILMA: *(Wide-eyed to audience.)* He's just smiling. I can see his teeth.

BUNNY: *(To off left.)* No sirree, bub. I'm sorry. *(Pause.)* And no, that's not my key. I said that is not my key. No. *(Pause.)* Not it is not. No. Would you please go away.

WILMA: Bunny, let's get some men up here.

BUNNY: I can handle this, Wilma.

WILMA: *(To audience.)* She seems to think she can handle this.

BUNNY: *(To off left.)* All right then, *when* have I seen you before? Speak. Can you speak? You know, words and things. *(Pause.)* When? Names and dates, please. Chapter and verse.

WILMA: Oh, Bunny, don't bother.

BUNNY: I have to pin this thing *down,* Wilma. *(To audience.)* It's the only way he'll go away. *(To off left.)* When have we…met? *(Pause.)* Name a day. Any day. Monday, Tuesday, Wednesday. January, February, March. Go on. Name a day.

WILMA: *(To audience.)* He's just—shrugging his shoulders. And scratching.

BUNNY: *(To Wilma.)* All right, Wilma, *you* pick a day.

WILMA: Me?

BUNNY: Since apparently he won't. Pick any day you want. I can account for it.

WILMA: Oh, Bunny, please—

BUNNY: Name a day, Wilma!

WILMA: *(Weakly.)* Tuesday.

BUNNY: Tuesday. Good. *(To off left.)* Wilma thinks we met on a Tuesday. At what *time,* Wilma?

WILMA: Bunny, I didn't say you met—*(To audience.)* I didn't say—

BUNNY: At what time, Wilma?

WILMA: *(Cowed.)* Three P.M.

BUNNY: Good. So on Tuesday afternoons, at 3:00 P.M., I met this character in a hotel. Some foul, sleazy hotel, apparently, where you can bring in women…And where I suppose I gave myself to him in a moment of sublime surrender and then left my key…Oh, this is ridiculous.

WILMA: Of course it's ridiculous.

BUNNY: *(Walking away from stage left.)* Now Wilma, tell him where I am on Tuesday afternoons.

WILMA: All right. *(She goes to stage left; calls out.)* Mrs. Stuntz couldn't possibly have been with you on Tuesday afternoons because on Tuesday afternoons she—*(Turns to Bunny.)* Where are you on Tuesday afternoons?

BUNNY: You know, Wilma. *(To audience.)* Wilma knows.

WILMA: *(To audience.)* I *don't.* I really don't. I've forgotten.

BUNNY: On Tuesday afternoons, I drive Binkie all the way over to Westfield for his art lesson, *and* do the marketing, *and* drive back.

WILMA: Is that true?

BUNNY: Of course it's true, Wilma.

WILMA: Oh, I know it's *true;* I just hadn't heard it before.

BUNNY: I take Marge Jackson's little girl, too. I take Pammy Jackson. *(Looks out into the audience.)* Marge Jackson, are you out there? Would you come up and tell this man what I do Tuesday afternoons?

Would you tell him where I take your very talented little Pammy? *(Pause.)*

WILMA: I think Marge is down singing college songs.

BUNNY: *I'll* tell him then.

WILMA: Oh, I'll *tell* him, Bunny. I believe you. I just didn't know you did that on Tuesday afternoons.

BUNNY: Well, I do. I've saved all the paintings. There's one of a dragon.

WILMA: I just didn't know, that's all. *(She goes to the left.)* Mrs. Stuntz couldn't possibly have—

BUNNY: Would he like to see my calendar? I'll show him my engagement calendar. It has everything I've done. Meetings, coffees, carpool, dentists, errands, everything. *(Calling off left.)* Would you like to see that? Would that convince you that you've made a mistake? I think if you looked at it—*(To audience.)* I think if he looked at it, he'd realize that there's not a single time in my life that I could have possibly—*(Back to left.)* gone with you to some seamy, sleazy hotel. You can look at my calendar. Anybody can. I'm perfectly willing to make it public. It's right here in this—*(Goes to box, realizes that it is locked.)* box. *(Pause.)*

WILMA: It doesn't make any difference, Bunny—

BUNNY: *(Bitterly.)* It seems everything important in my life is locked in this box.

WILMA: *(Looking off left.)* He's holding out the key, Bunny.

BUNNY: *(Shaking her head.)* That's not the key. The key's at home. With Bill and the children. It's on the table by my bed.

WILMA: *(Looking off left.)* He's nodding—as if he knows that table, Bunny.

BUNNY: He does not know that table.

WILMA: *(Looking off left.)* He's nodding as if he knows that bed. *(Bunny stiffens, looks at Wilma, and strides off left. Wilma watches anxiously, There is the sound of a loud slap. Wilma gasps. Then two more slaps come in quick succession. Bunny comes reeling backwards onto the stage, holding her cheek, looking back offstage.)* Why, he—*(To audience.)* Let's have some *men* up here, for heaven's sake! She's—

BUNNY: *(Grimly.)* No, I'm all right. *(To audience.)* I said I'm all right.

WILMA: *(Starting off toward the audience.)* I'm going to call the police! He hit you!

BUNNY: *(Sitting down.)* That was because I hit him. *(To the left, sneeringly.)* Like some cheap, second-rate blonde in a B movie, I'm now resorting to slapping strange men. I've slipped to that level, apparently.

WILMA: Oh, Bunny, let's have him thrown out!

BUNNY: *(Talking to the left.)* Oh, sure. And you think that will get rid of him for good? Oh, I know this kind of character. He'll be on my neck for life unless I beat him my own way. He'll pull up alongside of me at traffic lights; he'll call on the telephone. Sly, cheap, insinuating, like a snake. And I've got to stare him down.

(Howie rushes on from the audience, now looking thoroughly rumpled, perhaps with lipstick on his face; he now carries a glass half full of liquor. He grabs Bunny by the waist.)

HOWIE: *(Singing, as he spins Bunny around.)* "And if there's one thing worse…in this universe…it's a woman…I said a woman…I mean a woman without a man…" *(Bunny breaks away.)* C'mon down, Bun. We got a great party.

WILMA: Oh golly! Just what the doctor ordered!

HOWIE: Sure! Listen! Doc Feldstein's playing shady songs on the piano. Marge Jackson's doing a way-out dance on a table. And me, I've been introducing myself to a newcomer in the corner!

BUNNY: Oh, Howie, Howie. You've all let go, haven't you?

HOWIE: Naw, Bun, we've all caught *on*. But we need you. C'mon down, Bun.

BUNNY: *(Shaking her head.)* I'm sorry, Howie. No.

HOWIE: We need an anchor man, Bun.

BUNNY: *(With a glance off left.)* No. *(Howie looks at her; then begins to sing a suggestive popular song to her, shuffling lewdly around her. He ends up with his arm around Wilma, who giggles sheepishly. Then he rushes off.)*

WILMA: Oh, Bunny, let's join the party. *(To audience.)* All of us. Let's all join the group downstairs. It sounds like such fun. *(To Bunny.)* Please, Bunny. You're not getting anywhere up here. It's too late to get started on a meeting…Our friends are down there, Bunny. Song and laughter and casual, harmless sex-play. *(To audience.)* We're all being party-poops, those of us who are left. Life goes on without us, down there, while we fuss around up here, worrying about some stupid man. There comes a point when we can become too serious, too obsessed with things. Come on. *(To Bunny.)* Come on, Bunny. Fill the cup, seize the hour, join the dance!

(Bunny shakes her head, staring out left.)

I'm going, Bunny. I feel like a good, stiff drink. And a little music. I'm going to join my friends. Are you coming?

(Bunny again shakes her head.)

Goodbye then, Bunny. *(Wilma exits through the audience; Bunny suddenly turns and gasps.)*

BUNNY: Oh, Wilma—*(Pause. She looks out over the audience, shading her eyes; by now, the lighting has become stark and theatrical. She stands in a harsh pool.)* Has she gone?…She has gone…Anybody left? I can't see very well. These lights—any familiar faces out there? Any? Oh there *must* be!…And anybody who is still here is my friend. I mean it. You're my friends, out there, whoever you are, because you came here and you stuck it out…*(She takes a deep breath, glances toward left, and then pulls her chair Downstage front. She sits in it, quietly. She speaks musingly, ironically—never sentimentally.)* So I'm going to be frank with you, friends. Since you stayed, I'll be frank. What if—what if I *have* seen this man before? What if—last Tuesday, for example—I *didn't* take Binkie to his art lesson? What if I was in the front of the house—gardening, say—cultivating my own garden—when he—this creature—happened to drive by in his red—Impala? What if his car makes such a racket that I naturally look up, and see this creature in his leather jacket, bombing by? Suppose he waves to me, and maybe I wave back, or *half* wave, uncertain, not knowing who he is. Suppose he drives around the block, thinking I've—what is that awful expression?—"given him the eye"? Back he comes, and there I am, crouched in the petunias. And so he pulls up to the curb, and I get the picture, and walk into the house, slamming the door. And the poor sap has had these dreams of glory ever since, till finally he follows me down here, and tries to embarrass me in front of all my friends at a public meeting. *(Stand up; speaks to left.)* Now, so long, sonny boy. *(Back to audience.)* There. That's it. That's my confession. I'm admitting what could, possibly, have happened. Now perhaps we can at least arrange for our next meeting. *(She goes to the table, starts to open her purse. Pause. Glances left, then back at audience. The lights are a little brighter on her now. She sits on the edge of the table.)* He's still there, friends…All right—we'll take it farther. Try this one. Suppose I go into the kitchen. Suppose there's a good, big fat leg of lamb in the oven, and I tritty-trot in there to baste it. Suppose Bill is, per usual, away and suppose the children are still at school. Suppose this character appears at the kitchen window, and leers at me, until I ask him please what in hell does he want. As if I didn't know. *(She speaks to left.)* Oh. You want to use the telephone? No, I don't think that's possible. I'm sorry, no. So please go away.

(Pause, as she glares off left.) Or—why not? I mean, there are neighbors around—friends, just like you people, out there, and the knife for the leg of lamb is handy—and I'm a little bored. So—yes. You may use the telephone. Come in. It's right here in the kitchen... Don't you want to use it after all? I didn't think so. Get out then. Now. *(Pause. She watches left, then turns to the audience. She has to peer against the light.)* He won't go, friends. He's still standing here. *(Takes a deep breath.)* All right. Picture this, if you will. *(Speaks to left.)* He's still there, slouched in my kitchen, leaning against the counter, chewing gum—*(She closes her eyes.)* And I am somewhat attracted to him. I'm admitting this. I'm making this public, which is apparently what I'm supposed to do. Dig we must, as they say—*(To audience.)* And all of you know what I mean, because you're the ones who came and stayed—to see. You want to see what's there, too, don't you, waiting in the wings? So all of us here, all of us in this room tonight, are a little in love with what is dark and shoddy and unpleasant. Yes. And I think it's good that we admit these things. Yes. I feel much better now that it's all out in the open. Recognizing the thing is—dealing with it, and of course then driving it out. *(She draws herself up proudly. Speaks to left.)* So sure. Yes. O.K. I'll admit out loud that I am attracted. And I'll even admit that in my own house—while we stood eyeing each other—something—physical might have happened— *(Long pause as she stares off left; then she shakes her head and turns again to audience.)* I said, something might have happened in that vacuum if the sounds of the world hadn't come flooding in. Here come the clichés, people, but thank God for clichés, say I...Suppose just then I hear two children fighting over a truck. Or I hear the Millworths' boxer barking at the mailman. And I shake my head. I say, "Thanks but no thanks." And I say to that man, "Get out, or I'll scream for all my friends!" And he gets out. But fast! *(She smiles at the audience.)* So there it is, isn't it? It's all out in the open. I've lied, I've told the truth, I've made a public confession of a nightmare. And now he should go. That's it. That's all. There isn't any more. I have values. So do you. We believe in things. We have families, friends, rules we can count on. We can afford to turn our backs on the—dark, seamy side of things. *(She turns her back on stage left.)* So let's go. Back to our homes. Back to our clean houses which are better than grubby hotel rooms. And we'll drive back in station wagons which really *do* make more sense than red Impalas: I mean, who do we want to im*pale*,

anyway? Oh, I believe in these things so strongly. I believe that attractive people are more attractive than unattractive people. I believe that children, with haircuts, in polo coats, going to see their grandmothers are more important than some cheap, cheap, cheap disgusting tussle with a strange man. I believe—*(She grabs the box off the table.)* I believe in everything here. What I've done. What I'm doing. What I hope to do. I believe in continuity and organization. I believe in a community of intelligent, responsible citizens, like you and me. So let's all, all go home! *(Pause. She closes her eyes.)* But it's not enough, is it? *(Puts box on table.)* I'm still here. *(Glances off left.)* And he's still there—*(Squints out at the audience.)* And you're still here... *(Perhaps a spot on her now, isolating her as she stands alone. She shields her eyes with her hand, and then suddenly lets her hand drop. She stares out into the light, slowly shaking her head.)* Oh, people—Oh, my friends... *(She lets out her breath in a long sigh.)* Hi. I'm Bunny Stuntz. And you're still here because you want to see the rape—of Bunny Stuntz. *(Pause. Silence. Then, from the left, a key on the end of a cheap, shiny chain is tossed out onto the stage, at her feet. She picks it up and dangles it out in front of the audience.)* See? See, friends? Can everyone see? It's a key. On the end of a chain. Snake-like, ain't it? *(She looks at the key, imitates a housewife in an advertisement.)* A key! Why, Bill, it's just what I needed! I've wanted one for so long. How ever did you guess? It's so smartly styled, so attractively priced! Wait, wait! Let's see whether it works on this exquisite little box I happen to have here— *(She trots to the box, inserts the key, turns it in the lock.)* Well whadya know, gang? The crummy little thing does the trick! *(She holds the box out to the audience, like a priestess, and slowly tips it forward. It is empty.)* Empty. That's also what you wanted, isn't it? *(She puts the box formally on the table, still open. She speaks coldly, bitterly.)* Famous last words now follow: I have been found damned in birth, damned in marriage, damned in my desires...Pray undo this button...It is a far, far better thing I do...Gently, sir, it's mother's day...
(She exits left, walking slowly, like a bride. Immediately, the sound of raucous laughter, as Wilma enters tipsily, carrying a glass of liquor. Howie leaps out at her from stage Right. Both are in disrepair.

WILMA: *(Caught and laughing.)* Howie, now stop it! I'm a married woman!

HOWIE: *(Grabbing her shoulders.)* You threw your doorkey into the center of the room, kid. I got it. See? *(He holds out the key.)*

WILMA: *(Sensuously.)* I know, Howie, but sweetie, that was just a game... *(She glances around.)* Where's Bunny? *(Pause. Wilma peers off left.)* I feel a draught....The outside door is open... *(She slides toward left. Howie watches. From off left, we hear the sound of a car starting and roaring off. Wilma turns to Howie slowly, straightening her dress.)* Bunny Stuntz is dead.

HOWIE: *(After a pause.)* You mean, she's—?

WILMA: *(Holding out her hand for her key.)* Dead. To us.

HOWIE: You mean, just because she's—?

WILMA: *(Holding out her hand.)* Dead. *(Howie drops her key into her hand. Wilma turns to the audience, speaks very efficiently.)* People: I regret to announce that Bunny Stuntz is dead. Now. Well, Howie, run downstairs and tell Marge Jackson to put on her clothes and drink black coffee. Then get on the telephone and call Bill Stuntz. Be tactful, Howie, and understanding. Then tell Doc Feldstein to hightail it over to Bill's with a sedative. *(Howie runs off into audience. Wilma picks up Bunny's box.)* And I think probably the best thing the rest of us can do is to go home calmly and quietly. I'll call you about the next meeting. Anybody who needs a ride come up and speak to me. I've got a large Ford station wagon with a rear seat which faces forward. *(She closes the box efficiently, picks it up along with Bunny's purse, and exits briskly into the audience as the houselights come up.)*

END OF PLAY

The Golden Fleece

A Play in One Act

Here I tried to combine my interest in the modern implications of a classical myth with my continuing need to involve an audience more immediately in an action.

ORIGINAL PRODUCTION

THE GOLDEN FLEECE was first produced in the Albee-Barr-Wilder Playwrights Unit at the Van Daur Theatre in 1967, directed by Jered Barclay. It was subsequently presented at the Mark Taper Forum in Los Angeles in 1968, again directed by Mr. Barclay, with Helen Westcott and Tim O'Connor in the cast.

THE CHARACTERS

BETTY, In her thirties
BILL, In his thirties
Other characters in the audience, if possible.

SETTING

No scenery, except for two chairs which will be brought out by the actors during the course of the play. There may also be an American flag and a plastic potted plant.

The Golden Fleece

While the house lights are still on, Betty and Bill enter up the aisle from the audience. They hang up their coats. Bill stands awkwardly, waiting for Betty, who may be seen just offstage combing her hair. Finally, Betty comes out and takes Bill's arm. Smiles. House lights down, stage lights on. They blink in the light.

BETTY: *(To audience; nervously.)* Tonight…on this stage…we are going to see the Golden Fleece. My husband and I have arranged everything. Jason and Medea will be here, and Jason will display the Fleece and tell us how he got it. And Medea will tell us how he got her.

BILL: And afterwards you can meet them. You can shake Jason's hand.

BETTY: Yes. And you can meet Medea. And you can touch the Golden Fleece.

BILL: They're a little late.

BETTY: Yes.

BILL: *(Softly; to Betty; indicating audience.)* They probably want to know how we arranged this.

BETTY: Yes. *(To audience.)* It took some doing.

BILL: But I sailed with Jason in the Navy.

BETTY: Yes. And I used that—Can you hear us? Out there?

VOICE: Yes, yes, fine.

BETTY: I used that connection to meet Medea.

BILL: And now she's great buddies with Medea.

BETTY: Well, we're friends. She's teaching me how to do pottery.

BILL: Betty brings home some great pots.

BETTY: Well, the point is I like Medea. And one day I said to her, "What about the Fleece, Medea? Could I see the Golden Fleece?" And she smiled mysteriously and said it was up to Jason. So I got Bill to call Jason.

BILL: And Jason laughed and said it was up to Medea.
(Both laugh.)

BETTY: And so then we thought, why not do it up brown? Why not...celebrate it? Why not share it with others, with other friends, with all of you?

BILL: I mean, how many times in your life can you see a Golden Fleece?

BETTY: It's more than that, Bill. It's much more than that. It's that we all...*need* to see it, these days. It will bring back so much that we've forgotten.
(Both begin to talk simultaneously.)

BETTY: And then we fussed about details. I asked Medea how she'd like to do it.

BILL: I told Jason I could show my slides. I've got some great Kodachrome slides of the trip.

BETTY: *(She wins out.)* And I thought maybe Medea would want to show some primitive pottery. Or sing authentic folk songs from her homeland.

BILL: But they both said no.

BETTY: Independently.

BILL: "Keep it simple," said Jason. "Keep it Greek."

BETTY: "Just give us a bare stage," said Medea. "Jason and I will fill it up."

BILL: So we rented this place—

BETTY: And notified all of you—

BILL: And here we are. On this blank stage.

BETTY: Waiting for Jason and Medea, and the Golden Fleece. *(Pause. Then the sound of a telephone ringing. They jump. Quickly.)* That's Jason.

BILL: I'll get it. *(He goes off quickly.)*

BETTY: *(Smiles; a bit nervous; to audience.)* Flat tire, probably. Or traffic. Jason has to drive all the way out from town, pick up Medea in the country, and bring her back in to us. *(Pause.)* You'll get the Fleece tonight. I promise you that. *(Pause.)* Bill and I will show you *some*-thing. If it kills us. *(Bill returns and whispers to her.)* Oh, no. *(Bill whispers.)* Oh, no. *(Bill whispers.)* Oh, I know. Darn it. *(Bill whispers. Irritatedly.)* I know that, Bill! *(To audience.)* Well. There we are. *(Pause.)*

BILL: He wants you to go out and get her.

BETTY: Right now?....*(Remembers audience.)* Oh. I'm sorry. Jason is tied up at work. So—

BILL: Medea's waiting.

BETTY: That's right. She doesn't have a telephone.

BILL: *(To audience; impatiently.)* She doesn't drive...She doesn't have a telephone—

BETTY: She doesn't *want* to drive. She doesn't *want* a telephone.

BILL: So go get her, and bring her in.

BETTY: Yes. All right. Is the Fleece with her?

BILL: I guess so.

BETTY: I'll go get her, then. *(She gets her coat, returns, stops, turns to Bill. He hands her the car keys.)* She's probably crawling up the walls.

BILL: She must be used to this. You know Jason.

BETTY: No, I don't, really. But I know Medea.

BILL: Go. *(She exits briskly, putting on her coat. Bill looks after her, and then looks at the audience. He smiles embarrassedly, and scratches his head. To audience.)* Don't worry. He'll show. He's an old friend. I sailed with him all over the Mediterranean. I was with him when he got the Golden Fleece. *(Pause.)* Oh, I know it's hard to believe now. I'm getting a little bald. I'm getting this gut. Huh, Howard? I wear these civilian clothes. But I was there. I pulled my oar. And then he promoted me to steersman. And so I steered. Right through the Dardanelles. On into the Black Sea. Dark skies. High waves. Shifting winds. But I kept that ship straight, so Jason could find his Fleece. *(Pause.)* You know sometimes when I'm pushing a pencil down at the office, when I'm counting the cash, I think about those days. I can feel that wooden tiller in my hand, and the push of the sea, and I can smell the wind again, and I wish...oh, well, we can't go back, can we? *(Pause.)* But I was good, then. I steered that ship into that dangerous harbor. Without a chart. Without a compass. I slid her right up on the beach. And Jason was standing on the bow, like a figurehead, and he turned to me, and he said, "Good man, Bill. Good man!" before he jumped ashore.

MAN'S VOICE: *(From audience.)* Can I ask a question?

BILL: Shoot.

MAN: Did you actually go ashore with Jason?

BILL: No. I didn't. I stayed with the ship. I had to stand watch. So I waited for Jason, while he explored, just as we're waiting now. Anyway, what was there to see ashore? A hot sun. A lot of gooks dancing around naked. Listen: you people don't know about ships. There's always work to be done on ships. We had to bring her home after all. And so I worked, while Jason looked around. And he showed up, finally. Late. Like now. Running. With Medea on one arm, and the Fleece on the other. But our sails were set, so they jumped aboard, and I had to steer a crazy course as the natives threw spears at us from the shore. But Jason had the Golden Fleece. And Medea.

MAN'S VOICE: Hey, Bill—how did they get the Golden Fleece?

BILL: The Fleece? Oh, I don't know the details. The Fleece came with Medea, that's all I know. She helped him get it, or it helped him get her. The point is, Jason got what he wanted and we brought him home.

(Pause.)

WOMAN'S VOICE: Uh…was there…rape involved?

BILL: Rape? *(He laughs.)* Oh listen, if that was rape, let's have more of it. Medea was crazy about him. We had fair weather all the way home, and Jason and Medea lay in the sun, up forward, on the Golden Fleece, screened by sails. And I swear, you guys, I had the tiller and I swear…that the whole ship shivered when they made love. And it was contagious! Every man on that ship was horny as a toad! And when we got home, why we tore the town apart! There are a lot of girls, a lot of girls, fellas, with bow legs because of that night! *(He laughs.)* Oh, those were the days, men! Those were the…*(Pause.)* Well, then I met Betty. And we got married. *(He points to his wedding ring.)* And Jason stood up with me, and handed me this ring, and now we're both settled down, with homes, and six kids between us. *(Pause.)* So he'll show. *(He looks off.)* And here comes the judge. Here comes the judge.

(Betty comes in quickly, panting.)

BETTY: Get me a chair, please.

BILL: Where's Medea?

BETTY: I'll tell you. Get me a chair. *(Bill goes off. Betty turns to audience.)* I'm exhausted. I'm drained.

(Bill comes back on with a chair. She sits down.)

BILL: Where's Medea?

BETTY: Out in the country. She won't come in. Except with Jason.

BILL: *(Impatiently.)* Jason's tied up.

BETTY: Oh, he's tied up, all right, all right.

BILL: What do you mean?

BETTY: Jason is tied up with a little friend, at the moment.

BILL: A little friend?

BETTY: A cutie pie. A little number. A girl.

BILL: No.

BETTY: Oh, yes. And Medea also said that this girl is not the first.

BILL: Not the first?

BETTY: Not by a long shot. This girl is just the latest of a long, long list.

BILL: Why, that—

BETTY: Oh, yes. This has been going on, with one girl or another, since a year after they were married.

BILL: Why, that son of a—

BETTY: Oh, yes. Jason has come and gone his merry way almost from the beginning. And the Golden Fleece…he's been spending it on other women.

BILL: Why, that son of a gun! *(Pause. He looks at her.)* I never knew that.

BETTY: Nobody knew that. She has never said a word.

BILL: She has never—

BETTY: Said one word. Until tonight.

BILL: She has said plenty to him, I'll bet. Knowing Medea.

BETTY: You don't know Medea. She has never mentioned it to him. She has let him do it.

BILL: She has let him—?

BETTY: Do it.

(Long pause.)

BILL: Think of that…*(To audience.)* Think of that, you guys.

BETTY: *(Sarcastically, to audience.)* Oh, yes! Think of that, you girls. *(She looks at Bill.)* And then start thinking about the Golden Fleece.

BILL: But it's…gone now.

BETTY: It has not gone. It is torn a little. It is tarnished a little. But it is still there, I'm convinced of it. And we're going to see it.

BILL: But how?

BETTY: Now, Bill, let me think. *(Pause; she thinks.)* Don't you see what's going on?

BILL: No.

BETTY: I do…I'm beginning to see it all…I think Jason and Medea have decided to…test each other.

BILL: Test?

BETTY: Exactly. Test. Each other. Through us. We are the audience, and they want us to witness a huge—test.

BILL: You've lost me, Betty.

BETTY: No. No, listen. *(To audience.)* Listen, everybody. I think…Jason was purposely late. I think…he wants us to know he's got a girl. He is spreading his tail like a peacock!

BILL: Oh, Betty—

BETTY: Yes, yes. And Medea was waiting for me, Bill! She knew I'd come. *(To audience.)* Oh, I think we've started something here, people. I think we've started a mating dance between two great whooping cranes!

BILL: And what happens next?

BETTY: It's obvious. Jason must get her, and bring her in. To us.

BILL: Which means—

BETTY: No more girls! She is calling his bluff…of course! Medea wants a new marriage, in public, in front of all of us. She wants Jason to stand beside her, with the Fleece between them, and declare proudly and publicly that he'll cherish her from this day forward! *(Triumphantly; to audience.)* Oh, that's it, people!

BILL: Jason won't buy that.

BETTY: Of course he will. He wants her to take a stand. And she's taken it. And here we are.

(Pause.)

BILL: *(Carefully.)* Who tells Jason to get Medea?

BETTY: You do, darling.

BILL: Forget it.

BETTY: I promised Medea you would.

BILL: I'm not going to get caught in the middle of this.

BETTY: But we're messengers, Bill.

BILL: *(Whispering angrily.)* I do that at work. I don't do it here.

BETTY: *(Smiling.)* Do it, Bill.

BILL: What would I say to the guy?

BETTY: You say, "Jason, go home."

BILL: Like a flunkey—

BETTY: Like a friend.

BILL: We're not friends.

BETTY: He was your best man!

BILL: We've grown apart.

BETTY: *He's* grown apart. You've stayed *with* it. Be his steersman, again, and steer him home. *(Indicates the audience.)* Look! here's your ship. We're all aboard. And Jason and Medea are the mainstay! If those two big beautiful people can't make it, then we'll all go under. So take the helm, Bill.

BILL: *(After a pause.)* Why do I always have to steer?

BETTY: It's your job, Bill. Now, come on. Anchors aweigh, Bill. Please.

BILL: Where is he?

BETTY: At the Downtown Motel. *(She hands him the car keys. Bill gets his coat, and starts off. She calls after him.)* Hey! *(He stops. She goes to him and gives him a big kiss, and then smiles at the audience.)*

BILL: Wow. *(He looks at the audience embarrassedly.)*

BETTY: That was just so you'll come back, sailor.

BILL: I'll be back. Grrr. *(He exits. She watches him go, and then turns toward the audience and sits down.)*

BETTY: *(Sighing.)* Medea, Medea, Medea...I am fascinated by that woman...I've known her all these years, and she has never mentioned this thing about Jason. She has kept it all to herself...Why? She worships Jason. She gave up everything for him. She was a princess, or something, in the old country, and she gave it all up, for him. The Fleece was hers, you know. Oh yes, it was her Fleece. And when she saw Jason with his blond hair and jaunty ways, why, she just handed it over to him, and they sailed away. She doesn't hear a word from home now. Nothing. Jason is all she has...Jason and the children.

WOMAN'S VOICE: *(From the audience.)* Betty, it sounds as though she's pretty content with Jason.

BETTY: Yes. I think that's right. I think that's why she bought that place out there in the country. To be alone with him. She won't even come in for dinner. Crabmeat casserole? That's not for Medea.

WOMAN: What do you do with Medea?

BETTY: *(Cups her ear.)* Me? Oh well. I go out there during the day. When Jason's not home. I love it actually. I...need it, really. Whenever I get fed to the *teeth* with all...this stuff...whenever the children get me down...why, then I just throw them in the car, and out we go, out to Medea's. And my kids play with her kids. And Medea and I do pottery. I just sink my fingers into that dark, red, wet clay. And then I watch it spin round and round on a wheel, and I pat it and poke it like mad, and I never know how it will come out...But there's always a shape. I must have shapes. *(Pause.)* Oh, she's got acres of land out there, and deep woods, and a barn, and animals, and a vegetable garden. And she handles it all herself. She makes blankets from the sheep's wool, and cans vegetables, and makes her own special cider from the apple orchard. Oh, it's wonderful, out there. Every season is different. It's not like…this.

Woman: Do you and Medea talk?

BETTY: *(Cups her ear.)* Do we talk? Why of course we talk…Or at least I do. Medea listens. The children play in the barn, and Medea and I sit by the fire, and she gives me a hot glass of cider, and I chatter away, just as I'm chattering now. And she…listens. So carefully, people. And she nods so…knowingly. There are things going on behind her dark eyes…I envy the woman, that's all. I envy her. She's…in touch with something we'll never touch. *(Pause; then quickly and brightly.)* Oh, I forgot. I have Medea's children. Yes. When I was out there, she insisted I take them. She had them all ready. *(Pause.)* I…don't know why exactly. She was adamant about it. *(Pause; then smiles.)* Yes I do know. Tonight she wants a second honeymoon. She wants the children out of the way. *(Pause.)* So we've got them. My mother is sitting for the whole tribe. I put them in our bed. Bill and I can sleep on the couch. It's the least we can do for Jason and Medea. *(She looks off.)* Ah! Home is the sailor, home from the sea…

(Bill comes back on. He whistles "Anchors Aweigh." His tie is loose. Pause.)

BILL: *(A little defiantly.)* Jason is going away with her.

BETTY: What? With Medea?

BILL: With the girl. With that gorgeous girl.

BETTY: Well, *go on*, for heaven sake! Tell!

BILL: I went to the Downtown Motel. I knocked. He opened the door immediately. *(Pause.)* He expected me.

BETTY: You see? He knew!

BILL: Oh, sure. He knew I'd show up. He knew what I'd say. And after I said it, he knew what to do. He picked up the telephone, and got two tickets on the night flight to Los Angeles.

BETTY: To Los Angeles?

BILL: He'll fly into the sun. With that golden girl.

BETTY: Why, that no-good—

BILL: Hold it!

BETTY: I said, that lousy, no-good—

BILL: I said hold it! *(Pause; then Betty smiles sweetly.)*

BETTY: You've been drinking.

BILL: Jason and I had a drink together, yes.

BETTY: Where? In some bar? Oh, I can see it. Palsy-walsy, buddy-buddy. Old Navy days in some bar. While we all waited here.

BILL: No. We had a drink in the motel room. All of us.
(Pause.)

BETTY: All of you? All? You drank with that girl?

BILL: We all sat on the bed and drank.
(Pause.)

BETTY: Perhaps you'd like to sit again. *(Indicates offstage.)* Out there. Where you can pull yourself together.

BILL: *(Through a grin.)* I'll sit when I want to sit.
(Pause. They look at each other.)

BETTY: *(To audience; through her teeth.)* I could kill that Jason. I could throttle him!

BILL: *(To audience.)* Jason is a good man.

BETTY: *(To audience.)* Jason is not a good man.

BILL: *(To audience.)* Jason is a great man.

BETTY: *(To audience.)* Jason is a big, fat stinker!

BILL: *(Wheeling on her, threateningly.)* Watch it, kid. You're talking about my best friend.
(Pause. She looks at him, sighs, and goes to her chair. She sits down and closes her eyes and folds her hands on her lap.)

BETTY: *(Quietly; sarcastically; eyes closed.)* Sweetheart...

BILL: *(Equally sarcastic.)* Yes, darling...

BETTY: Sweetheart, I wonder if you'd say why you think your good friend Jason is such a good man. Do you think you could do that for the group, dear?

BILL: Sure. *(He turns and immediately walks out. She opens her eyes and sees that he is gone. She jumps up, panicky. He returns immediately, carrying a chair. He sets it up a distance away from her chair. Both sit down. Pause.)* Why I think Jason is a good man...

BETTY: Yes, dear. Jason. You know. The one who is leaving his family in the lurch.

BILL: Oh, *that* Jason.

BETTY: Yes, that one. Your best friend Jason.

BILL: Ah. Now I remember: I only spent a relatively short time with Jason.

BETTY: Yes. Sitting on a bed with some babe. Yes.

BILL: Yes. We just hacked around. You know.

BETTY: Yes. I know. And it was all just a little bit out of your league. Wasn't it?

BILL: Maybe...But I learned one thing.

BETTY: And what's that?

BILL: I learned that Jason is one helluva lot like me.

(Pause.)

BETTY: Why is Jason running out on Medea?

BILL: Because she's forcing him to.

BETTY: She's forcing him to choose.

BILL: He doesn't want to choose.

BETTY: Well, he's got to.

BILL: So he's chosen.

BETTY: Some babe.

BILL: A gorgeous girl!

BETTY: He doesn't love Medea!

BILL: Sure he does.

BETTY: He doesn't love his children!

BILL: Sure he does.

BETTY: I don't believe that.

BILL: He does. And he loves the girl. And he'll love Los Angeles.

BETTY: Then I don't know what love means!

BILL: I do. And so does Jason.

(Long pause.)

BETTY: *(Getting up.)* Well. We're out of it now.

BILL: You think so?

BETTY: Oh, yes. We've done what we can. The rest is up to them.

BILL: We're not out of it, baby.

BETTY: Oh, yes, oh, yes.

BILL: Oh, no...Go tell Medea!

(Pause.)

BETTY: Jason will tell Medea.

BILL: No, he won't.

BETTY: Then he's a coward.

BILL: Your turn, baby.

BETTY: No.

BILL: I told Jason you would.

BETTY: I won't.

BILL: We threw the ball in, kid. Let's keep it going.

BETTY: I'm frightened.

BILL: Of Medea?

BETTY: No...Yes...You don't know her.

BILL: Ah, but you do. She's your best friend.

BETTY: No, no, she isn't. Not really. I don't know what she'll do.

BILL: Go find out.

BETTY: Bill, I want to stop this.

BILL: Stop? Now?

BETTY: Yes. I want to stop. I want to go home.

BILL: To do what?

BETTY: Bill, we're in this over our heads now. It's none of our beeswax now. I—I think we did some good, actually. We—brought things to a boil. And now our job, it seems to me, is to get out of it, and stay out of it.

BILL: *(Sarcastically.)* But we're messengers, Betty!

BETTY: No, Bill, no, I...don't like it here. It's...empty up here. *(She looks at him.)* Bill, what I thought we'd do is...call it a day...We'll join all our friends... *(Indicates audience.)* at Howard Johnson's or something...and then, Bill, when we get home...I'll give you a glass of Ovaltine, and a piece of cherry pie, just the way I used to when we were first married. Remember that, Bill?

BILL: Yeah, I remember—

BETTY: So I'll give you that, and then we'll... *(Smiles at the audience.)* just go to bed. Hmmmmm? Hmm. Bill?

BILL: *(Weakening.)* You mean, just—

BETTY: Go to bed. And we can sleep late in the morning, Bill, because Mother's there, and she'll get up the—*(Pause; thinks.)* We'll move Medea's children down to the couch.

BILL: Medea's children?

BETTY: She asked me to take them.

BILL: Medea's children are now in our bed?

BETTY: They will be on the couch.

BILL: *(Exploding.)* Children in my bed! Always some goddam kid in my bed! Diapers in the john! Toys on the stairs! Food on the floor! Cats crapping in the fireplace! Dogs barfing on the rug!

BETTY: *(Very quietly.)* What...exactly...are you talking about?

BILL: I'm talking about children in my bed! I'm talking about greasy hotdogs, and spilled milk, and a decibel level beyond human tolerance! I'm talking about a broken stereo set, and stacks of doctor's bills, and crumby crayoned pictures all over the goddam white walls!

BETTY: *(Grimly.)* You are talking about your home.

BILL: *(Grimly.)* Yes, I am.

BETTY: I take it you don't like your home.

BILL: Not at the moment. *(Pause.)* I like it here. *(Pause.)* I can breathe here. *(Pause.)* I can talk here. I can hear myself think. *(Pause.)* There's nothing on the floor, here, to trip me up. *(He begins to move around the stage in a sort of shuffle.)* There are no tinker toys here…*(Moves more easily.)* No tricycles…No erector sets to gouge my shins and tear my pants. *(He lifts his feet.)* No silly putty ground into the rug! *(He looks down.)* No crumby homemade pottery! *(He pantomimes kicking a pot out at the audience.)* Crash! *(He dances.)* I'm free here. It's the wide-open spaces. I can do anything I want here. I can be the fastest gun in the West! *(He pantomimes shooting her.)* Save the last bullets for the women and children!…Or d'Artagnan! *(He pantomimes a sword fight, almost cutting off her head.)* "Monday, Monday…Tuesday, Tuesday…Wednesday, Wednesday…" *(He ends with a big finish. She looks at him and slowly turns toward the audience.)*

BETTY: That was…lovely. *(Pauses; she holds out her hand.)* Keys, please! *(He makes her grope for them in his pockets. When she gets them, he gooses her.)* I will now take Medea's children back to their mother.

BILL: Yes. Do that.

BETTY: I will wake those poor children, who have already been awakened once tonight, and I will bundle them into the car, and take them to Medea.

BILL: Good. Fine. Get them out of my bed. And change the sheets, will you!

BETTY: Those children will need a mother now. They will need all the mothering they can get now—

BILL: *(Shouting.)* Can't even get a good night's sleep!

BETTY: And Medea will want her children now. She'll want them home. I will tell Medea—

BILL: Tell her that Jason is goddam tired of finding children in his bed, and so he's flying away with a beautiful girl into the Golden West!

BETTY: *No I will not tell Medea that!* I will tell her that she is *lucky!* Lucky because she is free. Free to start a new life with the children. A life where she doesn't have to worry about some stupid, idiot *Man!*

BILL: Good! Tell her that!

BETTY: I will also tell her to hold Jason up for everything he's got! She gave up everything for him. Now let him cough up for her. And for the children. Oh, Medea is a lucky lady! She's going to be free, free, free! *(She starts off.)*

BILL: Jason too, baby! Jason too!

BETTY: *(Wheeling on him.)* Oh, no! Not Jason! This is going to cost him the whole goddam Golden Fleece! *(She strides out.)*

BILL: *(Calling after her.)* You don't know what the Fleece is, kid! *(Pause; he looks at the audience.)* I do. I've just seen it. *(He comes downstage, determinedly.)* And I'll tell you about it! *(He shields his eyes and looks out.)* This is for the men. You women can shove off. Go home to the kiddies. This is going to be much too raunchy for you. *(Pause.)* This is stag, girls. Scram, please. *(Pause; presumably the women don't go.)* O.K. Stick around, then. Don't say I didn't warn you. *(Pause.)* Anyway, you girls won't understand this. Only men will understand this. So here goes, fellas. I'll tell you about the Golden Fleece…He met me at the door. And get this: he just had a towel around him. So I said I'd wait outside. "Hell no," said Jason. "Come on in." And he gave me a great big bear hug for old time's sake. And I could feel his beard—he wears a beard again—I could feel it against my cheek. *(Looks out; points his finger.)* I know what you're going to say, buddy. It was nothing like that. It was hearty, man to man. Like a huddle in a football game. So I went in. *(Refuses another question.)* Hold your water, fella. I'm getting to her…She was in the bed. Jason introduced me to her, and when she held out her hand, the sheet fell away and I could see two of the biggest, most beautiful…I mean, there they *were!* Just winking and blinking at me, and she didn't even bother to cover them up! So I just stood there, slowly shaking her hand, and trying not to look at those two, big, soft, pink *breasts!*

MAN'S VOICE: *(From audience.)* Hey, Bill, how old was she?

BILL: About twenty-two or three. *(Pause.)* Blonde hair. Long and blonde. Sort of in her eyes. Which were blue. Got the picture? O.K. *(He takes a deep breath.)* So. Jason broke out the Scotch, and we all sat on the bed and had a drink. I felt like a visiting minister sitting there with my legs crossed, holding a glass in my hot little hand, trying to keep my beady little eyes away from those bazoolis. I mean, they were still un*covered*, guys! But after a while, I felt easy. We sat and talked about everything under the sun. And…they were like two kids, laughing at everything, and pretty soon I was laughing too, and the girl, when she laughed, why her boobies jiggled up and down like they were beckoning me, saying come and get it, and I just wanted to reach over and grab them, and then by golly, I *did!* And we all laughed all the more.

WOMAN: Did you bother to mention Medea?

BILL: *(Grimly.)* Yes, madam, I did. I mentioned Medea. *(Pause.)* And oh, boy, did that put a damper on things. *(Pause.)* Jason just looked at his drink. The girl pulled the sheet up to her chin. It was very quiet. And then Jason got up, and called the airlines, and got two tickets for Los Angeles. *(Pause.)* And then suddenly we were all laughing again, and then— *(Pause.)* I don't know whether to tell you this part or not. *(Pause.)* I wish you women would get the hell out. *(Pause.)* Never mind. It will do you good. O.K. So we got Medea off our back, and we were hacking around, and suddenly I got the urge to take off my clothes. So I did. I got up. And I took off my clothes! Yessir! Every stitch. And they cheered, those two! They applauded, Jason and his girl! And Jason put a record on his portable, and we all danced, naked as jaybirds, drunk as skunks, we all danced to the Mamas and the Papas... *(He sings "Monday, Monday..." and then he stops.)* And then I remembered this little gold ring on my finger. *(Pause.)* And I thought of my wife. *(Pause.)* And my kids. *(Pause.)* And all of you, sitting here. *(Pause.)* So I got dressed. I said goodbye. I shook hands. I took one last little squeeze of those... *(Pause.)* And I left. *(He looks longingly off right.)* And I guess they're still there. Those two blond beautiful naked people. Dancing to the Mamas and Papas. Waiting to fly to Los Angeles.

(Betty comes on from the left. She carries a bulky bag. She looks at him coldly, and turns to the audience.)

BETTY: I've told Medea everything. She is sending this bag to the girl.

BILL: What is it? A bomb?

BETTY: *(Not looking at him; grimly patient.)* No. It is not a bomb. It is a dress. *(She opens the bag, holds out the dress; it is long, reddish-gold, luxurious, menacing.)* Medea is sending this dress to Jason's girl.

BILL: I don't get it.

BETTY: No. You don't. *(To audience.)* Medea was waiting for me, of course. She knew I'd bring back the children. She hugged them wildly. And then she took them into her bedroom, and came back with this dress. It's her native costume. She wore it when she sailed away with Jason. And now she wants the girl to wear it.

BILL: Oh, come off it.

BETTY: You don't understand.

BILL: No, I don't.

BETTY: You don't, because you're a man. We women understand. Every woman here understands.

BILL: And every man here doesn't.

BETTY: *(With a sigh.)* Ladies: Medea wants to say something with this dress. To me, and to the girl, and to all women everywhere. *(She holds it in front of her own body.)*

BILL: Could you—uh—translate it? Into words? for us guys?

BETTY: *(With a patient sigh.)* Medea is saying—how would you men put it?—"Welcome to the Club?" She is saying that Jason—men—don't really count. She is saying that what counts, in the end, is this old, old dress...which has come all the way across the sea from Medea's dark homeland. And which will go all the way across this land to sunny California. And it connects all us women, across all the distance. It binds, it ties together Medea, and me, and the girl, more than marriage ever could. *(She holds it out to the audience.)* This is the Golden Fleece, really. This is the important thing.

BILL: I see—

BETTY: No, you don't see. Because it can't be seen. *(She puts it carefully back in the bag.)* It's something to feel. And men can't feel it.

BILL: *(He glances off right; then he looks at his wedding ring. Rubbing the ring.)* So this little ring...doesn't mean much?

BETTY: *(Patting the bag.)* Not compared to this.

BILL: *(Glances off right again; starts to sing softly.)* "Monday, Monday..." *(He looks at Betty. Then he takes off his ring, holds it up to his eyes, and squints at her through it.)* Silly little things...these rings....

BETTY: *(Carefully.)* Oh, they have their uses...They're insurance, after all. *(She looks at him.)* They guarantee support. No matter what. *(Long pause.)*

BILL: Well, I'll take that package on over.

BETTY: I'll do it.

BILL: *(Reaching for it.)* It's my job.

BETTY: *(Holding onto it.)* Oh, no. This is woman's work.

BILL: *(Tugging at it.)* I said—

BETTY: I said *No!*

BILL: *(Poking her with his finger.)* That motel is my territory, baby.

BETTY: I promised...*(Poking him back.)* Medea!

BILL: *(Poking her harder.)* Jason's my best friend!

BETTY: Medea is mine!

(With a sudden lunge, she straight-arms him, and starts running off with the bag. He grabs her, and lifts her up; she kicks and struggles. She lands an effective kick, and starts off again. He tackles her. She falls on the floor. He pins her like a wrestler. Then he looks up with horror at the audience, letting go of her arms. She smacks him on the head with the bag. He twists her nose. She smacks him. Pause. Both pant. He lets her go and gets up. She extends her hand feebly. He helps her up. She lets him have it in the gut. He moves toward her, fist raised. She retreats. He slugs her, grabs the bag, and starts out.)

BILL: I'm going to Los Angeles. *(He storms out.)*

BETTY: *(Shrieking after him.)* I'm moving in with Medea! *(She rubs her jaw. She looks at the audience.)* No, no. I'm all right. Keep your seats, please. Keep your *seats!* I said I'm all *right,* thank you. *(She gets to her feet, panting.)* I'm fine. *(She staggers a little.)* I'm perfectly fine. He didn't hurt me. He's too *weak!*...That does it, of course. *(She shouts off.)* That does it, buster! *(She throws her coat onto the floor.)* I'm moving in with Medea! I'm taking the children, and out we go! Tonight! We'll sleep in the barn. If anyone else wants to come, she's welcome. Any woman, any mother, is welcome out there with Medea! Come on! And bring the children! *(Looks out.)* Oh, you're so wrong, lady! Children do not need fathers! What is a father these days? What does he do? Does he teach them how to hunt? Does he show them how to plow? Where is he, most of the time? Gone! Out of it! As that father...*(She points off.)* is out of it now!...This, this is your life girls! This! Right here. This bleak, barren stage, halfway between Jason and Medea, where we stand around trying to explain ourselves! Oh, let's go back to Medea where we belong! *(Her eyes dart around the audience.)* Oh, I know what you're going to say! *(Sarcastically.)* We mustn't forget schools! *(Vehemently.)* Well, the hell with schools! The hell with those smelly buses, and that crazy arithmetic, and all those sappy things they learn about American democracy! We'll run our own schools out at Medea's. We'll teach them farming and animal husbandry. They'll learn how to sink some roots in the ground. They'll see lambs born. They'll get milk from cows, and eggs from the chickens, and fresh peas from the pea patch! And at night, when they're asleep, all together, all in the hay, we women will churn butter, and spin wool, and Medea will tell us old folk tales around the fire. *(She smiles.)* And men can come to Medea's. Not husbands. Men. Visiting hours will be at night, in the spring. We'll meet you in the fields, in the woods, in the barn, and we'll never see your faces, or your silly bodies! Oh yes, we'll have men. Any men, all men. Black men, white men, old men, young men. Come, and then go! And that's all I have to say about men! *(She comes close to the edge of the stage, croons to the audience.)* But women! My women! Come with me to Medea. Wake the children. Wrap them in swaddling clothes. Lay them in the manger, among the cattle and sheep, and we'll all begin again...

(Bill comes on slowly from the right. Betty sees him, turns heel, and starts out, grimly.)

BILL: *(Quietly.)* Jason has gone back to Medea.

(Pause. Betty comes back on.)

BETTY: I don't believe that. That's not true.

BILL: *(Grimly patient, to audience.)* Jason has gone back to Medea.

BETTY: If Jason crawled back on his hands and knees, he'd get—nothing! Let him stay with his girl.

BILL: There's no girl now.

BETTY: No girl?

BILL: *(Looking at her.)* The girl is out of it.

BETTY: Did she wear the dress?

BILL: Yes.

BETTY: Then why—?

BILL: I don't know.

BETTY: *(Grimly.)* The suspense is killing me.

BILL: *(To audience.)* I took the dress to the girl. She laughed, and wanted to try it on. As a joke. But Jason took it away from her.

BETTY: He probably wanted to try it on himself.

BILL: *(Ignoring her.)* The girl insisted.

BETTY: She had to wear it.

BILL: She tried it on. She slipped it over her head, holding up her arms, and as it slid down, I took one last look... *(He turns defiantly to Betty.)* at her beautiful breasts.

BETTY: *(Very calmly.)* Oh, I'm sure. *(To audience.)* He sneaks into porno movies during his lunch hour.

BILL: Once!

BETTY: *(She holds up three fingers to the audience.)* Go on about the dress, dear.

BILL: *(With a grim sigh.)* When she got the dress on, Jason just stood and stared at her.

BETTY: Because she looked so lovely.

BILL: She looked like Medea!

BETTY: Exactly! Oh, I knew it!

BILL: Jason shouted at her: "Take it off! Take the goddam thing off!"

BETTY: Because he remembered Medea!

BILL: But the girl panicked. She couldn't get it off.

BETTY: Because it fit too well!

BILL: Her hair got caught in the zipper, and she writhed and struggled as if the dress were on fire—

BETTY: Medea's dress!

BILL: And Jason tried to pull it off. And the girl lost her balance. They rolled on the floor, the girl clawing at the dress, Jason pulling at it, and she was screaming at him, and he hit her—hard—and then she lay still. And he ripped the dress off her, and walked out of the motel. The girl lay there, shivering. I threw a blanket over her. And came back here. And Jason went back to Medea.

BETTY: Because—

BILL: Because she has the Golden Fleece.

BETTY: *(Triumphantly.)* Ah, I knew it, I knew it! The dress did it! Medea was telling him, with the dress, that he'll always fall in love with the same woman! It's always Medea! *(To audience.)* Oh, haven't you seen it? The second wife just like the first. It's the old story...*(She turns back to Bill.)* So he's gone home! For the Golden Fleece! Which is their old love.

(Pause.)

BILL: I don't think so.

BETTY: Oh, yes. The Golden Fleece is their old love!

BILL: I don't think so.

(Pause.)

BETTY: *(Carefully.)* What do you think, then? What is the Golden Fleece? To you?

BILL: The children.

BETTY: The children?

BILL: Those golden-haired kids. *(Carefully.)* They're what it's all about, I think.

BETTY: Jason loves—

BILL: His children.

BETTY: *(Shaking her head.)* He's never shown it.

BILL: He will now. He remembered them.

BETTY: And he remembered Medea.

BILL: A little.

BETTY: And he loves Medea.

BILL: He'll live with Medea.

BETTY: And love her.

BILL: *(Shaking his head.)* Not in the old way.

BETTY: Why not?

BILL: Because he's changed since then.

BETTY: More girls?

BILL: More life.

BETTY: Medea wants all or nothing.

BILL: Jason wants…more.

BETTY: Then he doesn't belong at home.
      (Pause.)

BILL: Then he'll see the kids on weekends.

BETTY: Oh, no.

BILL: He has a father's right.

BETTY: And she has a mother's.

BILL: He has the law.

BETTY: What law?

BILL: He gets them in the summer.

BETTY: *(Contemptuously.)* Oh, that law.

BILL: He'll take those kids.

BETTY: Steal them? Kidnap them?

BILL: To a new life.

BETTY: He's too old.

BILL: Younger than you think.

BETTY: Then Medea has another law. She'll teach the children to hate
      him.
      (Pause.)

BILL: She wouldn't do that.

BETTY: You don't know Medea. *(Pause; the sudden sound a telephone ring-ing.)* Ah. There's your pal. Calling from the neighbors' to tell you that
      all's well.

BILL: He wants me to meet him at the airport. He'll have his kids.
      (More ringing.)

BETTY: He's coming here with Medea to prove his love.
      (More ringing.)

BILL: What Jason does, I'll do.

BETTY: Fair enough. The same with me and Medea. *(More ringing. He exits. She comes downstage; to audience.)* Medea will forgive and forget. Because she's a big woman. Oh, there will be...tension. I admit that. The children will suffer, for a while. Their marks will go down, and they'll act up. But at least they will sleep in their own beds all night long. *(Pause; she smiles.)* And when we're sixty we'll talk about all this. And laugh.

(Bill comes on. He stares at Betty blankly.)

BILL: That was the police. *(Pause.)* Medea has killed her children. *(Pause.)* She was waiting for Jason at the door. *(Pause.)* She shot them down, like animals, before his eyes. *(Pause.)* The police asked if we knew why. *(Pause.)* Do we?

BETTY: *(Backing away. She doubles up for a scream, then shakes her head, speaks very quietly.)* I hardly know that woman!

(She straightens up. He takes her arm. They exit slowly through the audience, unable even to say good-bye.)

END OF PLAY

The David Show

A Play in One Act

Turning from Greek myths to the Bible, I here tried to say something about contemporary politics and the television medium. I'm not sure I knew enough about either.

Original Production

THE DAVID SHOW was originally produced as a two-act play at the Players Theatre in New York City in November of 1969. It had Tom Keena, Jay Barney, Holland Taylor, Glenn Keher, Ira Lewis, and Milton Earl Forrest in the cast, and was directed by Ben Tarver. It was reviewed as a one-act on a double bill with THE GOLDEN FLEECE the following year, this time directed by Jered Barclay, with a different cast, except for Ms. Taylor. The evening was entitled THOUGHT IN LIVING COLOR and opened at the Actor's Playhouse on Sheridan Square.

The Characters

SAMUEL
DAVID
SAUL
JONATHAN
HAM
BATHSHEBA

The David Show

The play takes place in a television studio. The control booth is on the right. There are various lights, monitors, cameras, cables, and other equipment distributed around, all focused on a throne upstage, on some steps. Behind the throne are two crossed and tasseled flags: The Stars and Stripes, and a white flag with a gold Star of David on it. To the left is a prop table, covered by a dust cloth. After the audience is seated and the house lights dim, we hear a voice over a loudspeaker.

VOICE: All right. That's one hour. Exactly. No Metzo-Metzo. Let us push, but not hurry. *(Samuel enters: a dignified old man with an interdenominational priest's stole over his suit. He blinks in the bright lights, peering out at the audience.)* Hey, Frank. Pick up on five-five. Look, if we…
(Voice fades out. Samuel addresses the audience directly.)
SAMUEL: Ah, good. You're here. I'm Samuel. A prophet of God. And frankly I'm not used to this. I belong in the temple. I crowned King Saul in the temple. In candlelight. With incense. And the music of the psalms. But David wants me to crown him here. Here, in this…television studio. Under these hot lights. In this make-up. In this costume. Because David doesn't like the temple. Too many shadows and echoes and reverberations, David says. So here we are. And we'll have to make the most of it. *(He glances offstage.)* David is in his dressing room, conferring with his staff, preparing for this run-through. Yes. David wants me to run through it. In an hour, when the technical people get back from their dinner break, they will tape us. And tomorrow night, when all the bugs are out of us, they will send us into every home in the country. David will be crowned king

on every channel, edited down to perfection. And all you can do then is watch. But you can do more tonight. Because tonight David must fight a battle. And that's why I'm glad you're here. He must do it…what's his word…"live." Yes. Face to face. Yes. In front of you, the Chosen Few, the Children of Israel. So I'm counting on you to stay with me, Samuel, your prophet. Stay with me here, even here, even in this wilderness, among these machines. For he hath prepared his throne for judgment, and we shall judge him. And we must take this David, David, the Elected One, and turn him into a king, even in an hour.

(David's voice is heard over a speaker.)

DAVID'S VOICE: Ah, Samuel…

SAMUEL: *(Confused; looking around.)* Ah, David…

DAVID'S VOICE: Are you at home out there now? Can you see, old friend?

SAMUEL: I can see, young friend.

DAVID: *(Entering.)* So can I…Who's out there? *(Calling offstage.)* Hey! This was supposed to be closed! Only staff, and a few friends!

SAMUEL: *(Indicating audience.)* These are friends, David…

DAVID: I know my friends…*(Peering out, but all smiles.)* I see strangers out there.

SAMUEL: These are your constituents, David. I told the door people to let them in.

DAVID: *(Looking at him.)* You told—

SAMUEL: Shall I tell them to go? Shall I tell them you prefer secrecy?

DAVID: *(Hastily.)* No! *(Suddenly, brightly.)* Let them stay.

SAMUEL: *(To audience.)* You may stay.

DAVID: Yes…Because we're all friends here tonight. *(To audience.)* Friends: When I was elected king, and I had to make a decision about the crowning, I said to myself, "Who else but Samuel?" *(Feelingly; hand on Samuel's shoulder.)* You're the custodian of the past, old friend. You're the last of the Mohicans.

SAMUEL: Thank you, David.

DAVID: Yessir. You crowned Saul. You'll crown me, by God…Well. Now to work. *(All business.)* We have one hour, Samuel. Repeat, one hour until the union comes back from their break. My lighting man and my sound man have stayed on, thank God. And my staff is in the conference room working on my crowning speech. But that's it. Frank, turn on monitor two. Good. So, we're on our own, old friend, until dress rehearsal. And these good people—

SAMUEL: The Children of Israel—

DAVID: *(Beaming.)* Ahh. The Children of Israel! Well, the Children of Israel will be patient with us, I'm sure, as we work out the bugs.

SAMUEL: I'm counting on them to be patient.

DAVID: *(After a glance at him.)* Yes. So let's give them a show, Samuel. But let's do it tastefully. Nothing brassy. Now…I thought…The cameras will…slowly…dolly in…on me…kneeling…*(He kneels.)* And you standing beside me. Frank, give me my light. *(Samuel does.)* And a little in back…*(Samuel steps back.)* And we are praying. To the God of our own choice. *(Both pray.)* Yes. And after that, you turn slowly and walk majestically up right—over there—Do it, Samuel.… *(Samuel starts.)* The camera will follow you to that table… Good…Stop, turn—Good—There's your mark! and let the camera take in those various artifacts. Remember? Those are the things I've been associated with, over the years.

SAMUEL: *(Removing the cover of the table.)* These are your props.

DAVID: Well, yes—

SAMUEL: And I hold up your props, one by one, and identify them.

DAVID: Yes! Exactly.

SAMUEL: All right…*(To audience, removing the dust cloth on the prop table.)* Children of Israel: behold the props of David's past! *(We see a small harp, a sling, a spear.)*

DAVID: The memorabilia of my past, I think. Memorabilia is better.

SAMUEL: *(Intoning, holding them up, one by one.)* The sling he used when he was a shepherd…The harp he played so sweetly for Saul…And the spear Saul gave him when he found favor in Saul's sight…

DAVID: Yes. Good. Now you move toward the throne…

SAMUEL: Yes. Oh David, such a story goes with these—memorabilia.

DAVID: *(Modestly.)* A very simple story, actually.

SAMUEL: On the contrary, on the contrary. A very complicated story. *(Pause.)* I should tell your story.

DAVID: *(Smiling.)* They've heard it, Samuel.

SAMUEL: But they should hear it again and again…Because it always says something new.

DAVID: *(Getting up on one knee.)* What would you say?

SAMUEL: I'd say that in the beginning, God created a little shepherd with a big dream.

DAVID: Yes. Good. Because I did dream. I dreamed of fighting a great battle with some huge giant, and killing him with my sling.

SAMUEL: But you never did.

DAVID: *(Laughing.)* Giants are kind of hard to find these days.

SAMUEL: I'd say this sling is just a toy.

DAVID: Oh, it taught me to be patient. While I waited.

SAMUEL: Waited for what?

DAVID: The call. To leave the farm.

SAMUEL: Which you did. Immediately.

DAVID: Of course. God called me.

SAMUEL: Moses said, "Why me?"

DAVID: That's because Moses lived in the days when God called ambiguously. Through fires and from high mountains.

SAMUEL: But God called clearly to you.

DAVID: Yes! And he calls clearly to every young man who takes the time to listen. God spoke to me on a sunny day in a flat pasture in Bethlehem. He advised me to get a good education. He urged me to find my slot in life. He encouraged me to shoot for the top. And that's what I've done. God helps those who help themselves. *(Pause.)* There's my story, Samuel. And you're welcome to tell it on television.

SAMUEL: Have you thought of Norman Vincent Peale?

DAVID: I want you, Samuel.

SAMUEL: Thank you, David.

DAVID: Good, fine. *(He resumes kneeling.)* Then after your little speech, you move slowly to the throne…Camera 2 follows you…good…and the incumbent will be sitting there…Save the lights, Frank. *(Calls off right.)* We're ready for Saul now! Ham! Ham! *(Ham comes on, a Negro.)* We're ready for Saul, Ham! He should be in the costume room. *(Ham nods and exits slowly.)*

SAMUEL: *(To audience.)* Ham works for David.

DAVID: *(To audience.)* And I work for Ham…Now, Samuel, you slowly take the crown off the head of King Saul.

SAMUEL: I crowned Saul in the temple…I hate to uncrown him here.

DAVID: The Lord moves in strange and devious ways, Samuel.

SAMUEL: I hope so, David.

(Voices and noise offstage: "Saul…Here's the king…" Clatter as if something was broken. Then Saul backs on, middle-aged, heavy, red-faced, explosive. He wears an elaborate breastplate, and a crown. He stops and rubs his eyes futilely in the bright light.)

SAUL: Jesus Christ! These lights!

DAVID: You sit in the throne, Saul.

SAUL: You're goddam right I sit in the throne. (*He strides to the throne and sits in it defiantly. Then he sees Samuel, and gets up.*) Hello, Sam.

SAMUEL: Hello, Saul…

(*They shake hands warmly, Samuel looks at him. Saul runs his hand along his brow.*)

SAUL: They put make-up on me, Sam. Some clown came at me with a goddam powder-puff.

SAMUEL: It's for the lights, Saul.

SAUL: It's for the show, Sam. All shows these days. They're choosing…(*A glance at David.*) entertainers to lead them. (*Then he controls himself.*)

SAMUEL: You sit on your throne, Saul.

SAUL: Anyway, I'm tired, Sam.

SAMUEL: So sit, Saul.

DAVID: (*Looking from one to the other.*) Are we ready to go on, gentlemen?…Could we recommence? Samuel, if you could reach over and gently take the crown—

SAMUEL: No, David. Have him give it to you.

DAVID: But the priest is supposed to.

SAMUEL: But on television, David, we should be nondenominational.

DAVID: I see…Yes…All right. Saul, we thought it would be appropriate if you—

SAUL: *You* take it off, kid! Come on, just try it!

SAMUEL: Why don't you play for him, David?

DAVID: Play for him?

SAMUEL: Yes. Play for him. Sing him your song.

DAVID: (*Looking at his watch.*) Now?

SAUL: Play for me, David. (*He sits on the throne.*)

SAMUEL: (*Holding out the harp.*) The Children of Israel will enjoy it…Or have you forgotten how to play?

DAVID: No, I haven't forgotten how to play. (*David exits, reappears immediately with an electric guitar with a cord running offstage.*) May I have permission to play for you, Saul?

SAUL: Permission granted. Play.

(*David lip-synchronizes to an amplified recording of "Home on the Range".*)

SAUL: (*Confused; getting up.*) Hold it. Hold it! *Hold* it! What is this? Disneyland?

(*David signals to "cut."*)

SAMUEL: Play for him live, David.

DAVID: Live?

SAUL: Yes, live. And sit where you used to sit. Sit at my feet.
   (David sings "live.")

SAUL: *(Interrupting him.)* Home on the Range! You made your home
   right on this *throne,* boy!

DAVID: Just a song, Saul.

SAUL: You always had your eye on this crown.

DAVID: *(More to audience, strumming sweetly.)* Every boy dreams of becoming king...

SAUL: *(Exploding to Samuel.)* Oh, he's a far cry from Samson, who caught
   lions with his bare hands!

DAVID: No one's claiming to be—

SAUL: A far cry from me, then!

DAVID: You're not Samson, Saul.

SAUL: No. I'm not Samson! *(Takes the spear from the prop table.)* But I
   know how it feels to shove this spear between a man's ribs. I made
   myself king! I hacked out this land with my own weapons! *(Jabs with
   spear.)* There were enemies all around us. Hittites, Injuns, Commu-
   nists! And I, Saul, killed my thousands, and became king! *(Looks at
   Samuel.)* And now you want me to hand over this crown... *(Sneeringly.)* to David, the Elected One! Oh, Jesus... *(Pause; he remembers
   the audience.)* I'm hot. I'm dripping. These goddam lights.

DAVID: It's that armor, Saul. I advised you not to wear it. It's old-fashioned.

SAUL: You didn't think so once. You asked if you could try it on, once
   upon a time.

DAVID: I was a boy then.

SAUL: *(To Samuel, laughing.)* He wanted to wear it, Sam. He wanted to
   wear my armor. I said, sure, here, kid, try it on. *(He laughs.)* It was
   too big for him. It was huge for him. He looked like a brave little tai-
   lor in the armor of a king!

DAVID: I was still growing then.

SAUL: You think it would fit you now?

DAVID: *(Laughing.)* Oh, I don't know—

SAUL: Want to try it on?

DAVID: *(Walking away.)* Oh, Lord—

SAUL: It still wouldn't fit.

DAVID: *(Turning.)* All right. I'll try it on, Saul, if you want.

SAUL: I want. *(David tries to undo Saul's armor. Saul winks at Samuel.*

Then, with an easy gesture, Saul removes the armor and David puts it on. David takes the spear and struts downstage. Saul is now in his undershirt.) Ah ha! You see? You see, Sam? It's still too big for him! *(Watching David.)* Look at the country boy, Sam! Strutting around in *my* armor!

DAVID: It's moldy, Saul. It's tacky. It's...old.

SAUL: *(Imitating him.)* "It's moldy, Saul. It's tacky. It's old..." He's a little man, Sam. I used to say, "Kid, saddle your ass, and go back to Bethlehem." Take over your old man's sheep. There's a lot of good money in sheep. I subsidized the wool industry.

DAVID: I was through with sheep. I said then, I say now, with our yesterdays firmly behind us, we must point for tomorrow today.

SAUL: What the hell was that? I don't understand that. An eye for an eye. This I understand. But this boy...this nice, nice boy...standing there in the armor I gave him, blinking at my crown, him I don't understand. You want this crown? Fight for it! I killed my thousands for it! Who are you going to kill? Me? Good. Fine. Fight me.

DAVID: I have no weapons.

SAUL: O.K., sonny. Take mine. *(Tosses his spear at David, who catches it neatly.)* Fight me with that. Samson style. Bare hands. You are a little man! I'm a giant compared to you! *(They face each other.)*

DAVID: And should I lift my hand against the crown, Saul?

SAUL: *(Whipping off the crown.)* Oh, touché. Here. Hold my hat, Sam! *(Throws crown to Samuel.)* Now. Put 'em up, Kid! *(He stands in an archaic fisticuffs stance.)*

DAVID: *(Shaking his head sadly.)* Oh, Saul if you had a mirror...if you could see yourself, as others see you...
   (He walks away. Saul looks out at the audience, realizes he is armorless, crownless, in public. He turns to Samuel.)

SAUL: The spirit of God has left me.

SAMUEL: I crowned you, Saul.

SAUL: My son Jonathan—he hates me.

SAMUEL: No, Saul...

SAUL: My wife, Sam. She—drinks.

SAMUEL: You've had a long day, friend.

SAUL: No, it's common knowledge. She drinks all day in the Rose Room.

SAMUEL: You're still king, Saul. Until I crown another.

SAUL: *(Looking at David.)* Oh, it galls me, Sam...

SAMUEL: You're still king tonight, Saul.

(Saul draws himself up.)

DAVID: There's a couch in my dressing room. You can lie down there if you like.

SAUL: I'll do what I want to do. I'm still king. Right, Sam?

SAMUEL: Right, old friend.

SAUL: Yessir. I'm still king around here tonight.

(He exits and we hear another crash. David stands in the armor and with the spear. He looks at Samuel, and then turns quickly to the audience.)

DAVID: Let me take this opportunity to say that there goes a great man. A great soldier has just marched off into the wings. If we had time, we'd dub in a death march. For we must always remember the battle he fought, so that we might be free of battles...*(He unbuckles his breastplate.)* He's...obsolete, that's all. I am reminded of Tennyson, *The Idylls of the King...(He puts the armor on the prop table, regards it elegiacally.)* "The old order changeth, yielding place to...the contemporary..."

SAMUEL: *(Wryly.)* They tell me Tennyson is obsolete, David.

DAVID: *(Grimly, looking at Samuel.)* Lots of things are obsolete, Samuel...*(He turns brightly to audience.)* There are no more villains these days. No bad guys...No big, bad giants...Fee, fi, ho, hum. *(He fakes a yawn.)*

SAMUEL: *(Holding the crown.)* And if there are no villains, who are the heroes, David?

DAVID: *(Slowly, carefully.)* Those who don't need villains to win.
(Pause.)

SAMUEL: That's a deep one, David. I'd save it for Educational Television.

DAVID: Maybe I will.

SAMUEL: Well...I'm holding the crown.

DAVID: *(Now all business.)* Yes. Saul has given it to you, and you take it, and give it to—
(Jonathan comes up the aisle, dressed as a hippie.)

JONATHAN: Me. Man, give it to me!

DAVID: Yes. To Jonathan. To my great friend Jonathan. *(Extends his hand.)* Who is right on cue.

JONATHAN: *(Ignoring the hand.)* I was early. Man. Sam said not to be late. So hi, Sam, here I am. *(He shakes hands with Samuel. David whispers to him. Jonathan responds loudly.)* Oh, I won't let it hit the fan, Dave.

DAVID: *(Warningly.)* Are you *with* me, Jonathan?

JONATHAN: I'm always with you, Dave.

DAVID: Good man. *(To Samuel.)* Now, Samuel: Jonathan will publicly reject the crown, once and for all.

JONATHAN: *(To audience.)* Yes. I'm the crown prince. The son of Saul. And I inherit—the earth.

DAVID: You don't want the crown, Jonathan.

JONATHAN: Naw. Hate crowns. Never wear 'em. *(David smiles.)* You—um—gave my Daddy Warbucks quite a time, Dave.

DAVID: The spirit of God has left him, Jonathan.

JONATHAN: Uh-huh. I watched. I'm a watcher these days. I watch things. I watch movies. I watch girls. You name it, I'll watch it. Just think tomorrow, on television, I'll be watching myself. Sounds kind of perverse, doesn't it?

DAVID: You make it sound that way, Jonathan. *(Genially; to audience.)* Jonathan loves the seamy side of things.

JONATHAN: I seem to see the seams…*(Pause; then briskly.)* Well now, Dave: What's the action here, baby?

DAVID: Very simple. Saul hands Samuel the crown. Samuel hands it to you, and you reject it.

JONATHAN: Gotcha. *(He gooses David and goes to Samuel.)*

DAVID: You'll be wearing a shirt, right, Jonathan?

JONATHAN: I am wearing a shirt, Dave. *(Lifts up his shirt, shows his stomach.)* See? No shirt. *(Jams down his shirt.)* Shirt. *(To Samuel.)* Hand me the crown, Sam.

(Samuel hands him the crown. Jonathan immediately hands it back.)

DAVID: Could you do it again, please? It looks a little…too quick.

JONATHAN: You don't think it's appropriate?

DAVID: No, I don't.

JONATHAN: O.K.

(He turns to Samuel. Samuel hands him the crown. Jonathan takes it, mimicking a slow-motion film, and laboriously hands it back to Samuel.)

DAVID: Oh, for God's sake! Come on, Jonathan.

JONATHAN: I dunno, Dave. Goshgollygeewhiz. Just can't seem to get it right, fella.

SAMUEL: Perhaps Jonathan should make a speech, David.

DAVID: Jonathan?

SAMUEL: Perhaps I should give him the crown, and he should hold it, and say why he doesn't want it.

DAVID: Would you like to give a *short* speech? would that help?

(Jonathan has disappeared. His voice is heard over speaker.)

JONATHAN'S VOICE: Unaccustomed as I am to public speaking…I dig it!

DAVID: All right then.

(Jonathan returns just as suddenly. Samuel hands Jonathan the crown. Jonathan takes it.)

JONATHAN: Children of Israel: I think David should wear this crown. It is exquisitely styled for gay occasions. Take David here. He has broken every record, broken every record, broken every record…

DAVID: *(Eyes closed.)* Jonathan…

JONATHAN: Something simpler? More from the heart? All right. You're the king.

DAVID: *(Infinite patience.)* Try it again, and again, and again…buddy.

JONATHAN: *(After a pause.)* Why I don't want this crown? Because it has sat too long on the bald heads of old men. They have stained it with the sweat of their slaves, they have smeared it with the blood of their neighbors, and they have patched and glued and mended it with their own calcified, worm-eaten, shriveled *Shit. (He throws the crown to Samuel disgustedly.)* So, man, I don't want to wear it. *(He wipes off his hands.)*

DAVID: That was a little rough, Jonathan.

JONATHAN: Was it? Should I have said ca-ca? Poo-poo? Number two?

DAVID: Samuel, tell him that was a little rough…For the television public…with the children watching…Tell him, Samuel.

SAMUEL: I'm not sure he'd listen to me.

DAVID: All right now, Jonathan—

JONATHAN: Behold I am vile. What shall I answer thee?…That's from the psalms, David.

DAVID: I know what it's from.

JONATHAN: The psalm I wrote, and you sang, in your checkered career.

DAVID: You wrote some of them.

JONATHAN: I wrote the ones that caught on. I wrote most of them. I wrote the angry ones. The ones that put you in line for your big, fat, gold commercial ones. I put you on the map, baby, and now you can't even remember my words.

DAVID: Of course I remember.

JONATHAN: Those were the days when there were giants to kill, David!

DAVID: Did Samuel tell you to talk about giants?

JONATHAN: You don't believe those psalms any more.

DAVID: There is a time for singing and a time for...not singing, Jonathan.

JONATHAN: You copped out on us, David.

DAVID: *(To Jonathan.)* I never—*(To audience.)* I never copped out.

JONATHAN: You did! You lost the way! *(Passionately.)* Oh, man, don't bring me down! Here's our scene—right here! Right now!—There's a giant here, and you and I can kill him!

DAVID: *(Contemptuously.)* What giant?

JONATHAN: The big guy! The fat cat! The Philistine! *(He wheels on the audience.)* Anyone, ANY ONE of these giants hiding under the shadow of this goddam crown! Here...*(He grabs the crown, draws his hand back as if to hurl it at the audience.)* Let 'em have it!

(David grabs is arm; they struggle tautly for the crown.)

DAVID: *(Through his teeth as they fight.)* You see the world through dark glasses, Jonathan. We've been given this Eden, and all you can do is thrash around in the good, green grass, looking for a snake! *(He wrests the crown from Jonathan, gives it to Samuel. Jonathan lies on the stage; David speaks to the audience.)* He would have burned this flag, people! *Burned* it! This symbol of our promised land! If that's what it means to kill giants, then I swear I shall kill none! *(David goes back to Jonathan.)* Jonathan, you needed psychiatric help. I got it for you. And I paid the bills! Now, you've had a rough family life, we all know that, and you're taking it out on the world! So let's not fight giants any more because then the real evil is done!

(Pause.)

JONATHAN: *(Whistling.)* Bring on the dog act!

DAVID: O.K., Jonathan, that's it. Out! You're out of the picture! Permanently! *(Pause.)* Unless you do it right.

(They look at each other.)

JONATHAN: Hand me the crown, Sam. *(He does it right. They look at each other.)* Was that right? Hmm? did I do it right?...Oh, goody, goody.

DAVID: That was right. And you'll do it right in dress rehearsal, and you'll do it right for the taping, right, Jonathan?

JONATHAN: Right. Right. Oh, right. Right. Right. Right. *(He exits.)*

DAVID: Now, Samuel. I will kneel. *(He does.)* And you will put the crown on my head.

SAMUEL: Now?

DAVID: *(Closing his eyes.)* Now.

SAMUEL: But something's missing.

DAVID: Nothing's missing.

SAMUEL: David, forgive me, but there is. I feel you and I are trying to assemble a sort of...machine...

DAVID: Not a machine.

SAMUEL: Yes a machine! And I want every piece to fit! And that's why I'm very much concerned... *(Glances offstage.)* that there's a piece missing.

DAVID: Ah. Giants. You are now talking about—
(Enter Bathsheba, in a little black dress.)

BATHSHEBA: I think he's talking about me.

DAVID: *(Aghast.)* Bathsheba!

BATHSHEBA: I know damn well he's talking about me. I'm the missing piece.

DAVID: I'll handle this, Bathsheba.

BATHSHEBA: Now, now, David. I was invited. Telephone call from Foxy Grandpa here at the crack of dawn. So, ready or not, here I am.

SAMUEL: *(Smiling, shaking his head.)* Bathsheba, the Philistine!

DAVID: Don't dignify that with an answer, Bathsheba.

BATHSHEBA: Well, it's better than WASP. Why is everybody so ethnic these days? Look what's happening: the Irish get all the votes, the Negroes sing all the songs, the Italians eat all the food, *(She wheels on Samuel again.)* and the *Jews* control the theatre.

DAVID: Bathsheba, none of your little jokes, please.

BATHSHEBA: *(To audience.)* Excuse us for just a moment, please. *(To David, in a whisper.)* Oh *David.* Get rid of Samuel. He's too tricky. Now I've brought along a good god-is-dead Episcopalian, and he'll crown you immediately, no questions asked. *(Calling out.)* George! Where the hell *are* you?

DAVID: I want Samuel.

BATHSHEBA: Why? All he does is argue. They all do. I've seen a million dinner parties mangled by one argumentative Jew.

DAVID: I want Samuel! He crowned Saul. He'll crown me. I need a tradition!

BATHSHEBA: Then why won't he do it?

DAVID: I don't know...

BATHSHEBA: I do. *(Calls off.)* Ham, darling, bring me my purse, please. *(To David.)* I know what he wants. *(Ham comes out with her purse; she rummages in it.)* I know exactly what he wants... *(To Ham.)* Thank you, darling. *(Ham exits. She holds out ten dollars to Samuel.)* Money. Typical. Here you are, Samuel. Now get a good grip on that crown and plunk it right smack on David's head.

DAVID: *(Stepping in; taking the money.)* Bathsheba! He's a man of God!

BATHSHEBA: And I'm a woman of means! *(To audience.)* If you've got it spend it. And I spend mine on David.
(David instinctively pockets the money.)

SAMUEL: Then you are indebted to this lady.

DAVID: *(Handing the money back to Bathsheba.)* I am indebted to no one. I am my own man.

BATHSHEBA: Of course you are. Honestly, Samuel, I don't lend David money—I give him money.

DAVID: *(Quickly.)* I say no, as I have said before, that I have received help along the way from friends...friends who have preferred to remain nameless...Friends such as this kind lady here. *(Pause.)* It is never a good idea to name names. People get besieged by frantic appeals...

BATHSHEBA: God. True enough. The National Sharecroppers. Boy's Town. The Democratic Party—

DAVID: *(Going right on.)* So in the past, I have avoided—names. But all your badgering, Samuel, has forced this good lady to forget herself, and speak in public on my behalf.

BATHSHEBA: *Forget myself?* I've been dying to come out.

DAVID: I'm naturally very appreciative that you did, Bathsheba. But no—

BATHSHEBA: I mean, everyone knows about us, anyway. The David and Bathsheba stories—

DAVID: I don't believe I've heard any such stories...

BATHSHEBA: *(Looking at him.)* Uh-oh. I've embarrassed you, haven't I.

DAVID: No, no, no, no.

BATHSHEBA: *(To audience.)* I think I've embarrassed him.

DAVID: No, no, no, no, no.

BATHSHEBA: I was his private life, and I made myself public.

SAMUEL: I've heard those stories, David. They say you stood on a high place, and watched Bathsheba bathing. They say you lusted after her. They say there was a husband involved.

BATHSHEBA: Now that makes it sound perfectly ghastly. Save the day, David.

DAVID: It was not like that, Samuel. I'll tell you how it was.

BATHSHEBA: So will I...Let's gird up our loins, and tell it as it should be told

SAMUEL: *(Taking out a notebook.)* Do you mind if I take notes? So I'll remember for my speech.

DAVID: Fine. Lights, Frank. Give me my pink! *(Lights change.)* After I broke with Jonathan and the Movement—

BATHSHEBA: Thank God—

DAVID: I was recording my Christmas album in the studio.

BATHSHEBA: I adore the Christmas album.

DAVID: And between numbers, I wandered out on the fire escape for some air—

SAMUEL: Ah. The high place.

DAVID: Yes. And from there, I looked down. I saw an old brownstone house, surrounded by high buildings—

BATHSHEBA: My grandmother's house. *(Jonathan enters.)*

JONATHAN: See the Philistine house!

BATHSHEBA: It has a lovely little garden in back. And a small pool.

DAVID: Beautiful and blue. Reflecting the sky. And when I looked down, I saw that pool. And in it—

BATHSHEBA: Was...Me...I...Me.

HAM: *(Entering.)* Whooo-eeeee.

JONATHAN: See the beautiful Bathsheba.

SAMUEL: Bathing—

DAVID: Swimming—

BATHSHEBA: Skinny-dipping, actually. I love it.

HAM: Whooo-eeeee.

JONATHAN: See the beautiful naked Bathsheba.

DAVID: Swimming. Doing a firm Australian crawl. And I watched. Watched her climb out of the water. And sit on the diving board, and comb her hair, in the afternoon sun.

SAMUEL: And you lusted after her.

BATHSHEBA: Not lusted. Loved—

DAVID: Loved—the idea that here, in this city, in all this racket, someone could take off her clothes, and sit on a diving board, and comb her hair—

SAMUEL: Ah. It was the hair. The Rapunzel story. You were held by the hair.

JONATHAN: See David held by the hair.

DAVID: I was held by everything.

BATHSHEBA: He was held by *me*. He wanted—

DAVID: *(Quickly.)* I wanted—that. That hint of Eden and this innocent Eve. I wanted those green pastures by those still waters—

BATHSHEBA: I was anointing myself with oil—

DAVID: I went down to that old house, and rang the polished brass bell, and hoped she would meet me halfway.

JONATHAN: Boinggggg!

BATHSHEBA: I thought you were just a salesman.

DAVID: I had nothing to sell.

BATHSHEBA: I thought you were a Jehovah's Witness.

DAVID: I'm a Jew.

BATHSHEBA: You don't look like a Jew. You don't have those deep sad Jewish eyes.

DAVID: That's because I'm far-sighted. And I saw something lovely from a long way off.

BATHSHEBA: You see? Oh, boy. What could I do against that? How do you stop a freight train? The little engine that could.

SAMUEL: Did you try?

BATHSHEBA: Yes, I tried. I told David I was married. To a very nice Army officer. Uriah the Hittite. And I told him I was just visiting my grandmother.

DAVID: So I left.

BATHSHEBA: And then my husband was suddenly sent overseas.

DAVID: To fight for freedom. In the fertile crescent.

BATHSHEBA: And David keeps me company while he's gone.

DAVID: We have become fast friends.

JONATHAN: Friends with a Philistine.

HAM: Whooee.

DAVID: Is that impossible to understand these days? That a man and a woman can be friends? We meet at her grandmother's!

BATHSHEBA: He drops in.

DAVID: To have a cocktail with her, served in Steuben glass, on a silver tray, on a waxed coffee table. And she is reflected in all these things. I like that. I like her style, and she likes my seriousness of purpose.

JONATHAN: See David's seriousness of purpose.

DAVID: We are friends!

BATHSHEBA: Fast friends.

DAVID: Good friends. And there's the story, Samuel. And you can sell it to *Look Magazine*, for all I care. *(Jonathan sings the Merry Melodies finish.)*

SAMUEL: It's a charming story, David. It has such rich chords. All it needs is a happy ending.

BATHSHEBA: Thank you, sweetheart. You told that beautifully. You're worth every cent I gave you. *(She gives David a quick kiss.)*

DAVID: Now I'm going to tell more—

BATHSHEBA: More? Be careful.

DAVID: I'm making an announcement. *(Jonathan does trumpet imitation.)* I have decided…*(Jonathan does drum roll.)* to appoint this lady… *(Jonathan builds.)* official hostess at the palace. She will be in charge of all social functions. She may come and go as she pleases. There's a scoop for someone out there.

BATHSHEBA: *(Squealing all the while.)* DELICIOUS! Ham, darling, there's a package in the wings. Get it for me, will you, sweetie? Bergdorf box. David, for that, I'm going to give you a present.

DAVID: You mean you came prepared?

BATHSHEBA: I'm always prepared. *(Ham returns with a fancily wrapped package.)* Thank you, darling. *(She hands it to David.)* This is for you, David. Open it. *(David opens it; holds up a small golden calf.)* See? The golden calf. You had your eye on it at my grandmother's. Antique. Priceless. Keep it.

DAVID: No. I'll put it to work! I'll invest it in this great nation! *(He goes to the prop table.)* It belongs here, in full view! I have declared my life, I have declared my past, I have declared my income!

BATHSHEBA: *(Going to him.)* And you have declared me, David.

DAVID: *(Arm around her.)* I have declared everything! And I stand by everything.

SAMUEL: *(Moving in.)* Do you, David?

DAVID: Oh, yes, Samuel! Now I see what you've been up to. You've been initiating me, haven't you?

SAMUEL: Yes—

DAVID: Yes! This has been a sort of—ritual, hasn't it?

SAMUEL: Yes—

DAVID: Yes! And you've been asking me to recognize these—sacred objects!

SAMUEL: Yes—

DAVID: Yes! And you've been asking me to recognize my responsibilities to all these people!

SAMUEL: *(Passionately.)* Oh, yes, David! That's exactly what I've been trying to—

DAVID: Then I do! I will! Oh, now I see how we must end this ceremony! We must bring all these things together! *(He rushes to the flags.)* First: Hidden electric fans will unfurl these flags. Oh, Samuel, look: it's all here. This, the Star of David, and this, the Old Glory. I want the church and the state, I want the old and the new, I want the Jew and the WASP, the Negro and the White, and I want AUDIO! "The Battle Hymn of the Republic". Sung by the Mormon Tabernacle Choir. *(Calling off.)* Find it, Frank! And put it on! And I want you, my good friends, to form a semicircle around me—do it, friends—and hold hands. Yes. And sing. *(They do, the music begins.)* Because we're talking about community, people. The community of friends, the community of groups, and some day, people, some day, the community of nations. And then, Samuel, you can crown me again, with a U.N. flag behind me, and *(Exultantly.)* Arabs...Russians...Chinese...Indonesians...Eskimos will be holding hands, and singing under these bright clear lights. But for now, Samuel, come forward, *(David kneels.)* come forward, Samuel and crown me king. *(Samuel disgustedly slams the crown onto David's head. Shocked; then feeling the crown.)* Why, it's plastic. *(He removes it, looks at it.)* It's fake... *(He puts it down.)* It's disposable.

SAMUEL: Why, yes.

DAVID: But where's the real crown?

SAMUEL: In the temple. You can get away with this one.

DAVID: Get away—?

SAMUEL: On television.

DAVID: *(Calling off.)* Someone: Go to the temple and—

SAMUEL: I go to the temple, David! When I'm ready to go!

DAVID: I want a real crown, Samuel.

SAMUEL: You'll have to earn it.

DAVID: How? *How?*

SAMUEL: Fight a giant.

DAVID: Oh, sure. Fighting giants—false giants. That's what's tearing this country apart!

SAMUEL: What an interesting thought, David.

DAVID: My whole speech is based on it.

SAMUEL: Then I must hear that speech.

DAVID: It's not *finished* yet.

SAMUEL: Go finish it.

DAVID: Oh, Samuel, do you think I'm that dumb? Do you? Do you think I'd leave you alone out here, mugging, winking, turning people against me? Oh, you've tasted blood tonight, haven't you, old man? You've tried every cheap amateur trick in the book!

SAMUEL: Go work on your speech, David. I'll go to the temple. A real speech wins a real crown.

(Pause.)

DAVID: Ham, get coffee...*(Ham exits.)* Jonathan—

JONATHAN: Some must watch, and some must wait, Dave.

DAVID: Bathsheba...

BATHSHEBA: I'll entertain the troops, David. Now I'm hostess.

DAVID: *(Toward offstage; to staff.)* Frank, get my car around back...Harriet, I want everyone in my dressing room on the double.

SAMUEL: *(Quietly; to Bathsheba.)* Tell him, Bathsheba.

BATHSHEBA: Tell him *what*, dear man?

SAMUEL: Tell him about the telegram.

BATHSHEBA: How did you know about the—?

SAMUEL: Tell him tonight.

DAVID: *(Returning.)* Samuel, my car's waiting to take you to the temple. *(Samuel looks at Bathsheba and joins him.)* I want the real crown on my head at the end, Samuel. I really want that.

SAMUEL: So do I.

(They exit in opposite directions.)

JONATHAN: What telegram?

BATHSHEBA: I think you should get off the throne. That's David's throne. I'm the hostess now, Jonny, and I decide who sits where.

JONATHAN: I've got something for you to sit on.

BATHSHEBA: *All Right*, Jonathan. Let's have it out then.

JONATHAN: O.K., baby. *(He begins to unbutton.)*

BATHSHEBA: That's just the sort of thing we don't do, Jonny. *(She moves so as not to see. Jonathan covers his crotch; she peeks over her shoulder; he removes his hands; she sighs in relief.)* Now I know why you're sitting on the throne. We all know. And we all know why you've been so rude and unattractive all evening long. You're a Revolutionary, aren't you? Oh, yes you are. We're not stupid. We read James Reston. You want to destroy Society, and everybody else. And furthermore, you have a Military-Industrial Complex. We all know this.

JONATHAN: Up against the wall!

BATHSHEBA: Exactly. All right! Then tell me this. *(Jonathan begins to poke her breasts.)* I'm *serious*, Jonathan. *(She moves away.)* We'd all be interested. After you've destroyed us all, what do you propose to build on the rubble? Answer me that.

JONATHAN: *(With elocutional flair.)* A brick shithouse.

BATHSHEBA: You see. You see. He has nothing remotely constructive to say. Come on, Jonny, put up or shut up. Describe your new world. Please.

JONATHAN: (Seriously.) A world of peace...and freedom...and joy. With plenty of food and drink for all.

BATHSHEBA: Oh, but, Jonny! There *are!* We all want exactly the same thing, sweetie. What you describe sounds exactly like my coming-out party. (*Jonathan begins to fake a melodramatic death scene, as if he had been poisoned.*) Oh, for Pete's *sake*, Jonathan! O.K. That's that... You can't come to any palace parties. (*Jonathan gasps and groans.*) You are uninvited as of now. If you show up, we'll throw you in the pool. Lord knows you could use a bath.

JONATHAN: (*Suddenly "recovering."*) That's the stink of life, baby. Too bad you don't recognize it.

BATHSHEBA: (*Gasping for air.*) I recognize it. I recognize it. (*Jonathan suddenly kisses her on the nose. Ham enters.*)

HAM: Hi. I got coffee out there.

BATHSHEBA: (*Having pulled herself together.*) My, my, Ham, you look swell! All gussied up!

HAM: I'm in the show now. I'm going to be on TV.

BATHSHEBA: Of course! It's your big chance! There you'll be, alive and in color!

HAM: Yes'm.

BATHSHEBA: Now, join us, Ham. While David works on his speech. (*Pause; she sits on the platform.*) Sit down, Ham. (*Ham sits. She pats a place nearer.*) Next to me. (*Ham moves.*) Now. It's high time we got to know each other, Ham. What exactly do you do for David?

HAM: I bring in the black votes.

BATHSHEBA: I know that, silly billy. I mean, now that the vote's in.

HAM: I'm on the staff. I'm the boss backstage.

BATHSHEBA: Fine. Good. Now, I'll tell you something, Ham. When I'm in the palace, I'm going to do something for the Negroes... Blacks... whatever you are. You can count on that. What exactly do you want?

HAM: Well, ma'am, I sure would like a piece of that old golden calf.

JONATHAN: You said it, Ham.

HAM: (*Mock Uncle Tom.*) Yes'm. That ole gol'en calf would shorely do me up right.

BATHSHEBA: The Golden Calf?

HAM: My mama used to tell me about it. She had to polish it up twice a week.

BATHSHEBA: Why of *course!* You mother *cleans* for my grandmother. You're the Ham she's told me about.

HAM: I'm the Ham—

BATHSHEBA: She said you were a wonderful tap-dancer. Until you started rioting and burning buildings. Now why, Ham? What did it get you?

JONATHAN: A headful of scars from your goddam Philistine police.

BATHSHEBA: I don't believe that. Every time I'm stopped by the police on the Merritt Parkway…

JONATHAN: Show her your scars, Ham.

BATHSHEBA: Where? Ham, let me see. *(He shows her.)* Why, you poor *thing! (To audience.)* It's true! There's a great gash on his skull! It went all the way through the wool! *(To Ham.)* Why, I'm *furious* about this, I'm going to call the National Association…for…Cruelty to Colored People! Gosh, I'm mad. *(To audience.)* We have all been negligent and naughty. *(To Ham.)* How can we make it up to you, Ham?

HAM: Give me the calf.

BATHSHEBA: Darling, that's *David's* calf.

JONATHAN: See, Ham? No calf for Ham…*(He picks up the spear from the prop table.)* Without this! *(He tosses him the spear; Ham holds the spear, and grins and picks up the calf.)* Now sit in the throne, Ham.

BATHSHEBA: That's a no-no, Ham. That's David's throne.

JONATHAN: She's prejudiced, Ham.

BATHSHEBA: Sit in the throne, Ham. *(Ham does an elaborate tap dance up the steps to throne. He ends with a fine flourish, sitting on the throne, wearing the crown, carrying the spear, holding the calf.)*

JONATHAN: Hey, boy, look at you.

HAM: *Don't call me boy!*

BATHSHEBA: Why, Ham, you look just like Pharaoh—about to drive us all into the Red Sea!

JONATHAN: Not yet.

HAM: When do I get the real crown?

BATHSHEBA: Some day, Ham…

(Saul enters suddenly, in a bathrobe.)

SAUL: What is that Ethiopian doing on my throne? *(To Ham.)* You going to rape this white woman?

HAM: No!

BATHSHEBA: Some day, Ham…*(Ham raises the spear against Saul. David enters.)*

DAVID: Cool it, Ham.

HAM: I've been cooling it.

DAVID: *(Indicating offstage.)* Look, I've got—

HAM: Uh-huh. All the king's men out there. *(He tosses the spear angrily to David, who catches it. Ham sings softly and ironically.)* "He's got the whole world, in his hands."

DAVID: I set you up, Ham. You were hanging around the street corners. I gave you a job, Ham.

HAM: "He's got the whole world, in his hands…" *(He puts back the calf.)*

DAVID: And I'm going to promote you, Ham—

HAM: *(Taking off his coat and tie.)* "He's got the whole world, in his hand…" *(He reveals an African shirt underneath.)*

DAVID: And I'll get you a home, Ham. In the suburbs.

HAM: "The whole world in his hand…"

DAVID: *(Grabbing him.)* Where are you going?

HAM: *(Whirling on him.)* Back to Harlem, baby. I gave it to you, and now I'm going to take it back. Man, O, man! I'm going to be my brother's keeper. (He exits.)

(Pause. David calls off.)

DAVID: Someone! Harry! Bill! Go after him! Establish a dialogue! *(Wheels on Samuel.)* All right. Who started this?

(Everyone speaks at once.)

BATHSHEBA: Jonathan stirred him up.

JONATHAN: Crap.

SAUL: Who is this Philistine?

JONATHAN: Bathsheba the WASP.

DAVID: *(Shouting them down.)* Quiet, everyone. *(Silence.)*

SAUL: *(Under his breath.)* Bad news! I knew her grandmother.

DAVID: Don't worry. Ham will be back. He knows where the gravy is. It's all in my speech. O.K. now, everyone in position. Saul in the throne…Jonathan beside him. Bathsheba, you're off camera.

(Bathsheba moves grumpily to one side.)

SAUL: *(To Jonathan.)* You should be sitting here.

JONATHAN: I'm not the type.

SAUL: You are the type. You were a goddam prince.

DAVID: Gentlemen: may we—?

SAUL: *(To Jonathan.)* You could still be king. I'll buy you a suit and get you started.

JONATHAN: I am king, Dad. My self to me a kingdom is.

DAVID: Well said, Jon. Now may we—?

SAUL: You're just the patsy. Why do you think he keeps you around? Go on, go on spend the rest of your life knocking things down so he can look good picking them up.

JONATHAN: You don't understand our friendship. Does he, Dave?

SAUL: Some friendship, these two. They can't live without each other. They oughta get married, this David and Jonathan.

BATHSHEBA: Now that takes the cake in the bad taste department.

DAVID: Fellas: may we—?

JONATHAN: David and I—relate to each other, Dad. He does my job for me, I do his job for him.

SAUL: What job? You never had a job in your life.

BATHSHEBA: Yes. What job? Don't tell us you're in the C.I.A., Jonathan?

DAVID: Yes. What job? I'd like to know what job.

JONATHAN: I do your living for you, man.

BATHSHEBA: That'll be the day.

JONATHAN: You need me, Dave. Admit it.

DAVID: I wouldn't say…"need"…

JONATHAN: You *live* off me. Where were you last night, Dave?

BATHSHEBA: He was working on his speech last night.

JONATHAN: He was over at my *pad* last night.

DAVID: I took a short break.

JONATHAN: You were over at my pad, sitting at my feet, watching me smoke pot—

SAUL: Oh, for God's sake!

BATHSHEBA: *(To David.)* You said you were—

DAVID: I had a short Scotch and soda.

JONATHAN: You were watching me smoke grass, man, asking me how it felt, listening to me talk, pumping my brain!

DAVID: You've been talking to Samuel.

JONATHAN: Samuel's been talking to *me.*

BATHSHEBA: Change the subject, change the subject…

SAUL: Come on, Jon. Come home with me. I can still straighten you out.

JONATHAN: Can't, Dad. I'm his connection. *(To David.)* I'm your fix, man. I give you a good shot of warm life-blood every time you get cold. You need me, even to write a speech. The old man's right. You can't live without me. *(Arm around him.)* Behold the friendship of David and Jonathan!

DAVID: I don't need either one of you any more.

SAUL: Ah hah! You see? Now he shows his true colors. Come home with me, Jon.

JONATHAN: Screw the family bag. My scene's outside. *(To David.)* I'm splitting, Dave. And I'll really give you something to watch. *(Exits.)*

SAUL: You turned my boy into a goddam beatnik. *(Grabs the spear.)* I'm running again. On a clean, hard conservative ticket. I'll put a spear in every decent white home in the country. *(He exits.)*

BATHSHEBA: Mercy!

DAVID: They've all gone.

BATHSHEBA: I haven't gone. And frankly, I'm a little irritated. If you want to smoke pot, I'll *get* you some. It's a big, let-down anyway. I tried it on the Vineyard, and I must say that a couple of good martinis—

DAVID: Where's Samuel, goddammit?

BATHSHEBA: Probably with the rest of them. At some wailing wall. I'm sick unto death of all this Jewish self-laceration.

DAVID: I'm a Jew.

BATHSHEBA: Phooey.

DAVID: I'm Jewish, and proud of it.

BATHSHEBA: Oh, sweetheart, I'm not talking about superficial surgery. *(She kisses him.)* I'm talking about the human heart. You're a Philistine at heart because you don't feel guilty.

DAVID: Why should I feel guilty?

BATHSHEBA: See? You're a Philistine. Just like me. *(Pause. He looks at her, and then comes downstage.)*

DAVID: *(To audience.)* I have decided…to make this a simple ceremony. I will give my speech. And Samuel will crown me. And that's all.

BATHSHEBA: David…*(He looks at her.)* Make me queen.

DAVID: We're not married.

BATHSHEBA: We should be.

(Pause.)

DAVID: You're married already.

BATHSHEBA: Am I?

DAVID: Yes. I like your husband. I like Uriah. I like Hittites.

BATHSHEBA: We're free. He's dead, David.

DAVID: Well, you may feel—

BATHSHEBA: *(Reaching into her bag; handing him a telegram.)* This came a week ago. He was killed in battle. *(Pause. David takes the telegram, reads it, looks at her.)* I was going to tell you tomorrow. After your big moment. (Pause.) But Samuel thinks you should know tonight…

DAVID: Samuel?

BATHSHEBA: Oh, don't blame him. And don't blame yourself. My husband liked war. So you sent him to one. There you are.

DAVID: I did *not* send him!

BATHSHEBA: Well, I mean you knew people in high places. You made telephone calls.

DAVID: *They* sent him to war! Not me!

BATHSHEBA: Exactly! So don't feel guilty. He asked for it. He made his bed. Now sleep in it. He lost. You won.

DAVID: I didn't win anything.

(Pause.)

BATHSHEBA: Why, David, you won me...And you can marry me. Now. Oh, not on television, of course. That would be tasteless. But soon. Come on. Keep the ball in the air. Keep the air in the ball.

DAVID: I don't want to discuss—

BATHSHEBA: Oh, David, you're king now. You can get away with murder!

DAVID: *(Grabbing her by the shoulders.)* Please stop talking!

BATHSHEBA: Then you say something! Quick!

DAVID: What? What should I say?

BATHSHEBA: Say here and now, in front of all these charming people, with their beady little eyes, that you loved me from the day you saw me bathe...say that we have been proudly popping into bed ever since.

DAVID: I'll simply say—

BATHSHEBA: Say that you sent my husband to war so you could marry me!

DAVID: *(Shouting her down.) I will not say that! (Pause.)* Who do you think I am?

BATHSHEBA: *(Quietly.)* Well, I don't know...Tell us.

DAVID: *(He looks at her, looks at the audience. To audience.)* I am a man...of flesh and blood. I have...passions like other men. Like other men, I was tempted by a Philistine woman. And finally, after a long struggle, I fell.

BATHSHEBA: You fell, all right.

DAVID: I'm on my feet now.

BATHSHEBA: So am I...Oh, well, back to the diving board. I guess I'll have to take off all my clothes and slip back into that pool...Keep the Golden Calf, David. I'll just deduct it. For services rendered. *(She exits.)*

DAVID: Go on, Eve! Back to Eden! *(Samuel enters, carrying a simple box.)* I suppose you overheard all that.

SAMUEL: I didn't have to.

DAVID: Your machine. That machine you made. It ran perfectly. All by itself. Just the way you wanted. It ran right over me, old man.

SAMUEL: Did it?

DAVID: That the crown? *(Samuel nodes.)* I've got my speech.

SAMUEL: Twenty men wrote that speech.

DAVID: *(Nodding; crumpling it; throwing it away.)* And it doesn't say a goddam thing.

SAMUEL: David…

DAVID: *(Exploding.)* Oh, *boy!* Oh, boy, oh, boy. You've cleaned me out, old man! *No* speech, *No* friends, no crown, nothing! I'll be lucky if I last beyond tonight! Was it fun for you? Did you get your kicks? Oh, I know: you loved it!

SAMUEL: David, I HATED it. These cameras, this costume, these lurid lights, that dramatic dash to the temple for this poor simple old crown. I hated it all.

DAVID: Then why didn't you make it easy? What do you want of me? What in God's name do you WANT?

SAMUEL: I want to know who you are.

DAVID: Oh, God, Samuel—

SAMUEL: *(Grabbing him.)* David, fight Goliath!

DAVID: *(Laughing.)* Who is Goliath? Your giant?

SAMUEL: *Fight* him. Take him *on.*

DAVID: Go get him then. Go get your giant.

SAMUEL: *(Starting off.)* You bring him on. I'll watch, with the Children of Israel.

DAVID: Hey, wait!

SAMUEL: Come ON, DAVID! It's all up to you!

DAVID: *(Alone.)* Me. *(Thinks.)* Me? *(Gets an idea, snaps his fingers.)* Me! Of course! Now I've got my ceremony! *(Calls offstage, enthusiastically.)* Frank, give me sound! I want the sound of a giant heading our way! *(A Goliath sound begins, slow at first, getting louder and faster as the scene continues: wild and electronic.)* Beautiful! I like that…I can do something with that! Someone take notes! We'll be doing this on tape in half an hour! *(To audience.)* First, I challenge the giant, proudly, publicly. *(Shouts out.)* I challenge thee, Goliath! *(Rips off coat*

and tie.) Now I improvise. No set speech. Human. Real. To contrast with the electronics. *(Displays his shirt, rolls up sleeves.)* Shirt sleeves. I've done what I've done through good hard work. That'll bring Saul around. *(Takes off shoes and socks.)* Then, I refer to my roots. For the Bible Belt. Barefoot boy. I know the land. "My feet were rooted in God's green pastures." Camera two...long shot. I want the feet. Good. *(He thinks.)* Then I modulate to Harlem. "I don't know how it feels to be black, but by God, I know what it feels like to be poor." And Ham will come back into the fold. *(Calls off.)* Good. Good suspense. *(Another idea.)* On to the radical element. Students. Hippies. I'll sing one of Jonathan's psalms. "Where have all the flowers gone", walk to camera... And the Left is with me. Next: the swimming pool set. I'll need body make-up. Frank, tell the girl! I'll refer to my personal life. "Better to have loved and lost..." The Philistines will smile. And then, oh, this will be sensational...I'll take off my pants....No...Yes. This is where it's at, anyway. *(Stands in his shorts. Calls off.)* Find me a loin cloth! Real leather! Like...Tarzan's! *(To audience.)* And then I stand here, kind of humble, kind of proud, human, vulnerable in my nakedness, and I—mention the war. And I admit, that I, I personally, feel responsible for—for those who died on our behalf. Now, Frank, build it, build it....And whoever's on lights, when I say "now," I want a total blackout, and then a spot on me. O.K., build, build, Goliath, Goliath, Goliath, *now!*
(Blackout. Then a small spot which hits him so as to cast a large shadow behind. He blinks, looks at his shadow, spreads out his arms, turns to the audience, beaming.)

DAVID: SEN-SA-TIONAL! *(Revels in his shadow.)* There's your villain. There's your giant. And I, David, am facing up to it on television! *(Goes to the prop table.)* Facing up to it, and fighting it down! *(Takes his sling.)* With a simple sling, and a smooth white stone! I confront Goliath, like this! *(He stands imitating a traditional statue, i.e. the Olympic Zeus.)* Or maybe like this. *(He tries another pose; perhaps a bullfighter.)* No, like this. *(He finds the Michelangelo pose.)* There! That feels...authentic! *(Then he's all business again; calling off.)* O.K., now I twirl my sling and aim at the light. I'm twirling, I'm twirling...*(To audience; as he twirls his sling.)* And here comes the kill...Here's where I really get down to the nitty-gritty...I shout out one last line...something original...something unforgettable... something that will say exactly who I am and what I stand for...

something that will bring every American to his feet, cheering...
something that will...something...*(He stops twirling; the sling hangs
limp; the stone drops on the stage floor.)* Something...*(He looks at the
audience, then, furtively, towards offstage.)* Kill it...I said, kill it...Kill
it! *(He backs away from the light as there is a sudden blackout. Then music comes up: David's recording of "Home on the Range," or possibly of
"The Star Spangled Banner.")*

END OF PLAY

The Problem

A Play in One Act

This could be categorized as a tentative excursion into the absurdist genre.

ORIGINAL PRODUCTION

THE PROBLEM was first produced professionally at the King's Head Theatre in London in 1970. It ultimately opened in New York at the Soho Repertory Theatre in 1975, directed by Penelope Hirsch.

CAST OF CHARACTERS

THE HUSBAND, in his thirties
THE WIFE, also in her thirties

SETTING

The suggestion of a study. A chair, a footstool, possibly a bookcase behind.

The Problem

At curtain, the Husband is sitting in the chair, feet up on the footstool, reading a book, smoking a pipe, taking notes into a notebook comfortably propped on his knee. After a moment, the Wife comes in, hugely pregnant. She stands looking at him. He continues to read.

WIFE: Hey.

HUSBAND: *(Not looking at her.)* I'm reading, dear.

WIFE: *(Sticking out her stomach.)* I know. But look at me.

HUSBAND: *(Still reading.)* I'm preparing for a class, dear.

WIFE: I know, but just look. *(She crosses to him, stands by his chair, and sticks out her stomach.)* Just take a gander.

HUSBAND: *(Turns his head and looks right into her stomach. He starts, takes off his glasses, looks again, and then looks up into her face.)* Well, well.

WIFE: Yes.

HUSBAND: Surprise, surprise.

WIFE: Yes.

HUSBAND: Merry Christmas.

WIFE: Exactly. *(Pause.)*

HUSBAND: Why have I never noticed before?

WIFE: Because I wear loose-fitting clothes.

HUSBAND: That's true.

WIFE: Clothes without waists. Merri-mekkos. Sack dresses. Granny gowns.

HUSBAND: That's true.

WIFE: Large, shapeless flannel nightgowns.

HUSBAND: True enough.

WIFE: So only now, tonight, does it seem to show.

HUSBAND: I see.

　　(Pause. They smile at each other. Then he looks at his watch.)

HUSBAND: I've got to teach a class in an hour.

WIFE: Oh, I know. And I've got to go out to a meeting on Open Housing.

HUSBAND: So...

WIFE: I just wanted you to know. *(Pause.)* So you could plan.

HUSBAND: Yes. I will. I'll plan accordingly. *(Smiles at her again, puts on his glasses, and returns to his book.)*

　　(She starts off and then stops.)

WIFE: Oh, there's one thing, though.

HUSBAND: *(Reading)* Mmmmmm. And what's that, dear?

WIFE: I don't know whether you've thought about this, or not.

HUSBAND: *(Looking up.)* State the problem. And I'll tell you whether I've thought about it.

WIFE: It's a little tricky.

HUSBAND: Well. We're married, after all.

WIFE: Yes. That's why it's a little tricky.

HUSBAND: Perhaps. But that's also why you should feel free to speak out.

WIFE: All right. *(Pause.)* You see, I'm not absolutely sure that *this*...*(She looks down at her stomach.)* is yours. *(Pause.)*

　　(He marks his place in his book, puts it down carefully, takes off his glasses, and then looks up.)

HUSBAND: Ah. So that's the problem.

WIFE: Yes. That's the problem.

HUSBAND: I think I'll trust you on this one, dear.

WIFE: That's sweet of you, darling. *(Pause.)* But do I trust myself?

HUSBAND: I think you should. So there we are.

WIFE: But...

HUSBAND: But what?

WIFE: The thing is...Now how do I put this?

HUSBAND: Speak frankly now.

WIFE: I'll try. The thing is...that you and I...haven't made love very much. Recently.

HUSBAND: Is that true?

WIFE: I think it is. Not very much. Not recently.

HUSBAND: Hmmm. Define "recently."

WIFE: Well, I mean...five years, more or less...give or take a month or two.

HUSBAND: Is that true?

WIFE: I think it is. *(Pause.)*

HUSBAND: *(Lighting his pipe.)* My gosh, has it been that long?

WIFE: Oh, yes.

HUSBAND: Well, well. And so...

WIFE: And so...

HUSBAND: And so you mind, obviously.

WIFE: Mind?

HUSBAND: Mind that we haven't. Much. Recently.

WIFE: Oh, no. Oh, no, no. I don't *mind.* Why should I mind?

HUSBAND: Well, then...

WIFE: *(Pointing to her stomach.)* I'm just thinking of *this,* that's all.

HUSBAND: Oh, I *see!*

WIFE: *(Smiling.)* You see?

HUSBAND: Of *course.* I see the connection! *(He slaps his head.)* Forgive me. I was thinking about my class.

WIFE: Oh, heavens. I forgive you. You love your work.

HUSBAND: Yes, but I'm with you now. I'm on your wavelength now.

WIFE: Oh, good.

HUSBAND: Yes, yes. I understand now. What you're really saying is...now stop me if I'm wrong...but what you're really saying is that you think someone else might have impregnated you.

WIFE: More or less. Yes.

HUSBAND: I see, I see, I see.

WIFE: It's possible, after all.

HUSBAND: Yes. It's possible.

WIFE: On these evenings that you have to go teach.

HUSBAND: Yes, or when you go out to your meetings.

WIFE: Yes. Exactly.

HUSBAND: So we do have a problem there, don't we?

WIFE: Yes. We really do.

(Pause; he looks at her, looks at her stomach, scratches his head, taps his teeth with a pencil, lights his pipe, twirls his glasses.)

HUSBAND: You know, darling...it occurs to me...that I should have made love to you more.

WIFE: Oh, no, no...

HUSBAND: I'm kicking myself now.

WIFE: Oh, don't, don't...

HUSBAND: I am. Things would have been much simpler.

WIFE: Oh, sweetheart, stop punishing yourself.

HUSBAND: But why didn't I? Darn it! Darn it all!

WIFE: Darling, you have your work.

HUSBAND: Oh, sure, but…

WIFE: You have your intellectual life…

HUSBAND: That's all very well, but…

WIFE: You had your book to get out…

HUSBAND: Yes, yes, but, darling, that doesn't really answer the question. The question is, why haven't I made love to you in the past five years? That's the question.

(Pause.)

WIFE: Well. You used to laugh too much, maybe.

HUSBAND: Laugh?

WIFE: Yes. In the old days. Whenever we started to make love, you'd start to chuckle.

HUSBAND: I did, didn't I? I remember now. *(He chuckles.)*

WIFE: Yes. You'd chuckle.

HUSBAND: *(Chuckling.)* Because the whole thing struck me as being slightly absurd. *(Chuckling.)* When you think about it. *(Chuckling.)* I should learn to control myself. *(He chuckles louder; controls himself stoically; then bursts into loud laughter; then forces himself to subside; looks at her.)* I'm sorry.

WIFE: Oh, don't be sorry. I was just as bad.

HUSBAND: Did you chuckle?

WIFE: No. Actually I'd cry.

HUSBAND: I don't remember your crying.

WIFE: Well, I'd whimper.

HUSBAND: Yes, yes! You would. You'd whimper. *(Chuckles.)*

WIFE: Well, I felt so sad! Making love. While all these horrible things are going on in the world.

HUSBAND: Yes. So you'd whimper. I remember now.

WIFE: Viet Nam…Urban blight…all that…I felt so guilty!

HUSBAND: And I felt so absurd.

WIFE: Yes. You chuckling, me whimpering…

HUSBAND: Yes. Oh, yes.

WIFE: And so it wasn't very conducive.

HUSBAND: Right. So we gave it up. That answers that. *(Pause; picks up his book and starts to read.)*

WIFE: But now there's this. *(Indicates her stomach.)*

HUSBAND: *(Reading; taking notes.)* Keep it.

WIFE: What?

HUSBAND: Keep it. Bear it. Bring it home.

WIFE: Oh, darling…

HUSBAND: Give it my name. Consider me its father.

WIFE: Oh, sweetheart.

HUSBAND: I've let you down. Now I'll make it up. Keep it.

WIFE: But I'm partly to blame.

HUSBAND: But I'm the man.

WIFE: You certainly are! You certainly are the man!

HUSBAND: And now I'm afraid that I must prepare for my class.

WIFE: Yes. And I've got to go to my meeting.
   (They smile at each other; then she starts out; then she stops, and stands reflectively. After a moment, he looks at her.)

HUSBAND: But you're not satisfied.

WIFE: Oh, I am, I am.

HUSBAND: Darling, we've been married ten years. You are not satisfied.

WIFE: You've got a class.

HUSBAND: My wife comes first. Come on. What's the problem now?

WIFE: I'm embarrassed even to bring it up.

HUSBAND: *(Tenderly.)* Come on. Out with it. Tell Daddy.

WIFE: All right. *(Pause.)* What if this…*(She looks at her stomach.)* turns out to be black?
   (Pause.)

HUSBAND: Black?

WIFE: Black. Or at least mulatto. Depending on how the chromosomes line up.

HUSBAND: *(Pause. Lights his pipe again.)* Mmmmm.

WIFE: You see? You see the problem?

HUSBAND: *(Nodding.)* Mmmmm.

WIFE: I mean, can you still act as its father if it's black?

HUSBAND: *(Puffing away.)* Mmmmmm. *(Looks at her wryly.)* Yes, well, that puts a different complexion on things.

WIFE: *(Giggling.)* Funny.

HUSBAND: *(Chuckling.)* That's a horse of a different color.

WIFE: *(Laughing.)* Now cut it out. You're awful. *(Stops laughing.)* Try to be serious.

HUSBAND: *(Pause. Settles down.)* Black, eh?

WIFE: I should have told you before.

HUSBAND: No, no. I should have assumed it.

WIFE: It just slipped my mind, I guess.

HUSBAND: I'm glad it did. That says something for America these days.

WIFE: Yes. But it's still a problem.

HUSBAND: In this case, yes. I'd say so. *(Pause.)* So you must let me think it out.

WIFE: But your class…

HUSBAND: I'll just be less prepared than I like to be. Which may be good. Which may be very good. Which may make things more lively and spontaneous. So let me think about this other problem. *(Puffs on his pipe.)*

(She stands watching him.)

HUSBAND: I could still adopt it.

WIFE: How?

HUSBAND: We could tell the world that you had a blue baby. Which died. And then we could bring home the black one. Which we say we adopted.

WIFE: That sounds awfully complicated.

HUSBAND: I know it.

WIFE: Awfully baroque.

HUSBAND: I know it.

WIFE: Besides, the real father might object. He might take pride in it himself.

HUSBAND: Need he know?

WIFE: Oh, yes. Because he'll see it, after all.

HUSBAND: You mean, he'll continue to come around.

WIFE: Oh, yes. After I'm home from the hospital. And capable of sexual intercourse again.

HUSBAND: I see.

WIFE: So that pretty well puts a damper on the adopting idea.

HUSBAND: Yes, it does. *(He thinks.)*

WIFE: But you have your class…

HUSBAND: No, no. Now wait a minute…*(He thinks carefully, then suddenly pounds his fist on the arm of his chair.)* Sweetheart, I'm going to be honest with you. *(Points to the footstool.)* Sit down.

WIFE: *(Looking at the footstool.)* I can't sit down. Your feet are there.

HUSBAND: I'll remove my feet. *(He does.)* Now sit down.

WIFE: All right. I'll sit down. *(Sits on the footstool in front of him.)*

HUSBAND: Now don't look at me. Face forward. Because this is going to be hard for me to tell, and hard for you to hear.

WIFE: All right. I won't look at you.

HUSBAND: And if I'm inarticulate about this, you must try to understand that this is a difficult thing for a man to tell his wife. I'm only doing it—I'm only telling you—because it seems to be the only way to solve this problem.

WIFE: *(Smoothing her skirt over her stomach.)* Yes. This problem.

HUSBAND: Now try not to interrupt, darling, unless you have to. Unless you're unclear about anything. Save your remarks and comments for the end. All right?

WIFE: I'll try.

HUSBAND: All right. *(He takes a deep breath.)* Now. To begin with, I've been lying to you this evening.

WIFE: Lying?

HUSBAND: Ssshhh. Lying. I don't have a class tonight. I've never had a class at night. I don't believe in evening classes. All these years I've been lying. The class that I've told you meets at night actually meets on Mondays, Wednesdays, and Fridays at 10 A.M.

WIFE: I see.

HUSBAND: You may well ask, therefore, where I go on these nights when I say I have classes. *(Pause.)* And that is what is so difficult to tell you. *(Pause.)* The fact is, I don't leave this house. Not really. Oh, I leave by the front door, all right. but I immediately circle around in back, and go down into the cellar by means of the bulkhead.

WIFE: I see.

HUSBAND: Now. What do I do in the cellar? You are probably asking yourself that. What do I do in the cellar?...Don't look at me, darling! *(Pause; then grimly.)* Here's what I do in the cellar. I make my way to a small space behind the furnace. And in that small space, I have hidden...certain things. *(Pause.)* What have I hidden? I'll tell you. *(He counts them off on his fingers.)* Some black theatrical make-up. A woolly wig. A complete change of clothes. And a mirror. That's what I have hidden in the cellar.

WIFE: I see...

HUSBAND: Yes. You see, my darling, or you're beginning to. When I go into the cellar, I set the mirror up on an adjacent water pipe. I strip myself to the buff. I daub myself from head to toe with that dusky make-up. I glue on that curly wig. I don the makeshift clothes. I leave the cellar. Go to the front door. Ring the bell. and reappear to you. So you see, my poor darling, I am your Negro visitor, and have been all along.

WIFE: You.

HUSBAND: Me.

WIFE: But—

HUSBAND: Oh, I know it sounds implausible. But remember how you always lower the lights. Remember, too, that I played Othello in high school. Somehow I was able to pass. I have deceived you for these past years. Deceived my own wife! Disguising myself as a Negro, and capitalizing on the sympathies you naturally feel for that unhappy race!

WIFE: But...why?

HUSBAND: Because I wanted to make love to you. And somehow this seemed to be the only way I could do it. You'll have to admit it worked.

WIFE: *(Looking at her stomach.)* Oh, yes. It worked.

HUSBAND: So out of all this depravity, at least a child will be born. And I was its father, after all.

WIFE: I'm somewhat...stunned...by all this.

HUSBAND: I know you are, darling. *(Gets up.)* Try to assimilate it while I'm gone.

WIFE: Gone?

HUSBAND: I'm going down to the cellar now.

WIFE: To put on your costume?

HUSBAND: No. To burn it.

WIFE: Burn it?

HUSBAND: Yes. It's all over now. Because you know. The mask is off. Any attempt to wear it again would be foolish. I'd be nothing but a self-conscious amateur. Our love life would be as absurd as it was before I found this way around it. So I'm going to destroy my role. *(Pause; he looks at her.)* And when I come back, I want you gone.

WIFE: Gone?

HUSBAND: You must leave me now.

WIFE: No.

HUSBAND: You must. Oh, my darling, this urge to love you is still in me. I don't know what...oblique form...it will take next. Take the child and go.

WIFE: Never.

HUSBAND: Please. Listen: I don't know what I'll think of next, in the cellar. I've got Genet down there. And a complete de Sade. I'll reread them both, looking for increasingly complicated arabesques of sexual perversion. I may reappear with a whip. Wearing riding boots. Or dressed as a woman. Get out, darling. Run to the suburbs. Give my child a normal home. Go!

WIFE: Normal? Normal? *(She laughs uneasily.)* What is normal?

HUSBAND: You're normal, my love.

WIFE: Me? Oh, my God, how little do you know! *(Grimly.)* Sit down. I have a tale to tell-o.

HUSBAND: Nothing you could say...

WIFE: Sit down.

HUSBAND: Nothing...

WIFE: I've known all along you were my dark lover!

HUSBAND: *(Sits down.)* You've known?

WIFE: From the beginning.

HUSBAND: But...how?

WIFE: Five years ago, when you announced to me that you had scheduled some evening classes, I became suspicious. And so when you left for the first class, I...followed you.

HUSBAND: Followed me?

WIFE: Yes. I followed my own husband. Followed you to that tacky little theater-supply shop downtown where you bought your disguise. Followed you back here. Followed you into the cellar, hid behind the hot water heater, watched you change into your poor, pathetic imitation of a Negro.

HUSBAND: You spied on me...

WIFE: Yes, I spied on you, my darling. Furtively, suspiciously, like some aging matron. But when I saw what you were doing, when I understood that you were doing it for me, my heart went out to you. With a great rush of longing, I dashed back upstairs, eager to receive you, but at the same time terrified that you would see that I recognized you. Frantically, I dimmed the lights, to make things easier for both of us.

HUSBAND: I thought it was because you were romantic.

WIFE: I know you did, darling. And I let you think that. But no: it was simply so I wouldn't give myself away.

HUSBAND: You were acting? The whole time?

WIFE: Yes. Wasn't I good? Pretending that you were someone new and strange? I, I, who am no actress, improvising like a professional during that whole scene!

HUSBAND: *(Shaking his head.)* It's hard to believe...You seemed so... excited!

WIFE: I was! I was terribly excited. I'll admit it. That strange, sly courtship, the banter, the give and take, with all those peculiar racial overtones. I threw myself into it with a vengeance. But then…when you carried me into the bedroom…everything changed.

HUSBAND: What do you mean? I was a tiger!

WIFE: You were, darling. You were a tiger. But I wasn't.

HUSBAND: You said you loved me.

WIFE: I was only pretending. I really hated you.

HUSBAND: Hated me?

WIFE: Hated myself. It was awful. I felt so guilty. All my old sexual agonies were magnified, as it were, by a gallery of mirrors. I wanted at least to whimper, as I did normally, with you, when you were white, but now you were black, I had to stifle my own sighs. Worse, I had to pretend, to play, to *fake* the most authentic experience a woman can have! And all the time, I felt like a thing, an object, a creature without a soul, a poor, pathetic concubine in the arms of an Ethiopian potentate. And when you left—finally left—I just lay on the bed, arms folded across my breast, like a stone carving on my own tomb. It took every ounce of energy I could muster to rise and greet you at the door when you returned from your supposed class.

(Pause.)

HUSBAND: So. For the past five years you have been through hell.

WIFE: No. After that first ghastly evening, I suffered nothing.

HUSBAND: You mean, you grew accustomed…

WIFE: I mean, I wasn't there.

HUSBAND: You weren't there?

WIFE: No. I left the house right after you went into the cellar.

HUSBAND: But then who…was here…with me?

WIFE: I got a substitute.

HUSBAND: I see.

WIFE: Oh, darling, try to understand. I simply could not endure another evening like that. The sham, the pretense—it revolted me. And yet I knew how much it meant to you! All the next day, I racked my brain trying to figure out something which would satisfy us both. I took a long walk. I wandered all over town. Finally, about an hour before I was due home, I saw a woman. Who looked a little like me. Same hair, same height…roughly the same age. It was at least a chance. Before I really knew what I was doing, I approached her and asked her whether she'd like to sleep with a Negro. Naturally she said she would. And so now, for the past five years, this good woman has come here while you were in the cellar changing your clothes, and in the dim light, she has pretended to be me.

HUSBAND: I see.

WIFE: Do you hate me very much?

HUSBAND: No. I don't hate you. But I must say I'm somewhat...surprised.

WIFE: I suspected you would be.

HUSBAND: But what about that? *(Points to her stomach.)*

WIFE: *(Clutching her stomach.)* Ah, this...

HUSBAND: Yes. That. Whose is that?

WIFE: Now bear with me, darling. On these nights while you're in the cellar, and while this good woman is preparing herself for your return, I go off with a real Negro. There it is. In a nutshell. His Cadillac pulls up quietly in front. He flashes his lights. And I sneak out, and drive off with him into the black ghetto. There, on an old mattress, infested with lice, nibbled at by rats, we make love. Love which for the first time in my life I can give myself up to, since I feel that with him I am expiating not only my own guilt, but the guilt of all America.

HUSBAND: I see. And so he is the father of that.

WIFE: No.

HUSBAND: No?

WIFE: Somehow, even that relationship wasn't enough. Somehow, in the ghetto, with all that soul music pulsing around me, all that frustration, all that anger, I still felt as if I were not playing my part. So I betrayed my lover for his friend. And his friend for another. And so on and so forth, with Puerto Ricans, Mexican-Americans, and Indians on relief. Oh, darling, for the past five years, I've been offering myself as an ecstatic white sacrifice to anyone with an income of less than five thousand.

HUSBAND: And so the father is...

WIFE: Social Injustice, on a large and general scale.

HUSBAND: I see.

WIFE: And now you'll leave me, won't you?

HUSBAND: Me? Leave you now? *(Laughs peculiarly.)* I want to stay more than ever. *(Cleans his pipe carefully.)* What would you say...if I said...that everything you've told me...excites me?

WIFE: Excites you?

HUSBAND: Sets my blood boiling. Gives me strange, wild frissons of desire…What would you say if I said that your ghetto experiences have lit a lurid light in my own loins?

WIFE: Really?

HUSBAND: *(Still cleaning his pipe; not looking at her.)* What would you say…if I said…that I suddenly want to exercise—how shall I put it?—a *droit de seigneur* on you? That I want to steal you from the peasants, and carry you into my bedroom, and ravage you with the reading lights going full blaze? *(Looks at her carefully.)* What would you say, if I said that?

(Pause; she looks at him coyly.)

WIFE: I'd say…do it.

HUSBAND: Mmmm.

WIFE: *(Hastily.)* And let me add this: Let me add that a woman, too, is capable of weird desires. This is hard to say, but looking at you now, slouched in that chair, surrounded by your books and papers, I suddenly have the strange urge to experience the stale comforts of bourgeois married love. They say that Americans in Paris, surfeited by the rich food, yearn for the simple hamburger. So it is with me. For you. Tonight.

HUSBAND: *(Getting up slowly.)* Then…

WIFE: *(Backing away from him.)* But there's still this! *(Indicating her stomach.)* This problem!

HUSBAND: *(Moving toward her.)* That's no problem.

WIFE: No problem?

HUSBAND: That's just the premise to the problem. Now we've solved the problem we no longer need the premise.

WIFE: I fail to follow.

HUSBAND: That's just the starting mechanism. Now the motor's going, we no longer need the starter.

WIFE: *(Looking down at her stomach.)* Oh.

HUSBAND: *(Stalking her.)* That's not really a baby you have in there.

WIFE: *(Backing away.)* Not really a baby?

HUSBAND: No. That's a balloon you have in there.

WIFE: A balloon?

HUSBAND: A balloon. Or a bladder. Or an old beach ball.

WIFE: It's a baby. I'm practically positive.

HUSBAND: No, no. Look. I'll show you. *(Takes the pointed metal prong of his pipe cleaner and gives her a quick, neat jab in the stomach.)* Touché!

(There is a pop, and then a hissing sound. She slowly deflates. They both watch.) You see? The problem was simply academic. *(Pause.)*

WIFE: *(Looking at him sheepishly.)* Aren't we awful?

HUSBAND: *(Going to his chair, closing his book, carefully marking the place.)* You started it.

WIFE: I know. It was my turn. You started the last one.

HUSBAND: *(Neatening his books and papers.)* Well, it's fun.

WIFE: Shouldn't we see a psychiatrist?

HUSBAND: *(Tapping out his pipe; putting his glasses in his glasses-case.)* Why? We're happy. *(Turns off his light. The stage is now lit only from a light offstage.)*

WIFE: But we're so de*praved!*

(He looks at her, then throws back his head and gives a long Tarzan-like whoop; then he pounds his chest like a gorilla; she giggles.)

WIFE: Quiet! You'll wake the children!

(He picks her up in his arms; she pummels him melodramatically; speaks in an English accent.)

WIFE: No, Tarzan! White men do not take women by force! No, Tarzan! White men *court* their women! They are civilized, Tarzan. It's very complicated. Do you understand what I am saying? Com-pli-ca-ted...Com-pli-...

(She giggles and kicks as he carries her offstage.)

END OF PLAY

Public Affairs

Part One
THE LOVE COURSE

THE LOVE COURSE and THE OPEN MEETING were written one after the other in the early seventies. I revised them years later, and put them together, where I hope they belong.

Original Production

Neither The Love Course nor The Open Meeting, to my knowledge, has had a reviewed production in New York City. The Love Course was done in England in the early seventies, and both have been performed in college theatres.

The Characters

Professor Carroway, a woman of certain age, who is professor of romantic literature at a large university.

Professor Burgess, a man of about the same age, who is professor of Renaissance literature at the same university.

Sally, a student of literature.

Mike, a student of electrical engineering.

Setting

The entire play takes place in, and during, a class in literature at a university. The audience is to be considered members of the class. The stage should suggest the teaching area: a wooden desk or table, with two or three simple chairs on either side, facing front. A blackboard behind, on which is written a list: Plato, Euripides, Dante, *Tristan et Iseult*, Shakespeare, *Madame Bovary*, *Wuthering Heights*, D.H. Lawrence, John Updike et al. Bracketing this list, and written in large letters, is "SAVE!!"

The Love Course

After the audience is seated, a loud school bell rings. Professor Burgess comes down the aisle toward the stage. He wears a sports coat and gray flannels, and carries a briefcase. Mike and Sally, two students who are sitting in the front row, get up to meet him. The following can be somewhat ad-libbed:

SALLY: Professor Burgess…
BURGESS: Hi, Sally…
SALLY: This is my friend Mike. Can he sit in on this class?
BURGESS: Certainly. Hello, Mike…
MIKE: Thanks, Professor Burgess.
    (Burgess goes on up toward the stage and waits, as Professor Carroway comes down the aisle, acknowledging the audience with soft greetings. She carries a stack of well-worn books, and wears something simple and slightly old-fashioned. Sally waylays her, too.)
SALLY: Professor Carroway…
CARROWAY: Ah. Good afternoon, Sally.
SALLY: This is the Mike I told you about.
MIKE: I've heard a lot about you, Professor Carroway.
CARROWAY: Thank you, and welcome.
    (She moves towards the stage where Burgess is waiting. She nods to him, then begins to settle her books and papers on the table. He comes behind the table to speak to her. They converse in whispers. This, again, might be somewhat ad-libbed.)
BURGESS: *(Whispering.)* I have to leave in a minute.
CARROWAY: *(Whispering.)* What? Surely not today…
BURGESS: The Curriculum Meeting…

CARROWAY: But this is our last class…

BURGESS: I'm sorry. *(Pause. He indicates class.)* You begin.

CARROWAY: Very well.

(He sits down on one of the chairs. She looks at him, looks at the class, comes downstage, and begins:)

CARROWAY: This is our last class on the literature of love. I don't mean simply for this term. This is the last class Professor Burgess and I will ever teach together. As you may know, I have accepted a position in the English Department at Mount Holyoke College for Women. And Professor Burgess has decided to join the administration of this university. So we will never teach together again. *(Glances at him.)* I am therefore especially eager on this, our last day, to bring the course together once and for all. I want to resolve, if we possibly can, all the great themes of love which have obsessed us and the Western World, from February up until now. *(Turns to Burgess.)* Professor Burgess I'm sure you have something to add.

BURGESS: Yes. *(Gets up.)* A few quick points before I go.

CARROWAY: *(To audience.)* He has to go to some meeting.

BURGESS: *(To audience.)* I have to go to the Curriculum Committee.

CARROWAY: Even though this is our last class.

BURGESS: They're revising the entire undergraduate curriculum.

CARROWAY: *(To audience.)* They want to make everything aggressively relevant.

BURGESS: I'm afraid I have to go.

CARROWAY: Oh don't be afraid.

BURGESS: I'm not afraid.

CARROWAY: Then go.

BURGESS: I will.

CARROWAY: I am naturally…very disappointed, that's all.

BURGESS: Surely you can handle this yourself: a quick review, a few questions, a discussion of the exam…

CARROWAY: *(Suddenly quite loud.)* I had planned to do more. In our last class. I had planned to do…everything! *(She goes and sits down, huffily.)* Well then, before you go, I hope at least you'll try to say goodbye.

(Pause.)

BURGESS: *(To audience; haltingly.)* Last fall, when Professor Carroway asked me to join her in teaching this course, I must confess I had some trepidation. She proposed that we deal with the literature of love from Plato all the way to the present. Now I'm a Renaissance Man...

CARROWAY: *(Under her breath.)* So I have heard and do, in part, believe...

BURGESS: *(After glancing at her.)* And Professor Carroway specializes in the Romantic period. Neither one of us had ever before focused on so specific a topic from so broad a perspective. And neither one of us had ever taught in...tandem before.

CARROWAY: *(Standing up.)* You are apologizing for the course!

BURGESS: I am not. I'm simply saying—

CARROWAY: You are apologizing for what we have done.

BURGESS: Dear lady, I am not! I've *loved* the Love Course! *(Covering his enthusiasm.)* I mean, it has been just the sort of course students seem to want. *(Pause.)* I am simply responding to the criticism which has arisen on the outside.

CARROWAY: What criticism?

BURGESS: Well, we have been accused, by some of our colleagues of...

CARROWAY: Of what? Of what?

BURGESS: Of being flamboyant and theatrical.

CARROWAY: *(Laughing.)* Oh dear.

BURGESS: And of straying far from the syllabus...

CARROWAY: Oh dear, oh dear...

BURGESS: Others say that all we've done is carry on private dialogue in public!

CARROWAY: And have you regretted it, Professor Burgess?

BURGESS: Not for a moment! I'm simply saying that some people have called our Love Course a little erotic—I mean, erratic.

CARROWAY: *(Laughing.)* Oh dear, oh dear, oh dear. Sigmund, wouldst thou were with us at this hour...Perhaps you'd *better* go to your meeting.

BURGESS: I will. I plan to. Good luck to all on the exam. *(He starts out.)*

CARROWAY: *(Suddenly getting up.)* I had planned...

(Burgess stops out of politeness.)

I had planned to read and discuss the first few lines of Shakespeare's *Antony and Cleopatra*.

BURGESS: Ah...

CARROWAY: *(To audience.)* It says worlds about what we've been up to.

BURGESS: *(To audience.)* I'm very fond of the first scene of *Antony and Cleopatra*.

CARROWAY: I know you are.

BURGESS: *(Quoting.)* "Here is my space...Kingdoms are clay..."

CARROWAY: I know. I know.

BURGESS: *(To audience.)* I once wrote an article about that first scene.

CARROWAY: *(To audience.)* "In his salad days,
When he was green in judgment, cold in blood."

BURGESS: It was a good article.

CARROWAY: It most certainly was. Much better, perhaps, than some of
your recent, earnest memoranda on the curriculum.

BURGESS: We have a responsibility to the students.

CARROWAY: We have a responsibility to Shakespeare.

BURGESS: One must try to keep a foot in both camps.

CARROWAY: *(To audience.)* "His legs bestrid the ocean; his rear'd arm,
Crested the world!"

BURGESS: *(Taking her up.)* "O Star of the East!
Where souls do couch on flowers, we'll hand in hand
And with out sprightly port make the ghosts gaze.
Dido and her Aeneas shall want troops,
And all the haunt be ours."

CARROWAY: Oh exactly! Are you sure you can't stay and teach the first
scene?
(Pause.)

BURGESS: *(Suddenly calling out.)* Someone...will someone do me a favor?
Will someone run over to the meeting...

CARROWAY: *(Calling out.)* Someone not regularly in the class...

BURGESS: And tell them I'll be a little late...

CARROWAY: I want our regular students here. Since it's the last class.

BURGESS: Is there anyone auditing, then?

SALLY: *(Appears in the aisle. Calling up.)* Mike says he'll do it.

CARROWAY: Oh yes. He's expendable.

BURGESS: Mike, would you run over to the conference room on the third
floor of the new science building, and tell them I've been temporar-
ily delayed.

CARROWAY: Say he has a class.

BURGESS: Say I'll be there soon.

CARROWAY: In an hour.

BURGESS: In a minute.

SALLY: Go on, Mike. Do it.

BURGESS: Will you, Mike? As a favor to me?

MIKE: Uh huh. *(He exits up the aisle.)*

CARROWAY: Thank you, Sally, for lending us your lover.

BURGESS: *(Now rummaging through his briefcase.)* Now where's my Shakespeare?

CARROWAY: I have mine. Look on with me.

(She holds out her book. He joins her, notices her book.)

BURGESS: All these notes in the margin...

CARROWAY: Oh I plan my classes. I prepare...

BURGESS: I can see you do.

(They might settle in their chairs behind the table here.)

CARROWAY: Well. *(To audience.)* After some preliminary—and I've always felt unnecessary talk—Antony and Cleopatra enter and take the stage. *(Reads.)* "If it be love indeed, tell me how much."

BURGESS: *(Reading.)* "There's beggary in the love that can be reckon'd."

CARROWAY: "I'll set a bourn how far to be belov'd."

BURGESS: "Then must thou needs find out new heaven, new earth."

(Pause.)

CARROWAY: *(To audience.)* Of course, she is asking him to describe his love.

BURGESS: *(To audience.)* Which he refuses to do.

CARROWAY: *(To him.)* Why?

BURGESS: Because to describe something is to...limit it. It's beggary, base and contemptible, to pin down a love like theirs.

CARROWAY: So she says she'll make up new rules, new boundaries. "I'll set a bourn," she says.

BURGESS: And he replies that she'd have to invent an entirely new world— "new heaven, new earth"—to encompass their love.

CARROWAY: Yes. *(Pause. Then to audience.)* But you see: they *have* described their love by *refusing* to describe it.

BURGESS: But we also get a shiver of foreboding. Because we know it can't last. Not in this world.

CARROWAY: Which is why they create their *own* world. Through language.

BURGESS: Which can't last either.

CARROWAY: Oh yes.

BURGESS: Oh no. The real world intrudes almost immediately. A messenger arrives from Rome.

CARROWAY: Who tells us that the real world is falling apart.

BURGESS: Not falling apart...

CARROWAY: Oh yes, oh yes. Collapsing completely. And we also hear...

for the first time…that there's a wife. *(She glances at him, then reads.)* "Fulvia perhaps is angry"…and later, "The shrill-tongued Fulvia scolds." *(To audience.)* Fulvia being the wife. *(Reading slyly.)* "Thou blushest, Antony…"

BURGESS: *(Quickly.)* But Antony replies—in some of Shakespeare's most sweeping poetry… *(He should be on his feet by now; reciting from memory.)* "Let Rome in Tiber melt and the wide arch

Of the rang'd empire fall! Here is my space.

Kingdoms are clay…The nobleness of life

Is to do thus…"

(Pause; he looks at her; then turns to audience.)

And at this point, he kisses her.

(Pause.)

According to the First Folio edition.

CARROWAY: Yes. I believe he does.

MIKE: *(Coming down the aisle.)* Professor Burgess…

(Burgess looks out.)

They want you there.

CARROWAY: Why?

MIKE: They said they need your vote.

BURGESS: I'd better go.

CARROWAY: Vote, and then come back.

BURGESS: There won't be time.

CARROWAY: There will be if you run!

BURGESS: I won't run, thank you very much. *(He comes down into the aisle, speaks to audience as he leaves.)* Good luck, people. I probably won't see you again.

CARROWAY: *(Calling after him.)* Nonsense! Antony comes back, and so will you. If you hurry! *(To audience.)* "And so he moved, with stately steps, and slow…"

(Burgess glances at her then leaves. Carroway closes her Shakespeare and comes to a decision. She goes to the stack of books on the table and takes up another book, old, leathery and worn. She looks at it affectionately then calls out to the audience.)

CARROWAY: You…Young man…Mike.

MIKE: *(Appears reluctantly in the aisle again.)* Me?

CARROWAY: You. Would you like to do the state some service?

MIKE: *(Shrugs.)* I guess.

CARROWAY: Come up here, please.

(Mike comes up on stage, uneasily, shy, embarrassed.)
Now. Do you see this book?
(Mike nods.)
This is my own personal annotated version of *Wuthering Heights.* I used this when I wrote my biography of Emily Brontë.
(Mike nods.)
Have you read my biography?
(Mike shakes his head.)
Have you read *Wuthering Heights?*
(Mike shakes his head.)
Then, poor soul, there is a great gap in your education which you could have repaired if you'd taken this course.

MIKE: Hey now wait a—

CARROWAY: Quiet, please. I'm about to give you instructions. Take this book to the Curriculum Meeting. Give it to Professor Burgess. Tell him I plan to end the class reading from it. *(Takes a bobby pin out of her hair, puts it in the book.)* Reading here. On this page. At this point. *(Hands him the book.)* Take it, and guard it with your life.
(Mike takes the book, and starts off, eager to be off the stage.)
Tell him…
(Mike stops.)
Tell him we began the class in his field. I'd like to end it in mine.

MIKE: I'll give him the book. *(He goes out, down the aisle.)*

CARROWAY: Now. While we're waiting, let's be aggressively Socratic. *(Calls out.)* Come up here, Sally, where we can all see and hear you.
(Sally comes up on stage; Carroway puts her arm around her and speaks to audience.)
Sally has been loyal from the beginning. Sally has loved this course. Indeed, when Sally heard that my contract was not being renewed, she wrote a letter in protest on my behalf. So let's listen, and learn from Sally. *(She gestures for Sally to sit down.)* Sally, why did you sign up for this course?

SALLY: To learn about love.

CARROWAY: Have you ever been in love?

SALLY: Yes. *(Pause.)* No.

CARROWAY: Make up your mind.

SALLY: I thought I was. But now I don't think so.

CARROWAY: Would you like to be?

SALLY: Oh yes.

CARROWAY: Why?

SALLY: Because…oh because…it sounds so great.

CARROWAY: Of course. These books do that for us. They've given us the words that make it great. *(To audience; indicating blackboard.)* Everyone thinks Wagner fell in love with Cosima Liszt, and then wrote *Tristan und Isolde.* Not true! Not true, people! Wagner wrote *Tristan* and thereby found the language which *enabled* him to fall in love. So it is with you, Sally. You are no longer in the cave! You are not longer blindly groping at the rank body of some pimply adolescent male! You have learned the language of love now. You are doomed to reach and strive and seek for something far more transcendent. Am I right, Sally?

SALLY: *(Nodding eagerly.)* Uh huh.

CARROWAY: Let's pursue the case further, Sally…Have you read all the books on the reading list?

SALLY: Oh yes.

CARROWAY: Did you like them?

SALLY: Oh yes. Most of them, anyway. Yes.

CARROWAY: Did you find anything in common with all of these books?

SALLY: *(Pause. Sally scrutinizes the list of the blackboard.)* It's kind of hard to keep them all in mind.

CARROWAY: Oh the mind, the mind. We're way beyond the mind, Sally. By now these books should be in your deep heart's soul.

SALLY: I know it.

CARROWAY: Then think, Sally. What are these books all about?

SALLY: They're about love.

CARROWAY: We know that, Sally. But what kind of love?

SALLY: *(Thinking like hell.)* Most of them are about…well, adultery.

CARROWAY: That's a grim, Puritanical word, Sally. They are about love beyond marriage.

SALLY: Yes…

CARROWAY: And what else are they about, Sally?

SALLY: Most of them…are about death.

CARROWAY: Precisely. *(Strides to the blackboard, begins ticking off the books.)* Phaedra, Beatrice, Isolde, Juliet, Emma Bovary, Catharine Earnshaw—all the great women die for love!

SALLY: Is that true?

CARROWAY: Of course it's true! There it is, on the board!

SALLY: *(Looking at the board.)* Lady Chatterley doesn't die.

CARROWAY: Well she ought to, Sally.

SALLY: And in the modern books…in John Updike and…others…people don't die.

CARROWAY: They *do,* Sally. The women do. They die the modern death. They die spiritually. Oh yes. Name a book, name a love story worthy of the name, that does not end with the death of the lady.

(Pause.)

SALLY: I can't.

CARROWAY: Then love in the Western World ends in what, Sally?

SALLY: Death.

CARROWAY: And do you still want to fall in love, Sally?

SALLY: Yes.

CARROWAY: Why?

SALLY: Because it must be worth it.

CARROWAY: Oh yes I think so. Yes I hope so. Yes. Despite all the risks, despite the fact that the woman is always sacrificed, it must be worth it. Yes. *(She looks out and sees Mike returning at the back of the room.)* Ah. Is that our messenger from Rome?

(Mike tries to take his seat.)

I'm speaking to you, sir. Are you our messenger from Rome?

MIKE: Huh?

CARROWAY: No, no. Don't sit *down.* Messengers never sit. They stand. And speak. Come up here. Tell us how things are in the real world.

SALLY: *(To Carroway.)* He's shy.

CARROWAY: Then he should learn not to be. Come up here, please.

(Mike reluctantly comes onto the stage.)

CARROWAY: Now tell us about the Curriculum Meeting. Who's in, who's out? Who was interrupting whom? What fateful edicts and what grim decrees were they determining?

(Pause.)

MIKE: I dunno.

SALLY: *(Starting to leave.)* We'd better—

CARROWAY: No, stay, Sally. Both stay. While we hear the messenger. *(To Mike.)* Tell me about Professor Burgess. Did you give him my book?

MIKE: Yes.

CARROWAY: You did?

MIKE: Yes.

CARROWAY: Did you tell him what I told you to tell him?

MIKE: Yes.

(Pause.)

CARROWAY: Well then, what did he say?

MIKE: He said thank you.

CARROWAY: He said…

MIKE: Thank you.

CARROWAY: *(Sarcastically; to audience.)* Oh these long-winded messengers! *(She wheels on Mike.)* Did he say he'd come back?

MIKE: No.

CARROWAY: No he didn't say, or no he wouldn't come back.

MIKE: He didn't say.

CARROWAY: Is that all?

SALLY: Professor Carroway, Mike's not in the course.

CARROWAY: He can speak, can't he? He has a tongue. *(To Mike.)* Did Professor Burgess look at the particular passage I indicated in my book?

MIKE: Yes.

CARROWAY: And? Did he say anything?

MIKE: No.

CARROWAY: Then what did he *do?* Did he tear the book asunder? Did he press it to his breast?

MIKE: He put it down.

CARROWAY: Down? Down where?

MIKE: On the table.

CARROWAY: You mean my book is simply sitting there, ignored, at that stupid meeting?

MIKE: Someone else picked it up and started looking at it.

CARROWAY: Someone *else?*

MIKE: I think she was his wife.

(Pause.)

CARROWAY: His wife.

SALLY: I think his wife is on the committee. I think she teaches in the Political Science department.

CARROWAY: No, Sally. No. She does *not* teach in the Political Science department. She is *connected* to the Political Science department through some academic nepotism which we will not go into. But she does not *teach* there. Unless you call sitting around in some seminar with two or three graduate students—unless you call that teaching. Which I do not. This, *this* is teaching.

(Mike tries to leave.)

Wait! I said, wait.

(Mike stops.)
So his wife was there. At this meeting.

MIKE: *(With increasing exasperation.)* Yes.

CARROWAY: What about his children? Were his children there? Did they contribute to the discussion? Did they have a vote?

MIKE: No.

CARROWAY: Did his children get their grubby little hands all over my personal copy of *Wuthering Heights?*

MIKE: There were no children at that meeting. *(He starts off again.)*

CARROWAY: Why are you slinking away?

MIKE: I'm not slinking.

CARROWAY: Then tell me more. What did his wife do, after she took my book?

MIKE: Do?

CARROWAY: *(To audience.)* "By heaven, he echoes me
As if there were a monster in this thought
Too hideous to be shown."

SALLY: Professor Carroway…

CARROWAY: What did the wife do with the book? Great heavens, have you ever taken a literature course in your *life?* Are you utterly incapable of description? What are you studying to *be?*

SALLY: He's just visiting, Professor Carroway. He…

CARROWAY: Quiet, Sally. I am educating your lover. You'll thank me for it one day. *(To Mike.)* What do you want to be, sir?

MIKE: An electrical engineer.

CARROWAY: Ah. Then we can look forward to more and better television sets. But what will be shown on them? Can you engineer that? And can you possibly engineer a description of what happened to my own personal copy of *Wuthering Heights?*

MIKE: *(Defiantly.)* She took the book.

CARROWAY: Yes. We know that.

MIKE: And she looked at it.

CARROWAY: Yes. Good. That's vivid. That's precise.

MIKE: And she smiled.
(Pause.)

CARROWAY: Smiled.

MIKE: Uh huh.

CARROWAY: Was that grunt meant to indicate the affirmative.

MIKE: *(Shouting.)* SHE SMILED AT THE BOOK!

CARROWAY: *(Suddenly all business.)* I am going to that meeting.

SALLY: Professor Carroway…

CARROWAY: I am going to retrieve my book!

SALLY: But Professor Carroway…

CARROWAY: *(Exiting down the aisle.)* And I also intend to make a little speech! *(Stops at exit.)* Sally, take the class. Read your excellent paper on Eleanor of Aquitaine and the Troubadour Poets. *There* was a woman who knew about love! *(She leaves.)*

SALLY: *(Calling after her.)* But I didn't *bring* that paper! *(To audience.)* I didn't bring that paper.

MIKE: *(Under his breath.)* Bitch.

SALLY: She's not.

MIKE: You're welcome to her.
(He starts off. Sally grabs his arm. The following dialogue starts sotto voce, and grows louder.)

SALLY: You're not leaving me up here.

MIKE: Damn right.

SALLY: Alone? All by myself?

MIKE: I've got work to do.

SALLY: You said you'd come to the class.

MIKE: I never said I'd teach it.

SALLY: She asked me to take over.

MIKE: She didn't ask me. *(By now he is almost off the stage.)*

SALLY: *(Louder, from stage.)* Thanks a lot, Mike! I mean just thanks a lot! *(To audience.)* Some man. Some friend. *(To Mike.)* Just…*leaving* me up here. Oh boy.

MIKE: *(Calling out; from the aisle.)* This is your course, not mine! I'm not even registered!

SALLY: That's right! Which is sad! Because you, especially, could learn so much from it! .

MIKE: *(Stopping; turning.)* O.K. *(He marches back up the aisle.)* O.K. *(He comes onto the stage, grabs a chair, plunks it down center, sits in it.)* O.K. *(He folds his arms.)* Teach me.

SALLY: *(Nervously.)* What?

MIKE: You drag me here, you set me up as a messenger boy, you let your pal Carroway give me a hard time, and now you say I've got a lot to learn. O.K., so now may I ask a few questions? *(Raises his hand, like a child.)* May I, Teach? May I?

SALLY: *(Coldly.)* Certainly. Ask away.

MIKE: First question: what is so goddam great about this course?

SALLY: Burgess and Carroway, that's what. Burgess and Carroway.

MIKE: And what's so great about them?

SALLY: If you can't feel it, I can't explain it.

MIKE: They're not even here.

SALLY: Which makes them all the greater.

MIKE: Why's that?

SALLY: Because even when they're gone, we can imagine them. They taught us how to imagine.

MIKE: I learn more in ten minutes in my major than I've learned here.

SALLY: About computers.

MIKE: What's wrong with computers?

SALLY: *(To audience.)* He loves computers.

MIKE: *(To audience.)* I like computers.

SALLY: You should learn about love.

MIKE: I know a thing or two.

SALLY: You should learn about me.

MIKE: I know about you.

SALLY: You don't. You just plain don't. You don't know me at all.
    (Pause.)

MIKE: *(Raising his hand again.)* O.K., then. Tell me.

SALLY: *Tell* you?

MIKE: Yeah. For example, tell me why you moved out on me?

SALLY: *(Embarrassed.)* Mike…

MIKE: I want to learn, Teach. Teach me. Suddenly, in the middle of the term, you move out of our apartment and back into the women's dorm. I want to know why?

SALLY: *(Whispering.)* Mike, this is a class…

MIKE: Right. So I want to know why.

SALLY: I moved out because… *(To audience.)* I decided not to share a room with Mike because I decided I didn't love him.

MIKE: That's not what you said then.

SALLY: Mike…

MIKE: You said… *(To audience.)* She said… *(Gestures to blackboard.)* She said that Tristan and Isolde only fell in love when they slept with a sword between them, and since we didn't have a sword, she moved back into the women's dorm.
    (Pause.)

SALLY: You make it sound so dumb.

MIKE: It was dumb. This whole course is dumb. No wonder they're no longer going to teach it. We had a good thing going till you took this course.

SALLY: It was not a good thing.

MIKE: It was the best.

SALLY: It was never love.

MIKE: I don't know what you call it, but we had...
    (Pause.)

SALLY: What, what did we have?

MIKE: I won't say.

SALLY: Because you can't. Because you can't find the words. Because it wasn't love.

MIKE: I can find the words.

SALLY: Then let's hear them. Let's hear what we had.
    (Mike says nothing; Sally turns to audience.)

SALLY: Oh you see? He can't even *talk*. We'd sit there, eyeing each other. I tried to get him to read. He wouldn't. He wouldn't read one of these books on this list. We had nothing in common, nothing to say to each other.

MIKE: We said a few things.

SALLY: Such as what?

MIKE: I know a couple of words you used to like.

SALLY: Such as *what?*

MIKE: Well there's one old Anglo-Saxon four-letter word you used to get a kick out of.
    (Pause.)

SALLY: *(Quietly.)* That's not enough. *(Pause.)* I thought it was but it isn't. *(Pause.)* There should be more than that.
    (Pause.)

MIKE: *(Raising his hand slowly.)* May I ask one more question, Teach?

SALLY: No.

MIKE: Just one?

SALLY: Go back to your computers. I'll handle the class by myself.

MIKE: Just a little one.

SALLY: No. I think we may have gotten too personal, in public.

MIKE: This is strictly a practical question.

SALLY: Practical?

MIKE: Shall I renew our lease for the summer? You see, I can't afford to carry it by myself.

SALLY: We'll discuss it later.

MIKE: So should I let it go, and move in with the guys down the street?

SALLY: *(Indicating audience.)* This is blackmail.

MIKE: The landlord wants to know. Shall I tell him we'll be moving out the books, and the tape deck, and the loft that we built ourselves? What'll I tell him?

SALLY: Tell him I want more. There should be more. Even in the summer, there should be more.

MIKE: Then I'll let it go.

(Carroway comes back hurriedly down the aisle, talking as she comes. She carries her book.)

CARROWAY: Shoo! Shoo! Exeunt omnes! Goodbye, young lovers, whoever you are! Out of my way! Clear the track! Give me the stage! I have something to say!

(Sally and Mike exit quickly into the audience. Carroway turns and faces the audience, catching her breath.)

CARROWAY: Class! I have just been... *(She searches for the words.)* Magnificent! I have just been superb! Oh, I wish you all could have been there! I wish you had followed me to the new science building, and accompanied me into the conference room, and stationed yourselves along the walls like a Greek chorus! Then you would have heard me sing my swan song! Then you would have seen this contemporary Cassandra plant her feet and throw back her head and launch into her last full-throated threnody! *(Comes forward.)* Let me tell you what I said and did!

BURGESS: *(Comes storming down the aisle, calling out to her as he comes.)* I'd like to speak to you alone.

CARROWAY: *(Drawing herself up.)* I am teaching a class.

BURGESS: I would like a minute with you in private.

CARROWAY: This is my last class!

BURGESS: *(Comes onto the stage.)* You *lied* to them, out there!

CARROWAY: That was no lie!

BURGESS: You told them we were lovers!

CARROWAY: Which is true!

BURGESS: Not true at all!

CARROWAY: Ever since Plato we've been in love.

BURGESS: You're insane!

CARROWAY: As all true lovers are!

BURGESS: *(To audience.)* We never even *met* outside of class!

CARROWAY: *(To audience.)* We never had to! Here's where we met! *(To Burgess.)* Here is our space!

BURGESS: *(To audience.)* The woman is mad!

CARROWAY: *(To Burgess.)* We were married here. We had children.

BURGESS: Oh God, oh God!

CARROWAY: Oh admit it. Think of Plato, think of the Symposium. *(She recites from memory.)* "There are those people who are pregnant in soul, and give birth to ideas. And these people maintain a much closer communion than the parents of children. They share between them children more beautiful and more immortal." *(She looks at him.)* That is how we were in class, and you know it. *(Pause.)* And that is what Plato calls love. *(Pause.)* And we based the course on it. We taught it. And it's true. *(Pause.)* Or if it isn't, then this whole semester has been one long lie. *(Pause.)* So say what you think.

BURGESS: *(Turning; slowly.)* I think you're a silly academic old maid. I think you made a fool of yourself, and of me, and of my wife, in front of the entire Curriculum Committee. They're still laughing out there, at both of us. And I think they're laughing in here as well.

CARROWAY: *(Aghast.)* No.

BURGESS: Yes. I'm sorry, but it's true. And now I think we should dismiss the class. And when you've recovered your wits, I am going to insist that you write an open letter to the university in general, explaining your remarks and apologizing for them.

CARROWAY: *(Reeling.)* No, no, no. *(She staggers off the stage.)* Someone...Sally...Help me. Please.

SALLY: *(Rushes to her aid. Shouting to Burgess.)* You are a stupid, *stupid,* STUPID MAN! *(Sally helps Carroway down the aisle and out.)*

BURGESS: *(After a long pause; to audience.)* Oh look: she barged, she *barged* into the meeting. In the middle of some remarks by Professor Blum of Biology, the door burst open and she barged right in. She insisted on joining the meeting. And she insisted on sitting next to me. I was at the far end, but she insisted. People had to get up and make room for her. Somebody had to get another chair. Professor Segal, who uses crutches, had to move over for her. So she could sit next to me. *(Pause.)* But that wasn't enough. Oh no. Before Professor Blum could resume his remarks, she leaned across me and in loud whispers demanded that my wife give her back her book. My wife, when she finally understood, complied. But not before Professor Blum had lost his thread, and everyone in the room was watching this ludicrous little scene!

(Pause.) But even that wasn't enough for your Professor Carroway. Suddenly she was on her feet, launching into a monstrous defense of this course. She said that she, that I, that you had learned more about love this term than we had ever known before. She recommended that every student in the university be required to take it. She recommended that every faculty member take it. She recommended particularly that my *wife* take it. And she said if we all took it, the world would be a far, far better place!

(Pause.) And then she walked out, edging her way out around the table, as we all sat stupefied and watched her go.

(Pause.) I rose to reply. But I couldn't make myself heard. Because of the laughter. Gales of laughter, waves of laughter, even old Professor Kurtz, of Physics, who has never cracked a smile, was shaking in his chair. And so I too, like your dear, dear Professor Carroway, had to edge my way out of that room. And come here.

SALLY: *(Appears in the aisle.)* Professor Carroway is dying.

BURGESS: Professor Carroway is not dying.

SALLY: She says she's dying. And I believe her.

BURGESS: She is naturally upset…

SALLY: She is dying the modern death. She is dying spiritually.

BURGESS: Where is that student? Where is that Mike?

MIKE: *(Calling out from the back.)* Right here!

BURGESS: Go find out what the story is, Mike.

MIKE: O.K. *(He goes out.)*

SALLY: *(Coming angrily onto the stage.)* I know what the story is. The story is—you killed her.

BURGESS: Because I asked for an apology?

SALLY: Because you voted against her tenure.

    (Pause.)

BURGESS: What makes her think that? Those meetings were secret.

SALLY: She said she could tell. By the way you behaved. *(To audience.)* He voted against her contract. Which, of course, made others vote against it. She has a book, and two articles, and won the teaching prize three years ago, but now she's going to die. At Mount Holyoke.

BURGESS: All right. I voted against her. But I got Holyoke to take her on.

SALLY: You traitor!

BURGESS: I had to. She's not for around here. She needs some small, quiet, conservative place in the country…

SALLY: Says who?

BURGESS: Says me! She has no sense of where we are! *(To audience)* She wanted to stop with *Wuthering Heights,* you know. "It's all there," she said. "We needn't go farther than that." But as you know, it's not all there. We're way beyond that. Marx, Freud, Darwin—they mean nothing to her. Science, mathematics, she holds them totally in contempt. I had to beg her to teach Lawrence. And you might remember what a disaster that class was.

SALLY: So you're sending her away.

BURGESS: We had to. Can you imagine her here for twenty more years?

SALLY: I can imagine her here forever!

BURGESS: She's too *much,* Sally!

SALLY: She's too much for *you,* Professor Burgess.

MIKE: *(Comes down the aisle.)* Professor Burgess...

BURGESS: How is she, Mike?

MIKE: She's O.K.

BURGESS: Of course she is.

MIKE: She's sitting in the lounge, smoking like a chimney.

BURGESS: Thanks, Mike.

MIKE: And sir: your wife is waiting outside. She says she has the car and she wants to go home.

BURGESS: Then that's it, class. There's my ride. *(He grabs his briefcase and starts off.)*

SALLY: You're running out?

BURGESS: I have to.

SALLY: Without even apologizing to Professor Carroway?

BURGESS: I'll talk to her on the way out.

SALLY: No! It should be here! Up here! In front of all of us! Unless you don't have the courage!

BURGESS: *(Pause. Burgess sighs and comes back on stage.)* All right. Tell Professor Carroway I am waiting for her to return. For mutual apologies. And mutual goodbyes.

SALLY: Gladly! *(She exits hurriedly down the aisle.)*

BURGESS: *(Calling out.)* And Mike...

MIKE: Yes sir.

BURGESS: Ask my wife to wait in the car while I say goodbye to Professor Carroway.

MIKE: O.K. *(Exits up the aisle.)*

BURGESS: *(To audience.)* You see? The course ends with the wife waiting offstage. We've forgotten wives in this course. We've forgotten marriage. *(Goes to the blackboard.)* Where is the *Odyssey* on this list? Where is Dickens? Where are the Penelopes, the Andromaches, the Portias? How can we talk about love and not talk about marriage? My God, what have we been *doing* for the past four months? Stumbling around in the dank fog of adultery. I'm beginning to breathe again. I'm beginning to—where's that Mike?

MIKE: *(In back.)* Here, sir.

BURGESS: Mike! Come up here, Mike! I want a *man* up here!

(Mike comes up onto the stage.)

BURGESS: Come on, Mike. I want a buddy, I want a pal, I want a little male bonding to go on up here. *(He gives Mike a chair.)* Sit down, Mike. No, I'm serious, pal, sit down.

(Mike does, awkwardly.)

BURGESS: Now we're talking about marriage, Mike. That's the topic on the table.

(Mike nods.)

Now look at me, Mike. Look at me carefully.

(Mike does.)

I'm a married man, Mike. You know that.

(Mike nods.)

BURGESS: Now answer this question, Mike, and answer it frankly. Do I seem happy, Mike?

(Mike looks at him.)

Come on, Mike. Be frank. Do I seem happy?

MIKE: No.

BURGESS: You are right! I am not happy. Not here, not up here I'm not. But *there,* out there, where my wife is, there I'm happy, Mike. I am eager, Mike, I am desperately eager to walk out of here, and get into that car, and kiss my wife, and hug my children in my own home! There's where I'm happy, Mike. Do you believe it, Mike?

MIKE: Well I…

BURGESS: Believe it, Mike. Believe it, for God's sake.

MIKE: O.K.

BURGESS: Take another tack. You live with Sally, don't you?

MIKE: Well we—

BURGESS: Sure you do. All you kids shack up. I know that. "Let copulation thrive!" I'm all for it.

MIKE: Thanks.

BURGESS: But you're not happy with her, are you, Mike?

MIKE: Well we—

BURGESS: You're not happy, she's not happy, and it's a mess, Mike. Admit it.

MIKE: O.K. I'll admit that.

BURGESS: It's a mess, and now I'll tell you how to clean it up, Mike. Marry her.

MIKE: Back off.

BURGESS: *Marry* her, Mike! That's where it's ultimately at, my friend. Get married, buddy. Go seek thyself a wife. There is a richness, a thickness in the married state which goes far, far beyond the excruciating self-tortures we've been inflicting on ourselves this term. Get married, Mike. Commit yourself to continuity. Have babies. Join the human race.

MIKE: I'm too young to die.

BURGESS: Die? You *live*, man! You stretch, you expand, you grow. Do you know the Rolling Stones, Mike?

MIKE: Of course I know the Rolling—

BURGESS: My kids introduced me to the Rolling Stones. My wife introduced me to paddle tennis. They bring things *in*, Mike. Oh there's a resonance in domesticity which all those books will never teach you. Wed her, and bed her, and make her thine forever.

SALLY: *(Comes down the aisle.)* Professor Carroway wants to teach *Wuthering Heights*.

BURGESS: Tell Professor Carroway I will simply shake her hand and say goodbye.

SALLY: I'll tell her you refuse to teach *Wuthering Heights. (Exits up the aisle.)*

BURGESS: See, Mike? How they turn sour? Now listen: go tell my wife that I have just sung her a love song. Ask her to wait a little longer. And then get that girl to marry you.

MIKE: I'll speak to your wife. *(He exits up the aisle.)*

BURGESS: *(Alone; to audience.)* I'll wait a few more minutes for Professor Carroway. *(Pause.)* I can't just walk away. *(Pause; looks around.)* Actually, I have to say I've grown a little fond of this room. *(Pause.)* This...space. *(Pause.)* We've had some good times in here, haven't we? All told. *(Sits on the desk, maybe.)* Some special times. *(Pause.)* Never, never in all my years of teaching have I taken such...risks. *(Pause.)* Remember the class on *Madame Bovary?* Oh my God, what a class! We flew, we flew in that class! We touched the stars in that class! We—*(Pause.)* It was too much, of course. Much too much. I had to take an aspirin when I got home. I had trouble getting to sleep after *Madame Bovary.* *(Pause.)* Well. Next year I'll be in administration, won't I? Oh boy, I'll tell you, we'll be making some major changes in the curriculum. Some real innovations, right on down the line. *(Pause; sadly.)* And I'll probably never teach again.

(Sally and Mike enter simultaneously in the aisle.)

SALLY: Professor Carroway—

MIKE: *(Simultaneously.)* Your wife—

(They glare at each other.)

SALLY: Professor Carroway says it's *Wuthering Heights* or nothing.

MIKE: Your wife says she can't wait around all day.

(Pause.)

BURGESS: Tell Professor Carroway I am willing to spend a few moments on "Wuthering Heights".

SALLY: Good. *(She goes out up the aisle.)*

BURGESS: *(To Mike.)* And tell my wife…*(Pause.)* Tell my wife…*(Pause.)* Just tell her: please.

MIKE: O.K. *(He exits up the aisle.)*

BURGESS: *(To audience.)* That it is, then. Just a quick crack at it. For old time's sake. It won't be *Madame Bovary.* I'm getting a little too old for *Madame Bovary.*

SALLY: *(Appears in the aisle.)* Professor Carroway is ready to teach.

(Carroway comes slowly down the aisle. She carries her book. She mounts the stage carefully, taking her time. Then she speaks quietly and carefully.)

CARROWAY: *(To audience.)* We thought, as a kind of coda on the course, we might read and discuss the final confrontation between Catharine Earnshaw and Heathcliffe in Emily Brontë's *Wuthering Heights. (To Burgess.)* Are we agreed?

BURGESS: Agreed.

CARROWAY: *(Opening her book; to Burgess.)* I have my book. You can look on with me.

BURGESS: No, no. *(Rummages quickly in his briefcase.)* I think I brought my own. *(He pulls out a bright paperback edition which should contrast with her old leathery volume.)* I did bring my own.

CARROWAY: I begin on page one ninety-six.

BURGESS: For those who have the Norton Critical Edition, we're on— *(He shuffles through the pages nervously.)* One thirty-two.

CARROWAY: *(To audience.)* Cathy is dying because of Heathcliffe...

BURGESS: *(To audience.)* Not *just* because of Heathcliffe...

CARROWAY: *(Grimly.)* She *thinks* because of Heathcliffe. And that's the important thing. What she thinks.

BURGESS: Yes. All right. Yes.

CARROWAY: *(To audience.)* Heathcliffe, after *years* of separation, has found his way to the dying Cathy's room. *(She reads.)* "And he could hardly bear, for downright agony, to look into her face..."

BURGESS: *(Looking at his book.)* Where are you? I have no idea where you are.

CARROWAY: *(Reading.)* "There was no prospect of ultimate recovery...She was fated, sure to die."

BURGESS: Ah. Found it.

CARROWAY: Then read.

BURGESS: *(Reading.)* "Oh Cathy! Oh my life! how can I bear it?" was the first sentence he uttered, in a tone—

CARROWAY: Just read Heathcliffe. *(Calling out into the audience.)* Sally! Come up here and read the Narrator!
(Sally comes up the aisle; Carroway turns to Burgess.)

CARROWAY: So we can concentrate on the dialogue.
(Sally comes up onto the stage; Carroway hands her the book.)

CARROWAY: Read there, Sally.

SALLY: *(Reading very prosaically.)* "And now he stared at her so earnestly that I thought the intensity of his gaze would bring tears into his eyes. But they—"

CARROWAY: *(Interrupting; knowing it by heart.)* "They burned with anguish. They did not melt." *(With passion, to Burgess.)* "You have broken my heart, Heathcliffe. You have killed me—and thriven on it, I think. How strong you are! How many years do you mean to live, after I am gone?"
(Pause. He looks at her, enrapt. Then quickly searches his book for the response. She turns to Sally.)

CARROWAY: Read.

SALLY: *(Reading.)* "Heathcliffe had knelt on one knee to embrace her..."

CARROWAY: *(To Burgess.)* Do it.

BURGESS: I'm not going to—

CARROWAY: *(Quickly.)* Go on, Sally.

SALLY: *(Reading.)* "Heathcliffe had knelt on one knee to embrace her; he attempted to rise, but she seized his hair and kept him down."

CARROWAY: *(Reciting from memory.)* "I wish I could hold you till we were both dead! I shouldn't care what you suffered. I care nothing for your sufferings. Why shouldn't you suffer? I do!"

MIKE: *(Enters down the aisle.)* Professor Burgess...

(Burgess comes to the edge of the stage, leans down. Mike whispers something to him. Burgess looks upset.)

CARROWAY: What's the matter?

BURGESS: Nothing.

CARROWAY: I said what's the matter?

BURGESS: My wife wants me to know she's watching in the rear.

CARROWAY: Good! Excellent!

(Mike retreats down the aisle; Carroway begins to recite again.)

CARROWAY: "Will you be happy when I am in the earth? Will you say twenty years hence, 'That's the grave of Catharine Earnshaw. I loved her long ago...I've loved many others since. My children are dearer to me than she was.' Will you say so, Heathcliffe?"

BURGESS: *(Reading very quietly.)* "Don't torture me until I'm as mad as yourself."

CARROWAY: Louder. People can't hear.

BURGESS: *(Very loudly.)* "DON'T TORTURE ME UNTIL I'M AS MAD AS YOURSELF!"

(Pause.)

CARROWAY: Read, Sally.

SALLY: *(Reading.)* "The two, to a cool spectator, made a strange and fearful picture."

CARROWAY: Skip to "She retained..."

SALLY: Um. *(Finds the place.)* "She retained in her closed fingers a portion of the locks she had been grasping..."

CARROWAY: *(To Burgess.)* Read.

BURGESS: *(Reading desperately.)* "You know you lie to say I have killed you. Is it not sufficient for your infernal selfishness that while you are at peace, I shall writhe in the torments of hell?"

CARROWAY: "I shall not be at peace."

(Mike again comes hurriedly down the aisle. Burgess again comes to the edge of the stage. Mike whispers to him, then leaves.)

What now?

BURGESS: My wife has just left.

CARROWAY: Run after her.

BURGESS: Yes!…No!…Yes!…Oh my God, why, why am I here? I've just missed my ride! I'll probably miss a meal! There will be hell to pay when I get home!

CARROWAY: The shrill-tongued Fulvia scolds.

BURGESS: No. She laughs. She laughs at you. She laughs at me when I mention you. Oh woman, what have you done to me? You have seduced me. With books! We have bathed in them, we have rolled in them, we have wallowed in them like lascivious Turks! Right now I should be home! I should be sitting at the kitchen table, talking to my wife, holding a cool beer, with beaded bubbles winking at the brim!

CARROWAY: Keats!

BURGESS: Yes, KEATS! And Shelley! And Brontë. Oh Lady, you are holding me in thrall! You're dragging me down! I'm drowning!

CARROWAY: Then swim to administration. Lie panting there, on that desert island.

BURGESS: What else can I do?

CARROWAY: *(Closing her eyes, reciting.)* "Heathcliffe, forgive me. Come here and kneel down. You never harmed me in your life. Nay, if you nurse anger, that will be worse to remember than any harsh words! Won't you come here? Do!"

SALLY: *(Reading.)* "Heathcliffe went to the back of her chair."

BURGESS: *(To Carroway, carefully.)* I'll come up to Holyoke. Commute. Once a week. So we can still teach the course.

CARROWAY: *(Shaking her head.)* Go on, Sally.

SALLY: *(Reading.)* "He leaned over, but not so far as to let her see his face…"

BURGESS: Or you could come down here. Be a visiting lecturer. I could arrange it.

CARROWAY: Go on, Sally.

SALLY: *(Reading.)* "She bent round to look at him; he would not permit it; turning abruptly, he walked to the fireplace, where he stood, silent, his back toward us."

BURGESS: *(Burgess has followed these directions almost instinctively.)* All right. I'll do what I can to have you reinstated here. I'll cite Affirmative Action. I'll get something going.

CARROWAY: "Oh you see, he would not relent a moment to keep me out of my grave. *That* is how I am loved!"

BURGESS: What do you want then?

CARROWAY: *(Now reciting more to herself.)* "Well never mind! That is not *my* Heathcliffe. I shall love mine yet and take him with me—he's in my soul.

BURGESS: Would you tell me what you want, please?

CARROWAY: "And the thing that irks me most is this shattered prison. I'm wearying to escape into that glorious world, not seeing it dimly through tears, and yearning for it through walls of an aching heart; but really with it, and in it."

BURGESS: For God's sake, woman, tell me what you *want!*

CARROWAY: *(To Sally.)* Read.

SALLY: *(Reading.)* "In her eagerness she rose and supported herself on the arm of the chair."

(Carroway does.)

"At that earnest appear, he turned to her, looking absolutely desperate."

(Burgess does.)

"His eyes wide, and wet at last, flashed fiercely on her, his breast heaved convulsively. An instant they held asunder; and then how they met I hardly saw, but Catharine made a spring, and he caught her, and they were locked in an embrace from which I thought my mistress would never be released alive."

(Sally looks up from her reading. Burgess and Carroway are kissing frantically. The book slowly lowers in Sally's hand. Softly.)

SALLY: Professor...Carroway.

(Then suddenly the bell rings for the end of class. Carroway breaks away from the embrace.)

BURGESS: *(Huskily.)* I meant what I said about getting you back here.

CARROWAY: Don't be silly. *(She begins briskly stacking her books.)*

BURGESS: I want to teach this course again.

CARROWAY: Once is enough, I think. *(To audience.)* Now the examination topic. I think you should write on Plato. *(To Burgess.)* Is Plato all right with you? We began there, we should end there.

(Burgess nods vaguely. She turns to the audience again.)

CARROWAY: Plato it is, then. The end of the *Symposium.* Where Socrates suggests that tragedy and comedy are ultimately the same thing. *(To Burgess.)* I think that should tie the knot, don't you?

(Burgess again nods vaguely. Carroway finishes stacking her books.)

CARROWAY: Sally, would you like to discuss Plato with me in my office?

SALLY: I—I'm not sure where my book is.

MIKE: *(From the aisle.)* I think it's in the apartment.

SALLY: *(To Carroway, with a shrug.)* I better go see.
  (She gives Carroway back her copy of Wuthering Heights, *and exits with Mike, down the aisle.)*

CARROWAY: *(Gathers her stack of books lovingly in her arms. She holds out her one free hand to Burgess.)* Goodbye, Professor Burgess.

BURGESS: *(Mechanically shaking hands.)* Goodbye, Professor Carroway.
  (Carroway exits briskly down the aisle. Burgess stands on stage watching her as the lights dim on the stage.)

END OF PLAY

Public Affairs

Part Two
THE OPEN MEETING

Original Production

Neither THE LOVE COURSE nor THE OPEN MEETING, to my knowledge, has had a reviewed production in New York City. THE LOVE COURSE was done in England in the early seventies, and both have been performed in college theatres.

The Characters

ROY, a middle–aged man
EDDIE, a young man
VERNA, a woman

The Setting

No curtain. A long functional table, facing front. Four chairs behind it. Upstage, two crossed flags: the Stars and Stripes, and some local flag. On the table, a pitcher of water on a tray, with four tumblers. Before each chair, four placards, reading from the stage right to left: Eddie, Dick, Verna, Roy.

The Open Meeting

While the house lights are still on, Eddie, Verna, and Roy come on. They stand upstage, to one side, arguing rather vehemently under their breath. Eddie is a young man, casually dressed, carrying a worn paperback entitled The Democratic Experience *into which are stuck a number of loose papers. Verna is an attractive middle-aged woman, dressed efficiently, carrying a commodious purse. Roy is older, in an expensive business suit, carrying an elegant attaché case. Their discussions continue for some time, becoming more and more heated, until Verna remembers the audience.*

VERNA: *(To audience.)* We're discussing whether or not to begin.
EDDIE: *(To audience.)* I think we should.
ROY: *(To audience.)* I think we shouldn't.
VERNA: *(To audience.)* I'm on the fence.
    (They turn to each other and begin arguing again. Finally:)
VERNA: *(To audience.)* The issue is whether or not to begin without Dick.
EDDIE: *(To audience.)* I think we should.
ROY: *(To audience.)* I think we shouldn't.
Verna. *(To audience.)* I'm still on the fence.
    (More ad-lib arguing, out of which Eddie's voice finally emerges.)
EDDIE: *(To Roy and Verna.)* Hey now look. This is May. It's our final meeting till fall. We've got a lot of ground to cover. It's about time we started sowing some seeds around here.
ROY: Without Dick?
EDDIE: Without Dick.
ROY: I don't buy that.
VERNA: *(To audience.)* I really am on the fence.
EDDIE: Maybe you'd like to explain your objections to the group, Roy.

ROY: I'd be glad to. We asked Dick to go down to Washington. We asked
him to meet with people in high places, sound them out, bring back
documents. Now Dick is still down there working on these things.
Until he comes up with answers, how can we possibly begin this
meeting without Dick?

EDDIE: I like to think, Roy, I like to think that just occasionally in this
country, in this so-called democracy, we can move ahead without either Dick or his documents.

VERNA: *(To audience.)* I could go either way.

EDDIE: I mean, what do you propose to do, Roy? Just stand around, eyeing each other, until Dick shows up?

ROY: I propose we cancel.

EDDIE: *Cancel?*

VERNA: Oh my!

ROY: Until Dick returns.

EDDIE: *(Defiantly taking his chair.)* Not me. I want to start this ball
rolling.

VERNA: Just like that?

EDDIE: Just like that.

ROY: Fine. Very well. You roll the ball any way you want to, Eddie. I myself intend to do something more constructive with my time. *(He
starts out.)*

EDDIE: Hold it, pal.

ROY: *(Stopping.)* Are you speaking to me, sir?

EDDIE: I've got something you might want to read, Roy. *(He rummages
through his papers.)* I've got something here which might interest
you...Ah. Here. *(Waves a piece of paper.)* Read this, Roy.

ROY: And what, pray tell, is that?

EDDIE: It's a note which was handed to me after our last meeting.

ROY: Ah. Well I am delighted you are receiving communications, Eddie.
You obviously are beginning to ingratiate yourself with the group.

EDDIE: *(Holding it out.)* Just read it, Roy.

ROY: *(Holding his ground.)* I am not at your beck and call, young man.

EDDIE: *(Waving it around.)* I dare you to read it, Roy.

VERNA: Perhaps I can help here. *(She takes the paper.)* Perhaps I can grease
the wheels of progress here. *(She crosses to Roy.)* Here, Roy.

ROY: Thank you, Verna. *(Takes the paper.)*

EDDIE: Read it, Roy.

ROY: I will read it in my own sweet time. *(Slowly reads it.)*

EDDIE: *(Low, to Verna.)* Notice how he is stalling.

VERNA: *(Low to Eddie.)* I won't take sides in this, Eddie. I really won't.

ROY: Who wrote this?

EDDIE: A friend, Roy.

ROY: *(Folding the letter.)* Some disgruntled job-seeker? Some left-leaning liberal?

EDDIE: I like to think it was a good friend.

ROY: You and I may have very different definitions of the word "good."

EDDIE: How about reading it out loud, Roy?

ROY: I don't see why I have to stand here, taking orders from the junior member of this panel. Is there any reason why I have to do that, Verna?

VERNA: Tell you what: I'll read it. *(Holds her hand for it.)* May I have it, please, Roy.

ROY: Verna, this is simply a...

VERNA: I'd like to read that piece of paper, if I may, Roy.

ROY: *(Reluctantly handing it over.)* Very well, Verna.

VERNA: *(Taking the paper.)* Now... *(She crosses down to the table, plunks down her purse, opens it.)* If I can find my glasses. *(She rummages in her purse.)* Eureka! *(She displays her glasses to the audience, then puts them on, opens the letter, clears her throat, reads carefully.)* Here we go. *(She reads.)* "Don't trust Dick."

EDDIE: See?

VERNA: Hmm.

ROY: Some crackpot.

VERNA: *(Reading it again.)* "Don't trust Dick."

ROY: Some trouble-maker.

EDDIE: You think so, Roy? What if I told you there are rumblings from others in this room about Dick.

ROY: Rumblings? From whom?

EDDIE: I'm not going to name names, Roy.

VERNA: People have the right to rumble, Roy.

ROY: Well it's nice to know that things are happening behind my back.

VERNA: *(Reading the note.)* "Don't trust Dick."

ROY: Now stop that, Verna! We all heard what it says.

VERNA: *(Low to Roy.)* Please don't raise your voice at me, Roy. I mean that.

ROY: Look, people. I'm not going to stand around here listening to Dick being disparaged by a bunch of disgruntled trouble-makers. Sorry, I've got better things to do with my time. *(Starts out again.)*

VERNA: Actually, Roy…

> *(Roy stops.)*

I also received a note after our last meeting. It was thrust into my lap by a woman.

EDDIE: By a woman?

VERNA: Just as we were breaking up. I remember being quite taken aback by what it said.

EDDIE: Taken aback?

VERNA: Yes, I found it quite disturbing.

> *(Roy has remained hovering on stage.)*

But go on, Roy. Leave, if you must. You shouldn't stay if you don't want to.

ROY: What did your note say, Verna?

VERNA: Well I'm not sure it's even germane to the discussion.

EDDIE: Let's read it and see.

VERNA: All right. Let's do that. *(Starts groping around her purse again.)* Let's see. I know I brought it. I remember thinking that it might come in handy during the evening. So when I changed purses, I distinctly remember putting it in the hall right by my car keys and, yes! Now. Who—whom do I give it to?

ROY and EDDIE: *(Simultaneously.)* Me!

VERNA: I'll read it myself. *(Looks around.)* Now where did I put my glasses?

ROY AND EDDIE: *(Pointing; simultaneously.)* There!

VERNA: *(Calmly.)* Thank you, gentlemen. *(She puts on her glasses, unfolds the note, and reads.)* Here's what it says: "Dick is a lousy lover." *(She looks from Eddie to Roy.)* I'll read it again: "Dick is a lousy lover."

> *(Pause.)*

EDDIE: Wow.

VERNA: *(To Eddie.)* You can see why I was somewhat taken aback.

EDDIE: I'm glad to see the sisterhood is at last speaking up, Verna.

ROY: Oh for Chrissake!

VERNA: Roy, I will not have you swearing.

ROY: But I mean, Jesus…

VERNA: I'm serious, Roy. I won't have it. It offends me, and I suspect it offends a number of other people in this room.

EDDIE: Yeah, Roy.

ROY: But that note has nothing to do with the issues!

VERNA: I already said I wasn't sure it was germane.

EDDIE: The remark is about Dick, isn't it?

VERNA: It most certainly is.

EDDIE: It's about Dick's attitude toward other people, isn't it.

VERNA: It's about Dick's attitude toward women.

EDDIE: Well then I think it's germane as hell, frankly. It implies that Dick has trouble relating to women.

VERNA: That's a very good point, Eddie. Very sensitive to women's needs.

ROY: Well I'll tell you one thing. I do not intend to stand around while the mainstay of this meeting is made light of, through a series of sly cracks and undocumented innuendoes. I will not be a party to that, and I suspect a number of other people here tonight feel equally uncomfortable. If Dick were here to defend himself, well and good. But since he's not here, since he's still in Washington, where he is working for our betterment and the betterment of democracy everywhere in the world, then I for one intend to go home and read a good book, and I invite everyone else to entertain the same notion. *(Starts out again.)*

EDDIE: Roy...

ROY: No, I'm sorry. Goodnight.

EDDIE: Roy, I just have one question. Then you can go.

ROY: *(Eyes closed; infinitely patient.)* Ask away.

EDDIE: Have you yourself recently received any sudden or unexpected communications about Dick?

ROY: No.

EDDIE: You sure, Roy?

ROY: I am sure.

EDDIE: Roy, when you and Verna and I were waiting in the wings, you were suddenly approached by a delivery person from Federal Express who put into your hands a large, stridently colored, glossy envelope, postmarked Washington, D.C., which required your immediate signature of receipt.

VERNA: That's true...I had forgotten that.

EDDIE: You signed for that envelope, Roy, and then you proceeded to slink off into a corner, where you opened it, read it furtively, gave a grim nod, crammed it into your briefcase, and then returned to our offstage deliberations.

VERNA: That's very well described, Eddie.

EDDIE: Was that letter about Dick, Roy?

(Pause.)

ROY: It was not.

EDDIE: May I ask what that letter was about then, Roy?

ROY: Eddie, my inquisitive young friend, I hope you'll forgive me if I choose not to discuss my private mail in an public forum.

VERNA: Yes, Eddie. We all have lives of our own.

EDDIE: All right. But I think it would allow a number of us here to feel more comfortable, Roy, if you let us read that letter, or at least gave us a brief paraphrase of its contents.

VERNA: Yes, Roy. I do think that would make life easier, all around.
    (Pause.)

ROY: If you must know, Eddie, that letter was from Dick.

VERNA: But I thought you said...

ROY: Eddie asked me if I had received a letter *about* Dick. I said no. Because it was *from* Dick. About something else. I believe I was being accurate in my response.

EDDIE: What did Dick's letter say, Roy?

ROY: Oh well, it was about some minor issue...

VERNA: Minor? When it arrives Federal Express at the last minute, right to this building?

ROY: Some personal business...Some legal technicalities having to do with various minor concerns...

EDDIE: May I read that letter, Roy?

ROY: You may not.

VERNA: May I read it, Roy?

ROY: I'd prefer you didn't, Verna.

VERNA: Then that's it.

EDDIE: WHAT?

VERNA: The subject is closed, Eddie. Roy and I outvote you on this one, I'm afraid. When it comes to questions of personal privacy, then I have to say that I stand fore square with the strictest interpretations of the law. Dick wrote that letter to Roy, not to us. And we have absolutely no right to learn its contents unless Roy is willing to make them public. Which he isn't. For reasons which are his own business.

ROY: Thank you, Verna.

VERNA: And now we should feel free to leave, Roy. And you should feel confident that your private life will remain just that. Private.

ROY: Thanks, Verna. *(He starts out again.)*

VERNA: *(To audience.)* Dick's letter obviously makes some totally uncalled for remarks about Roy's personal hygiene.

ROY: *(Stopping.)* It does NOT, Verna.

VERNA: Well then it probably makes some totally unnecessary insinuations about your tax returns, Roy.

ROY: It doesn't do that either!

VERNA: Well it must do something, Roy. Otherwise you'd let us read it.

ROY: ALL RIGHT! *(He comes down to his place, slams his briefcase onto the table, snaps it open angrily, takes out a Federal Express envelope, slams shut the case. He opens the envelope, takes out a crisp letter, read it, shakes his head, and then slams it down on the table.)* There. *(He walks upstage, sulkily.)*

(Eddie and Verna rush to the letter, and hover over it.)

VERNA: Today's date...

EDDIE: Washington, D.C....

VERNA: Handwritten...

EDDIE: In what looks like Dick's pinched, ungenerous penmanship.

VERNA: I'll read it: "Dear Roy..."

EDDIE: "Try to abort the meeting."

VERNA: "Affectionately, Dick."

EDDIE: "Try to abort the meeting."

VERNA: "Affectionately, Dick."

EDDIE: "Try to abort the meeting!"

VERNA: "Affectionately, Dick."

EDDIE: But "*abort* the meeting!" My God!

VERNA: I don't see what's so bad about that.

ROY: I don't either, frankly.

EDDIE: What? "Try to abort the meeting?" It means that Roy and Dick don't want this meeting to happen, Verna.

VERNA: Oh now...

EDDIE: They don't want any meetings to happen.

ROY: Oh look...

EDDIE: They'd be perfectly happy if none of us ever met again!

VERNA: Oh heavens, Eddie. Please!

EDDIE: I'm serious! Think of what Roy has done all winter long! With his tabling and postponing and subcommittees and points of order! Think of Dick; with his fact-finding trips and constantly increasing absentee record! What are these guys up to? I'll tell you what. They are systematically trying to undermine the group process!

ROY: Oh Good Lord!

EDDIE: Lookit, pal. Look at the evidence here. *(He lines up the three doc-*

uments on the table in front of him.) I get a note saying don't trust Dick. Verna gets a note saying Dick is a lousy lover. And then you, Roy, get a secret communication from Dick down in Washington asking you to abort the meeting. I don't see much of a willingness to move forward in any of these documents, now do you, Roy?

ROY: And why, Eddie, for the sake of argument, do you think Dick and I don't want things to "move forward," as you so lamely put it?

EDDIE: Because you're scared of what might come out.

VERNA: *(Rereading Roy's letter.)* "Affectionately, Dick." Did you and Dick have a sexual relationship, Roy?

ROY: We did NOT, Verna!

VERNA: Just *asking!* Honestly, Roy! No need to get so huffy!

EDDIE: I don't care whether they did or not. That's not the point. The point is that there are many things wrong with this country, many things radically, radically wrong, and it seems that Roy and Dick have spent the entire winter systematically preventing us from dealing with them.

(Pause.)

ROY: Well. *(Taking his seat.)* I can see I have to answer that.

VERNA: It might be helpful if you did, Roy. *(She takes her seat.)*

EDDIE: *(Sitting down as well.)* Let's hear it, Roy.

ROY: First, I'd like a glass of water, please, Verna.

VERNA: Yes. Oh yes, Roy. You deserve one, after having been in the hot seat for so long. *(Pours and gives him one.)*

ROY: *(Drinking his water.)* Good water. Excellent water. Is this bottled water, Verna?

VERNA: It well may be. I have no idea.

EDDIE: He's just buttering you up, Verna.

ROY: It is first-rate water, Verna, and I thank you for it.

VERNA: Thank you, Roy.

EDDIE: He just wants your vote, Verna.

ROY: I am simply commenting on the excellence of the water.

EDDIE: I can envision a time when we'd get good, sweet water, right from the tap.

ROY: Here we go…

EDDIE: I can envision a time when our reservoirs and our lakes and our rivers and our ground water would no longer be…

VERNA: That's enough, Eddie. Really. Now just simmer down…Now, Roy, I believe you had something to say to the group.

ROY: Yes, well, that is, I simply want to say that I as much as anyone believe that this nation should reap the benefits of the past even as we sow the seeds of the future. Yes, I see challenges ahead, but I view them as opportunities. Yes, mistakes have been made, but we must learn from our errors, and with both firmness and flexibility, with one eye on yesterday and the other on tomorrow, we must move firmly forward, bearing hope and freedom and democracy into all four corners of the globe.

EDDIE: Globes don't have corners, Roy.

ROY: It was a figure of—

EDDIE: It was a figure of bullshit, Roy.

VERNA: Now Eddie…

EDDIE: Are you paying Dick, Roy?

ROY: Am I paying Dick?

EDDIE: Or is Dick paying you? To distract us with that bullshit.

ROY: Now wait a minute—

EDDIE: Or are both of you on the payroll of someone else?

ROY: *(Getting up.)* I am not going to sit here and listen to—

VERNA: Now Eddie, stop! And Roy, please! Sit down…

ROY: I do not have to stay here and—

VERNA: Now wait. Now listen. Here's an idea. Why don't we telephone Dick down in Washington and clear things up?

EDDIE: Just telephone him?

VERNA: Exactly. Just call him up. Say, "Hi, Dick. All of us up here are just kind of sitting around wondering what the heck is going on down there."

ROY: You can't just do that to Dick, Verna.

VERNA: Why can't you?

ROY: Because he's a busy man. Because he's preoccupied.

EDDIE: *(Getting up.)* I'll do it. Right now.

ROY: No, all right. I'll do it.

EDDIE: What's his number, Roy?

ROY: I think I'd better do the telephoning around here.

EDDIE: Give me Dick's note there, Verna. Maybe it's on that.

VERNA: Eddie, I do not respond to people who just hold out their hands and say "gimme."

EDDIE: May I have Dick's note, please, Verna?

ROY: Don't give it to him, Verna.

EDDIE: *(Grabbing Dick's note.)* Let me just look at this here.

VERNA: Nor do I respond to people who grab, Eddie!

EDDIE: But his number's written right here. *(He starts out.)*

ROY: I want to do the telephoning, please.

VERNA: Let Eddie do it, Roy.

ROY: What? Why? Why him?

VERNA: Because he's younger.

ROY: But what will he say?

EDDIE: I'll simply say, Roy, that he should get the fuck back here toot sweet or we should know the reason why.

VERNA: No, Eddie. You will not say that. You will simply say that a number of us are becoming unhappy at what's happening in this country, and we would appreciate it if he'd come up here and share with us his thoughts on the subject. That's what you will say, Eddie. And if you say anything else, I'm going to be very, very mad.

EDDIE: I'll find my own words.

ROY: That's what worries us.

EDDIE: There's a word or two I'm saving for you, Roy!

VERNA: Just GO, Eddie!

> *(Eddie goes off. Pause. Roy sits moodily, Verna looks at him.)*

VERNA: Roy…

ROY: Mmm?

VERNA: *(Indicating where Eddie has gone.)* That was calculated, Roy.

ROY: What?

VERNA: That. Getting Eddie to call Washington. I thought that up.

ROY: Mmm.

VERNA: And I did it for a very specific purpose. I did it because I wanted to talk to you alone. *(Remembers audience; smiles.)* That is, without Eddie.

ROY: Mmm.

VERNA: *(Taking a deep breath.)* Roy…

EDDIE: *(Returns, stands by exit.)* I need a quarter. For the pay phone.

VERNA: Yes, all right, Eddie. I'll give you a quarter. *(Begins to rummage in her bag.)*

ROY: Kid hasn't even got a quarter.

EDDIE: I'll bet you've got plenty of quarters, Roy.

VERNA: *(Rummaging nervously.)* Where is that quarter? I know I had a quarter.

ROY: Yes I have plenty of quarters, Eddie. I earned them through good, hard work!

EDDIE: Robbing who, Roy? Who'd you rob for your dough?

VERNA: *(Desperately producing a quarter.)* Here! Here's a quarter! Now go call, Eddie!

ROY: You'll never see that quarter again, Verna.

EDDIE: How many quarters did it take to buy off Dick, Roy? *(He goes out.)*

ROY: *(Shouting after him.)* You couldn't even earn an honest dime!

EDDIE: *(Coming back in.)* I can envision a time when people could communicate freely and easily, back and forth, all over the earth, without enriching the coffers of the telephone company, Roy! *(Goes out again.)*

ROY: *(Calling after him.)* Communist! Fuzzy-headed pinko liberal wimp!

VERNA: Now stop it!

(Roy subsides moodily.)

That is exactly what I wanted to talk to you about, Roy.

ROY: What?

VERNA: That. There is something going on between you and Eddie.

ROY: What do you mean?

VERNA: There is something extremely nonproductive, Roy. I've sensed it. I think everybody in this room has sensed it.

ROY: That kid accused me of bribery.

VERNA: That is just a symptom, Roy. We all know that. That is just the culmination of something which has been going on all winter long.

ROY: The hell with him.

VERNA: I won't accept that as a solution, Roy. I'm sorry, but we're not fooling around now.

ROY: He irritates me.

VERNA: He's young, Roy. He's a mere babe. Now tolerate him.

ROY: I've tried.

VERNA: No, Roy. No. You have NOT tried. Not really. Oh now look, my friend. I'm on the fence here. I'm in the middle. I'll make no bones about it. My role is the role of too many women these days. Namely, to Keep. The. Peace. Well, that's what I've done through all these long, dark, gloomy, winter months. They say that in Spain, Roy, to keep the bulls from fighting, they put cows into the pens. All right, I guess that's what I am, Roy. A cow. Mooo, Roy. Mooo.

ROY: Oh now, Verna…

VERNA: No, I am. And Dick, well maybe Dick is a steer. But it's no fun, Roy. Many's the time I wanted to lock horns with all of you. There are women who do, these days. There are cows who now go into combat. But I didn't. I went on trying to pour, well, milk on the troubled waters. *(She pours herself a glass of water.)*

ROY: Verna, my dear friend…

VERNA: But I'm not sure I can do it much longer, Roy. I mean that. I'm getting torn apart by this tension. Look at my hand shake. Last week, after one of your battles with Eddie, I had to take a good stiff drink when I got home. I drank ALONE, Roy.

ROY: Verna…

VERNA: I'm not finished, Roy. Now you know, and I know, and I think everybody here knows, that there is something going on here. I don't know the name of it, and I'm not sure I want to know. But there is something under the surface here, and it is beginning to poison these meetings. They are becoming simply a ritual dance, a parody, a travesty of what they once were. And I won't have that, Roy. I simply won't have it. If the democratic experience is doomed to degenerate, then I want to get off the train.

ROY: But he—

VERNA: I'm almost finished, Roy. Now: all I want you to do is make an effort. I'm asking you personally to make a special effort. I'm asking you to fight whatever subterranean thing is tearing us all apart. When Eddie walks back into this room, I want you to treat him with warmth and affection, so that all of us can join hands in this thing the way we once did. There. I've said my say, Roy. And now I'd be very interested in your response.

ROY: Why don't you say these things to him?

VERNA: Because he's young, Roy. He doesn't know. And you do. Now. Promise me you'll make an effort. For the sake of all of us.

ROY: I'll…try.

VERNA: *(Kissing him on the cheek.)* Good. Oh, good, Roy. I know you won't regret it.

EDDIE: *(Comes angrily back into the room.)* Want to know what happened?

VERNA: Sit down, Eddie.

EDDIE: I said, do you want to know what happened?

VERNA: We only do, Eddie, if it's relevant. If it's not relevant, if it's unpleasant, if it could irritate or embarrass anyone in this room, then no, we do not want to hear what happened.

EDDIE: *(Angrily takes his seat.)* He put me on hold.

VERNA: He what?

EDDIE: *(Shouting.)* He put me on HOLD! He put me on HOLD!

VERNA: *(Covering her ears.)* Eddie, do not shout in my ear. I don't like it.

EDDIE: Dick put me on hold.

VERNA: Well. Maybe he was busy, Eddie.

EDDIE: He left me hanging on hold. Listening to Musak. Listening to the goddam love theme from *Doctor Zhivago.*

VERNA: Oh how ghastly!

EDDIE: Finally his assistant got on the line.

VERNA: His assistant?

EDDIE: He's got an assistant now.

VERNA: I'm not sure I like that.

ROY: What's wrong with that? The man's busy, he needs help…

VERNA: There's something about it I don't like, Roy.

EDDIE: Anyway, he put her on.

VERNA: Her? You said, "Her?" His assistant is a "her." I knew there was something.

ROY: Now Verna…

VERNA: It bothers me, Roy, and I suspect it bothers a number of people here. When we delegated Dick to go down there, I don't recall anything about hiring a female assistant. I may be wrong, we can check the minutes, but I don't recall anything about that.

ROY: It simply means that Dick is working overtime and needs help.

VERNA: It may mean that, Roy. It may mean something very, very different. *(To Eddie.)* What did this so-called assistant say to you, Eddie? When she took you off hold?

EDDIE: She asked me what I wanted.

VERNA: And you replied?

EDDIE: I said I wanted answers to a few questions.

VERNA: And she?

EDDIE: She said she'd try to answer them.

ROY: See? What's wrong with that? Girl was doing her job.

VERNA: Now wait, please, Roy…Go on, Eddie.

EDDIE: So I asked her point blank. I said, how come our country is turning into a second-rate economic power? How come we have created an impoverished, drug-ridden, hopelessly miseducated under-class, with one of the highest infant mortality rates among the industrialized nations? I said how come we continue to spend huge amounts of our national treasure on totally unnecessary military armaments, while we go on contaminating the natural environment, perhaps irreversibly, for the generations that follow us?

VERNA: And how did this so-called assistant respond to that?

EDDIE: Oh, she hemmed and hawed.

VERNA: I'll bet she did. That little bimbo.

ROY: Oh hey, come on, Verna. Those were tough questions to answer.

EDDIE: She also said something else, Roy.

ROY: Oh yes? What else did she say?

EDDIE: She said tell Roy to keep those contributions coming.

VERNA: She said that?

EDDIE: That's what she said: keep those contributions coming.

VERNA: Now that also bothers me.

EDDIE: It does me, too, I'll tell you.

VERNA: Roy, have you been sending money to Dick on the side?

ROY: Well I mean I've tried to see to it that he...

EDDIE: Let me put things a little clearer. No wonder Dick isn't here. No wonder he's goofing off in Washington with some second-rate bimbo. The thing is that Roy has bought him off!

ROY: *(Rising from his chair.)* Hey, now just a minute!

VERNA: *(Restraining Roy.)* Roy, you promised!

EDDIE: *(Pressing home.)* And the reason Roy bought Dick off is that he wants to continue exploiting the poor and polluting the earth!

VERNA: Just ignore it, Roy.

EDDIE: And the reason Roy wants to continue doing these things is that he is motivated, no, *consumed* by simple, selfish, irresponsible greed!

VERNA: Just change the subject, Roy. Move blithely onto another topic.

ROY: *(Brushing her off; standing up.)* No, Verna. I will not move blithely onto another topic! I'm going to answer that here and now!

VERNA: *(To Eddie; through her teeth.)* Do you know what I think, Eddie?

EDDIE: No. What do you think, Roy?

ROY: I think you want to make me look bad out here.

EDDIE: Oh really, Roy?

VERNA: I won't have this!

ROY: Do you know what else I think, Eddie?

EDDIE: What else do you think, Roy?

ROY: I don't think you even bothered to call Dick out there.

VERNA: I will not have this!

ROY: I think you just pretended to call Dick out there. I think what you really did out there was think up bad things to say about me. And I think you pocketed Verna's quarter!

VERNA: *(Covering her ears.)* I will not listen to this!

EDDIE: Roy, the only thing I'm going to pocket tonight is your fat ass!

VERNA: *(Pounding the table with her fists.)* No, no, no, NO! I want the subject changed, do you hear me? CHANGED! Nobody's interested in these personal remarks! Now stop it! Eddie, you obviously need a laxative. Now go TAKE one, for heaven's sake!

ROY: Yes, Eddie!

VERNA: *(Wheeling on Roy.)* And you, Roy, are obviously having trouble with your prostate again!

EDDIE: Yes, Roy!

VERNA: So cut it OUT! Honestly! I've never seen a meeting degenerate so completely! It's sophomoric! Now grow UP! Both of you!

ROY: It's up to him. One more crack from him and I leave. I'm serious. I've got better things to do with my time.

VERNA: Do you hear that, Eddie? Now it's up to you.

(Pause.)

EDDIE: *(Quietly.)* Roy...you know...in some ways, I respect you...

VERNA: Good, Eddie...

EDDIE: And come to think of it, you've run some good meetings this winter...

VERNA: Yes, he has, Eddie. Good...

EDDIE: Maybe you've held a little too much onto the status quo, maybe you've been a little too skeptical of change, but that's your right, Roy, that's your privilege, and in a funny way, I respect you for it...

VERNA: That's very well put, Eddie. That's very mature...

EDDIE: BUT, Roy...

ROY: Here it comes...

EDDIE: BUT, Roy...

ROY: Come on, come on. Out with it...

EDDIE: Even though I respect you, Roy, I don't think I can rest, I really don't think I can rest, Roy, until I have presented to this assembled multitude your left ball!

(Roy pushes his chair back from the table, stands up, and storms angrily out. Verna groans and buries her head in her hands. Finally she turns to Eddie.)

VERNA: Go apologize to that man!

EDDIE: No.

VERNA: I said go—

EDDIE: I said NO!

VERNA: I want to see Roy sitting in his chair!

EDDIE: I want to see Roy flat on the floor.

VERNA: Roy sat in this chair every week, all winter long. Wind, rain, and snow. There sat Roy.

EDDIE: Buying off Dick.

VERNA: I don't care. Dick ducked out. Roy stayed here. Here. Right in this seat. Feel. His seat is still warm from where he sat. Feel, Eddie.

EDDIE: Thanks but no thanks.

VERNA: Oh, and look! You made Roy so mad he left without his briefcase. (Picks it up.) Look at this. This lovely old leather. These personalized initials, unobtrusively engraved in gold leaf. *(She weighs it in her hand.)* Heavy...Heavy with homework...Work he planned to do on our behalf, Eddie...*(Puts it on the table.)* Oh and look at the wear and tear! Here is that spot where he fell in a puddle, hurrying to one of our meetings! And here is that gash from when he was attacked by knife-wielding muggers in the parking lot. *(She tenderly wipes it clean with her handkerchief.)* Oh Eddie, at least return his briefcase to him.

EDDIE: Let him come back and beg for it.

VERNA: Youth can be so cruel. *(She snaps open the briefcase, looks inside.)* Oh look. It breaks my heart. *(Withdraws a large sheaf of papers.)* Look at the work he's done over the years. Proposals, plans, budgets... *(Withdraws a large calendar.)* And look at this calendar. Carefully marked with the dates of all our meetings. Blank for the summer, of course. And then all marked up again for next September, itemizing all the possible topics for discussion. Oh, say what you want to say, Eddie. You're not as hard-working as this, and you never will be.

EDDIE: *(Defensively.)* I have a different style of approach.

VERNA: *(Continuing to poke around in the briefcase.)* Oh, and look at these notes he wrote to himself: "Must do this"... "Ought to do that"... You're mentioned in these notes, Eddie.

EDDIE: I am not.

VERNA: You are! *(Reads.)* "Remember to send Eddie a birthday card"... "Remember to buy Eddie a beer."... "Try to get Eddie a Government grant"...

EDDIE: Lay off, Verna. I feel bad enough as it is.

VERNA: *(Half withdrawing a folder.)* I know, but look at—*(She sees folder's title, stops, puts it quickly back into the briefcase, slams it shut.)*

EDDIE: What?

VERNA: *(Snapping the snaps on the briefcase.)* Nothing, Eddie.

EDDIE: You saw something in that briefcase, Verna.

VERNA: *(Trying to hide the briefcase behind her back.)* No, no...

EDDIE: *(Holding out his hand.)* Give me that briefcase, Verna.

VERNA: This is Roy's private property, Eddie.

EDDIE: Hand it over!

(They struggle for it; finally he wrests it away from her. She collapses into her chair. He slams it down on the table in front of him, snaps it open, searches through it.)

EDDIE: Now. Let's see. Papers, calendars, applications for government grants, and......ah hah! *(He pulls out the suspicious file, reads the cover.)* "For Dick's Eyes Only"...Ah hah. *(Opens the file, reads title page.)* "Plans to Turn America from a Democracy into an Oligarchy" AH-HAH!

VERNA: *(Exhaustedly.)* What's an oligarchy?

EDDIE: An Oligarchy is government by the rich, for the rich, and dedicated to the proposition that they get even richer.

VERNA: Oh Lord.

EDDIE: *(Reads through the file.)* Sure. Here it is...Tax breaks for the upper income brackets...Exorbitant salaries for corporation executives...sheltered retirement accounts...cut backs on health care for the poor...permits on exploiting the environment...It's all here, Verna...And finally, this note, at the end, written in what is obviously Dick's handwriting! *(He slams the note down in front of her.)* Read it, Verna. Read it and weep.

VERNA: *(Shaking her head.)* I can't read it.

EDDIE: *(Taking it up.)* Then I'll read it! *(Reads.)* "Sic Semper Liberalis"...Translate it, Verna.

VERNA: I can't translate it.

EDDIE: Then I'll do that, too... "Thus always with liberals"...Written in Dick's pinched, ungenerous hand...Do you still want me to go apologize to Roy, Verna?

VERNA: *(Quietly.)* Planted.

EDDIE: What?

VERNA: Planted! Someone could have planted that folder in Roy's briefcase.

EDDIE: Oh Verna...

VERNA: Why not? It's possible. Someone who hated Roy and the power structure he represents.

EDDIE: Are you accusing me, Verna?

VERNA: Not necessarily. I'm simply saying that in his country a man is innocent until he's proven guilty.

EDDIE: All right. We'll let him convict him*self*.

VERNA: I don't follow you, Eddie.

EDDIE: He'll convict himself in front of all these witnesses. *(Indicates audience.)* Listen. If Roy knows that this briefcase contains this incriminating folder, he'll come back for it almost immediately. The very fact that he comes back will prove he's guilty as sin.

VERNA: And if he doesn't come back? If he simply telephones and asks me to drop it by his office in the morning?

EDDIE: Then he's innocent, Verna, and I'll apologize to him personally.

VERNA: So we just...wait.

EDDIE: Yes. Wait. Wait while he drives home in his gas-guzzling, space-consuming stretch limousine, peering furtively behind the tinted glass, making guilty and intrusive calls on his mobile telephone. We wait while he pulls into his exclusive restricted, privately protected neighborhood and pulls into the driveway of his insultingly ostentatious home. We wait while he gets out, deactivates his burglar alarm system, and sidles into his customized kitchen to stuff his face on a late-night snack of fat and unnatural food. We wait while he lumbers into his over-decorated den, farts, and then settles into his over-stuffed chair to vicariously identify with a few minutes of violent commercial television. There he sits, festering, stewing, wallowing in his own depraved thoughts. Then suddenly he stiffens. He sits up. His beady, yellow little eyes narrow to slits. His tiny, tufted little ears prick to attention. He remembers! He remembers! He remembers he's forgotten his briefcase! And with a sickening squeal of anger, he scampers back here, as fast as his cloven hooves can carry him! And we'll be waiting!

VERNA: That last speech, was unnecessary, Eddie.

EDDIE: Necessary or not, baby, I made it, and I loved making it! And I'll make more of them to his fat face. *(Takes the incriminating folder, puts it on his chair.)* Oh, Verna, this is exhilarating! I suddenly feel as if we've opened a door to a room which has been closed for years! It's as if we were all stepping back into the cave, when we knew who we were! Come on, Roy! Come home! I'm going to eat you for breakfast!

(Pause.)

VERNA: I loved him, Eddie.

EDDIE: What?

VERNA: I loved him.

EDDIE: You loved ROY?

VERNA: It's hard to admit, particularly in public, but since this looks like our last meeting, I think it's time to tell all. *(Pause.)* We had a thing going, Roy and I. Last fall, after these meetings we'd drive out into the country. *(Pause.)* We made love. Under the harvest moon. Among the squash and pumpkins.

EDDIE: You made LOVE? With ROY?

VERNA: Yes, Eddie.

EDDIE: *(Turning upstage.)* I think I'm going to be sick.

VERNA: And I'll tell you something else, Eddie. Even before we ran these meetings, when Roy and I were both young, we copulated.

EDDIE: Roy was never young!

VERNA: He was, Eddie. He was once young. And liberal. And potent.

EDDIE: I never knew that.

VERNA: Oh there are lots of things you don't know, young man. For instance, I don't imagine you know that one spring, several years ago, he sired you in a newly planted cornfield.

EDDIE: You mean...Roy's my...father?

VERNA: If you want to put it that way.

EDDIE: And you're my...?

VERNA: If you want to pin things down.

EDDIE: I always thought my *parents*...were my parents.

VERNA: Well, they're not.

EDDIE: I didn't know that.

VERNA: Nor does Roy. But he always liked you, Eddie. Dick used to irritate him with all his greed and ambition, but Roy always spoke fondly of you.

EDDIE: Are you saying Dick is...my...brother? Out of you? By Roy?

VERNA: I'm saying lots of things, Eddie. I'm saying Roy had a special feeling for you. And he watched your passage into puberty with pride and affection.

EDDIE: Gosh.

VERNA: Yes. Gosh. You can say gosh now, when that poor man is thrashing around his home, looking for his briefcase!

EDDIE: You know, Verna. All this time I thought that you loved *me*.

VERNA: I did. I do.

EDDIE: No, but I mean, all this spring, ever since Groundhog Day, I've secretly been hoping that you and I could drive out into the corn-fields. And copulate.

VERNA: We can! We will!

EDDIE: But now I know about you and Roy, it changes everything. Every-thing becomes so much more complicated.

VERNA: But that's exactly what I'm *saying,* Eddie! All I'm trying to do is get you—get all of us—to think about these things! There's so much in*volved!* Everything goes way, way back!

EDDIE: I'm beginning to realize that.

VERNA: I hope so, Eddie. Because now I'm going to give you something very difficult to do. *(Opens her bag, begins to take out various things and put them on the table in front of her.)* I have sat here all winter long. *(Out come gloves and hat.)* I have tried to be an agreeable, ac-commodating woman. *(Out come lipstick, compact, perfume, a wig.)* I have tried to hold things together, night after night. I have used every device in the book. *(Liquor, scotch tape, a sewing kit.)* But I can't do it anymore. Times change. People grow old. Institutions become atrophied. We simply don't—meet anymore, you and Roy and I. We've got to make a clean, fresh start. We've got to get back to the essentials. *(Overturns her bag on the table, pouring out a cornucopia of seed packages.)* So you've got to do something about it, Eddie. *(Reaches down into the bottom of the bag, pulls out a small, shiny re-volver, holds it out to him.)* Ah! Here! Take this. Use it on Roy. Do it simply and cleanly. Aim for the heart. Nothing—primitive, please.

EDDIE: *(Not taking the gun.)* I can't kill my own father.

VERNA: Eddie, you've got to. *(She puts the gun down on the table.)* There comes a point when men must act, and women simply have to step out of the way. *(Begins scooping things back into her bag.)*

EDDIE: You're not leaving, are you?

VERNA: I'm afraid I must.

EDDIE: But where are you going?

VERNA: To take a bath.

EDDIE: There are no bathtubs in this building.

VERNA: There's running water somewhere upstairs.

EDDIE: Verna…

VERNA: Eddie, I think I hear Roy's stretch limousine pulling up to a side entrance. Now, please! Spread your wings and fly!

EDDIE: But Verna, if I do this, and if you get your bath, can we still drive out to the cornfields?

VERNA: Oh Eddie. Haven't you learned by now? I'm a woman. Doesn't that answer your question?

EDDIE: Yes, Verna, and I'm a man! That spring chicken, that young capon, that strutting little bantam cock who was crowing around here five minutes ago...He's grown up, Verna!

VERNA: Thank God! Otherwise these meetings have been fruitless, and we've all gotten absolutely nowhere! *(She goes out.)*

(A noise is heard off, on the opposite side. Eddie looks off, quickly takes the gun, puts it in his pocket, turns and faces where the sound came from. Roy enters. Pause.)

ROY: I...um...forgot my briefcase.

EDDIE: Yes...

ROY: I believe that is it, right there.

EDDIE: Yes...

ROY: I'll just pick it up, then.

EDDIE: All right.

ROY: *(Looking around.)* Where's Verna?

EDDIE: Taking a bath.

ROY: Taking a bath?

EDDIE: Trying to, Roy.

ROY: Then the meeting is...breaking up?

EDDIE: I'm afraid so. Yes.

ROY: *(Picks up his briefcase, starts off; stops; weighing it in his hand.)* This briefcase seems lighter somehow.

EDDIE: Oh yes?

ROY: *(Lifting it up and down.)* Lighter than when I brought it.

EDDIE: Oh really?

ROY: Maybe I'm just stronger.

EDDIE: I doubt that, Roy.

ROY: Or else everything isn't here.

EDDIE: Why don't you look and see?

ROY: All right. I will. *(Puts his briefcase on the table, snaps it open, pokes around inside.)*

EDDIE: *(After watching him for a while.)* Perhaps this is what you're looking for, Roy. *(Produces folder.)*

ROY: *(Goes to the folder, opens it, looks through it, closes it.)* These are not my papers.

EDDIE: Roy...

ROY: This is not my folder.

EDDIE: You came back for that folder, Roy.

ROY: I came back to clear my good name.

EDDIE: You said your briefcase felt lighter, Roy.

ROY: That was a ploy.

EDDIE: A ploy, Roy?

ROY: An excuse to stay around. A sop to my pride. I wanted to rejoin the group.

EDDIE: I don't believe that, Roy.

ROY: I want Verna.

EDDIE: Verna's irrelevant to the discussion, Roy.

ROY: *(Calling off.)* Verna!

EDDIE: She can't hear you, Roy.

ROY: *(Calling.)* A little help here, Verna!

EDDIE: The splashing of water, that's all she can hear.

ROY: I'll go find her then. *(He starts off.)*

EDDIE: *(Pulling out his gun.)* She gave me this, Roy.

ROY: She gave you that? That's *my* gun. And my father's before me. That's a family gun. She had no right to give it to you, unless you're my own flesh and…*(Pause; then quietly.)* Blood.

EDDIE: Hello, Pop.

ROY: You're not going to kill your old man, are ya, boy?

EDDIE: I'm afraid I have to.

ROY: Hey! Hey, kid! Come off it. I'm your pal. I'm your buddy, from way back.

EDDIE: Don't make it tough for me, Dad.

ROY: No, hey, listen, kid. It's not over yet. Want to make model airplanes together? Huh? Huh? I'll hit grounders to you with a fungo bat. I'll take you out in the woods, pal. You can shoot your first bear.

EDDIE: *(Painfully.)* Oh Dad…

ROY: No, hey, listen. Tell you what. We'll go out on the town, then. You and me, kid. Make the rounds, Have a few beers. Get loaded. Listen to some tunes. Then we'll give Verna a ring. O.K.? O.K., son? The three of us? You and me and Verna?

EDDIE: It's too late for all that, Dad. You should have thought of these things a long time ago. *(Points gun at Roy.)*

ROY: *(Protecting himself with his briefcase.)* Couldn't we at least work out a compromise? Suppose I plead nolo, and you assign me some sort of community service?

EDDIE: Dad, let me tell you something: if this were a closed session, I suppose you and I could sit down together and work out some sort of deal. But since it's an open meeting, I imagine everyone here wants and expects me to blow your brains out.

ROY: But why?

EDDIE: Because you have systematically betrayed our group, and the republic for which we stand. Now kneel, and pray, to the deity of your choice.

ROY: *(Dropping to his knees; praying.)* Quo vadis…e pluribus unum…sic semper liberalis…

EDDIE: *(To audience.)* Did you hear that last one? Is there any question NOW whether he's guilty?

ROY: *(Praying more desperately.)* Caveat emptor…semper paratus…non illegitimis corborundum.

EDDIE: *(Puts the gun to Roy's temple. A moment. Then he lowers it slowly.)* I can't do it. *(He goes and slumps in a chair.)*

ROY: *(Opening his eyes.)* You can't…?

EDDIE: Do it. Oh my God, is that what it all boils down to? The son killing the father while the mother waits offstage? Are we all caught in some grotesque Freudian parody, and is the democratic experience simply the sum of a series of petty patricides, commencing at the local level? How horrible to contemplate! How can I contribute to such a grim charade? How can I pull this trigger, except on myself? *(Closes his eyes; points gun at his own temple.)*

ROY: *(Slowing getting up; brushing himself off.)* Then I win.

EDDIE: Nobody wins, Roy. It's an absurd meaningless world.

ROY: Go see a psychiatrist, kid. And don't send me the bill, either. Get a job for a change. Start at the bottom, and stay there, for all I care. As for Verna, she's finished, pal. She's taken her last bath. That cheap two-timing whore! It's back into the kitchen for her. I'll have her waxing floors and darning socks. She'll be lucky if she has time to read *Good Housekeeping. (To audience.)* And now for you folks: No more meetings! No more gatherings in groups greater than three! No loitering, no littering, no fornication for seventeen days! I'm in control now, gang. Permanently! I call the shots. The sun will rise on my say so! The moon only shines if I approve. From here on in, I decide who gets into Harvard, who flies First Class, and who gets a good review in the *New York Times.*

EDDIE: *(Taking a bead on Roy with the gun.)* That does it, Roy! It's a meaningless world, Roy, but perhaps I can find meaning in an arbitrary act.

(He pulls the trigger. Roy reels back. Eddie shoots again and again, vindictively, as Roy reels, shudders, groans, collapses. Eddie crosses, kneels and puts the gun on Roy's chest, à la Tosca.)

VERNA: *(Comes out jauntily, in a fresh, flowered dress. She looks much younger. Brightly.)* Oh Eddie, you were wonderful!

EDDIE: *(Kneeling by the body.)* This is no time for crowing, Verna. I'm lost in a mood of sober contemplation and regret.

VERNA: Now don't be silly.

EDDIE: I've killed Roy, Verna.

VERNA: Nonsense. I put blanks in that revolver. I don't believe in the use of real bullets on stage.

EDDIE: But then...how...?

VERNA: Perhaps I'd better explain.

EDDIE: Perhaps you'd better.

VERNA: First of all, *I* shot Roy.

EDDIE: You?

VERNA: I took a bead on him from off in the wings. See that smoking gun out there, leaning against that radiator? I used that. But I didn't *kill* him, Eddie. I got him in the right buttock with one of those tranquilizing darts they use on rhinoceri in the game preserves of Kenya. *(She reaches down, pulls the dart out of Roy's rear; holds it up.)* See? *(She puts it in her purse.)* Oh, he'll be a little sore for a while, but he'll end up fine.

(Roy stirs.)

VERNA: Look. He's coming around.

EDDIE: I'm confused, Verna. I need further explanation.

VERNA: Here's what happened. While I was out there, taking a bath, Dick telephoned and wanted to know what was going on. I told him what we had accomplished so far. He felt the meeting was getting out of hand. So he suggested neutralizing Roy. He had the tranquilizing gun sent over by the local chapter of the CIA.

(Roy gets woozily to his feet, rubs his rear.)

EDDIE: So Dick was behind this?

VERNA: Exactly. He said these meetings are getting nowhere. He thinks we're constantly getting off the track. Enough is enough, he said.

EDDIE: I'm beginning to feel a little manipulated, Verna.

VERNA: I'm sure you do. But think how Roy must feel.

(Roy tries to sit down, can't.)

VERNA: Roy, darling, look what I have here. *(She takes an airplane ticket out of her purse.)* This is a plane ticket to Florida, sweetie pie. Business Class. Now you go down there and find yourself a nice condo on some backwater canal, and putter around happily ever after. Here you go, sweetheart. *(Hands him the ticket.)*

EDDIE: I suppose Dick also arranged for that plane ticket.

VERNA: No, I did. But Dick said he'd reimburse me later with taxpayer's money.

EDDIE: That irritates me too, Verna!

VERNA: Oh now, Eddie. Dick said he was perfectly willing to do favors for people, but in return he hoped we'd give up these open meetings, and leave the responsibilities of government to elected representatives like himself.

EDDIE: I consider all this extremely manipulative! It seems that Washington is totally pulling the strings. *(Puts his arm around Roy.)* I feel a new sympathy for Roy here, jerked around as he has been by Dick. You also, Verna, seem to have become putty in Dick's hands.

VERNA: You may have a point.

EDDIE: These meetings may be inefficient, they may be confused, they may take us in strange directions, but we should all, all of us, take steps to preserve their viability.

VERNA: Well they do help us let off steam, don't they?

ROY: *(Woozily.)* I want to go to Florida.

EDDIE: All right, old friend. I understand. Your days are over in this arena. I can see this is a battle my generation will have to fight by itself.

VERNA: *(Kissing Roy on the cheek.)* There's a taxi waiting to take you to the airport, lovey. Have a wonderful trip. And don't flirt with the Flight Attendants.

(Verna and Eddie point Roy gently offstage.)

Eddie, you mentioned something about taking steps.

EDDIE: Yes I did. I plan to go down to Washington and remind Dick, face to face, that democracy begins and ends at the grassroots level.

VERNA: Oh Eddie, don't go to Washington. I'm scared.

EDDIE: Are you scared Dick will have me killed?

VERNA: No, I'm scared you'll become just like him.

EDDIE: That will never happen, Verna.

VERNA: It might. After all, you're his brother.

EDDIE: I've learned tonight that every man is my brother, Verna. And ever woman, too.

VERNA: Maybe so, but that kind of thinking can turn you into a lousy lover.

EDDIE: It's a chance I'll have to take, Verna. Goodbye for now.

VERNA: Goodbye, Eddie.

(They kiss, then Eddie leaves. A pause. Then Verna turns to the audience.)

VERNA: Well. That's that. All told, I think this has been a very successful meeting. We'll see you in the fall. Meanwhile, if anyone's interested in getting out into those cornfields, please see me afterwards. I'm beginning to think we could use a little new blood around here. *(She goes off.)*

END OF PLAY

The Old One-Two

A Play in One Act

I tried to teach the Classical Tradition during the tumultuous sixties, and this play attempts to be funny about that experience. I returned more seriously to the same milieu with Another Antigone *a few years later.*

Original Production

The Old One-Two was first performed at Brandeis University in 1972, directed by Maggie Voss. It was produced professionally in London and recorded for BBC radio. To my knowledge, it has had no professional productions in the United States.

The Characters

Augustus Holder, Professor of Classics at an American university
Susan Green, a student.
The Dean

Setting

Four playing areas:

1. An old oaken lectern, facing out, from which Professor Holder addresses his class.
2. Professor Holder's office. A cluttered desk with books, notes, papers. A Greek bust on it. A telephone. A picture of the Parthenon behind. Two chairs, one behind the desk, one in front.
3. The Dean's office. A metal desk with push-button telephones, a dictaphone, an electric typewriter. Modern furniture, an abstract painting on the wall.
4. Susan Green's room in a dormitory. A wooden chair and institutional desk. Paperback books and records scattered around. Posters about peace and ecology on the wall. A wall dorm-line telephone.

The play takes place during the Fall of the current academic year.

The Old One-Two

As the houselights dim, Professor Holder comes out and goes to the lectern. He carries an old battered leather briefcase and a black umbrella. He wears an old-fashioned, rumpled dark suit, white shirt, dark tie. He is in his 50s, graying, and has an Old World charm about him. He leans his umbrella carefully against the lectern, places his briefcase on the lectern, and carefully removes a couple of books and lecture notes, arranging them on the lectern. He puts his briefcase neatly next to his umbrella. He puts on a pair of steel-rimmed glasses, surveys his notes, takes off the glasses, surveys the audience, and finally begins. He speaks with a slight foreign accent.

HOLDER: *(To audience.)* Good morning…This course is entitled Introduction to Humanities. Colon. The Classical Experience. *(A wry smile.)* It is known to students—affectionately, I hope—as The Old One-Two. *(Pause.)* Old, because I have taught it in this university for a great many years. *(Pause.)* One-Two because I teach it both semesters. In that way, those of you who fail it in the fall can repeat it in the spring. *(Pause.)* I should only add that this is a required course for all students in the liberal arts. Over the years, it has been attacked, occupied, ravaged, and abused. But it has stood. It stands. I will stand. Mutilated, but beautiful. Like the Parthenon.

(A pretty Girl, in casual clothes, carrying books and papers, gets up from her seat in one of the rear rows and edges her way out to the Center aisle. She may ad-lib "Excuse me…Sorry…" Holder sees her, over the top of his glasses; he watches her patiently and finally speaks.) Just a minute, please.

(The Girl continues toward the door.)

I said just a minute, please.

(The Girl stops.)

What's the difficulty, please?

GIRL: I'm in the wrong course.

HOLDER: You are in the right course.

GIRL: No, I mean wrong for me.

HOLDER: How do you know?

GIRL: How do I *know?*

HOLDER: *(Patiently.)* How do you know this course is wrong for you?

GIRL: Oh. Well, you see I'm interested in Urban Studies.

HOLDER: Good. Here you will study Athens and Rome. Sit down, please.

GIRL: Oh no. I mean contemporary urban problems.

> *(Pause. He waits.)*
>
> Like traffic patterns…
>
> *(He still waits.)*
>
> And slums…

HOLDER: You want to study traffic? You want to study slums?

GIRL: Exactly.

HOLDER: Oh dear. Well. Study what you want. But first you must have the Classical Experience.

GIRL: But I don't want the Classical Experience.

HOLDER: That's not the point. The gods of this university, in their infinite wisdom, long ago decreed that you cannot know yourself until you know your tradition. You cannot study traffic and slums until you study Homer and Sophocles. You cannot be taken seriously as an educated person—until you have taken me. *(Pause.)*

GIRL: *(Suddenly defiant.)* I'll see the Dean.

HOLDER: He'll send you back.

GIRL: The *new* Dean?

HOLDER: Any Dean.

GIRL: I'll take a substitute.

HOLDER: There are no substitutes.

GIRL: I'll petition, I'll appeal.

HOLDER: *(Shaking his head.)* No petition, no appeal.

GIRL: Why that's absolutely, totally unfair!

HOLDER: Ah ha! There! You see what you've learned? Already you've arrived at a primitive conception of Greek tragedy! Think about that. And sit down.

GIRL: No, I won't. I won't think about that. And I won't sit down, either. And I won't study the Greeks. I'm going to find a way out of The Old One-Two!

> *(She walks out. We hear a door slam in the rear. Holder sighs, and speaks to the audience.)*

HOLDER: During the term, you will read a number of Greek plays. And in them, you will discover several splendid young heroines. Antigone, Polyxena, Iphigenia...*(He loves these words.)*...all these maidens will you meet. And you will see them stand up bravely to authority. And go to their death for it, singing fine, pure, triumphant songs. And you will realize that there is a great tradition of personal protest in our culture. And you will recall this recent exhibition, and you will see it as a poor, sad parody of that tradition. And you will shudder with shame. *(He returns to his notes, is now all business.)* Your first paper, on Homer, of at least two thousand words, will be due a week from Monday. I personally will read and grade your work. Try hard! Like the Greeks we study, I believe in fate, struggle, honor, and sudden death. Plan your weekends accordingly. *(He holds up a battered, leathery volume, stuffed with notes.)* Now Homer. *The Odyssey.* I translate from the Greek. *(He reads, carefully translating.)* "Sing inside of me, Muse, and through me only let the story be told..."

(The lights fade out on Holder and the lectern; they fade up on the Dean, in his office. He is in his early thirties, modishly dressed, and at this point is answering an intercom in his office.)

DEAN: O.K. Send her in.

(The Girl comes in.)

Hi.

SUSAN: I'm—

DEAN: Susan Green. I know. I heard all about you. I'm the new Dean. *(He shakes her hand enthusiastically.)* Now here's what I've done. I've reserved a room for you at the student center. Big enough for a reasonably large crowd. I've scheduled it for seven-thirty. I thought that was a good time: after the meal and before the movies. My secretary will help you run off announcements on the Xerox, and then I'll dig up people to help you post them on bulletin boards around the campus. O.K.?

SUSAN: But I don't want that.

DEAN: You don't want to have a protest meeting?

SUSAN: No, I just want to get out of the course.

DEAN: Oh, gee. I thought you were going to protest.

SUSAN: Uh uh. Not me. I'm not the type. *(Pause.)*

DEAN: *(Sitting down, sadly.)* Darn.

SUSAN: I want to change to the social sciences.

DEAN: You, too, huh? I mean we're losing half our students because of that course, and no one even wants to protest.

SUSAN: Why don't you fire him?

DEAN: Can't. He's got tenure.

SUSAN: Why don't you get rid of the course?

DEAN: Can't. There are too many old men around this place who think it's essential.

SUSAN: But the students hate it.

DEAN: They don't show it. They either get out of it, like you, or else re-tire to their room and write a two thousand word paper, without a whimper. God. Where is the spirit of the sixties? I'm going back to teaching Romantic poetry. There's more excitement in Wordsworth's "Daffodils" than there is in the corridors of power these days. Well, many thanks, anyway, for lighting a small temporary candle in a dark Nixon world.

SUSAN: If we protested, what would you do?

DEAN: Oh, I'd have an excuse to break up the course.

SUSAN: Break it up?

DEAN: Sure. Kids could choose. You could take Professor Birnbaum on Culture and Counterculture. You could take Miss Russell on Sex and Sexuality. You could take Mr. Johnson on Black Power. *(He shows her a catalogue.)*

SUSAN: Oh what fabulous courses!

DEAN: They could be. But I'll have to cancel all three of them if we con-tinue to lose our enrollment. *(Pause.)*

SUSAN: All right. Then I *will* protest. I will call that meeting.

(The Dean looks at her, goes to her, gives her a big hug.)

DEAN: There! That's what we did in the sixties. And if you mention any of this to anyone else, I'll deny it ever happened. Now get going, baby. The Xerox is waiting. You do your part, I'll do mine, and we'll have this place swinging in six months.

(She goes out. He dials the telephone quickly, all the while humming "Hey Jude.")

DEAN: Let me speak to the treasurer, please. *(More "Hey Jude.")* Bill?…It's me…You know that crazy fascist alumnus who wants to give money to The Old One-Two…Listen, I think I've got a way we can use it now…Supposing Holder gets tired and wants a rest…

(The lights fade on him, and fade up on Holder, who is also on the tele-phone.)

HOLDER: Hello, Darling…I'm coming home early today. Will you meet the four o'clock bus?…Yes. A bad day…The Old One-Two…The usual flurry of complaints at the beginning of the term. This time, a silly young girl. I wonder if I'm getting too old to play the villain…Goodbye, darling. See you at four.

(Holder hangs up, puts on his overcoat, grabs his briefcase, and exits as the lights dim on his office. The lights come up on the lectern. Susan Green comes nervously down the aisle.)

SUSAN: *(Nervously; to audience.)* Before the bell rings, before he gets here…*(Glances off.)*…I'm supposed to say…for the people who couldn't make the meeting last night…well, we met, and took a vote, and decided not to write that first paper. Hear that, everyone?…It's a strike. O.K.? We're striking…And anyone who finks out, anyone who writes that paper, will hear about it. From me. O.K.? *(Pause; glances off again.)* And I was elected to tell him.

(Pause. She stands nervously in the aisle. Then the bell rings. Holder comes out, briefcase and all. He seems not to see her, and sets up his books and notes as usual. Finally, when he is all set, he calls out to her.)

HOLDER: Now. Who are you?

SUSAN: You know who I am.

HOLDER: Ah so I do. Forgive me. You all look alike. The hair, the clothes…I'm particularly fascinated by the clothes. This yearning of upper middle class American children for the bucolic. It's charmingly decadent. We went through it in Europe in the 18th century. The French call it "nostalgie de la boue"—longing for the gutter. You, as I recall, long for the slums.

SUSAN: *(Suddenly.)* We refuse to write the first paper. *(Pause.)*

HOLDER: Come up here, please. *(Pause.)*

SUSAN: All right. *(She starts for the stage.)*

HOLDER: I want everyone to see and hear you.

SUSAN: All right. *(She mounts the stage, stands near the edge.)*

HOLDER: *(To Susan.)* Now. Repeat what you said.

SUSAN: We refuse to write the first paper.

HOLDER: Who refuses?

SUSAN: We. *(Indicating audience.)* Us.

HOLDER: "We" is correct. The nominative case. The subject of the verb "refuse."

SUSAN: Well, we do.

HOLDER: The first paper.

SUSAN: Yes.

HOLDER: On Homer?

SUSAN: Yes. On Homer. We refuse to write it.

HOLDER: Why?

SUSAN: Because…two thousand words is too much.

HOLDER: Too much? On Homer?

SUSAN: We have other things to do.

HOLDER: Such as what?

SUSAN: Other courses. Other activities.

HOLDER: I know the courses. I've heard of the activities. I hear the major activity is avoiding work for the courses.

SUSAN: That's just plain wrong.

HOLDER: Well, well. You feel that these activities, these courses are important?

SUSAN: Yes.

HOLDER: More important than Homer?

SUSAN: Yes.

HOLDER: *(With a sigh.)* Oh dear. And you speak for the whole class?

SUSAN: Yes.

HOLDER: And so I've got to speak for Homer, don't I? *(Holder paces back and forth, scratching his head, thinking.)* Or rather: Homer should speak for himself. As he has for three thousand years.

SUSAN: We feel—

HOLDER: Wait, wait. I'm thinking…There is an incident, in Book Two, of the *Iliad*, where an insolent soldier tries to persuade the Greeks to leave Troy. The Lord Odysseus listens to the man, and then hits him over the head with a sceptre. The soldier collapses, the rebellion subsides and everyone falls into line on behalf of the Greeks. *(He turns to her proudly.)* There it is. Right in Homer. So…A week from Monday, I will ask for the papers. And anyone who does not hand one in, appropriately typed, with a minimum of misspellings, gets hit over the head with an F. For Fail. Then you will understand Homer.

SUSAN: I think…

HOLDER: Write *down* what you think. About Homer. And stop playing these silly games! *(Now all business, he goes to the lectern, speaks to the audience.)* Now in the time remaining, let us consider that passage in *The Odyssey*— *(Nodding offhandedly to Susan.)* you may sit down— *(To audience.)* where Odysseus lies exhausted on the beach from his struggles in the sea… *(She stands there helplessly as the lights dim on them and the lectern.)*

(Lights up on Holder's office. The Dean enters, paces, pokes through a book or two. Finally Holder comes in, sees him.)

HOLDER: Ah. Mein Dean.

DEAN: Where the hell have you been? I've called all over campus.

HOLDER: I got the message. *(He reaches into his pocket, brings out a fistful of little pink slips which he lets flutter one by one into the wastebasket.)* See the Dean…Call the Dean…please see or call the Dean…*(He throws the rest away.)* You rule the paper empire, Agamemnon.

DEAN: *(Patiently.)* Where were you?

HOLDER: Jogging. I jog. In the gym. Sound mind, sound body. Every day, after class, I jog two miles around the track. It's quite invigorating now that women use the athletic facilities. But then I always take a cold shower, and read the Stoics. *(Sits down behind his desk.)* Or else see my Dean.

DEAN: Gus…

HOLDER: Now be calm. Their strike is broken. Strike! I abuse the dignity of American labor by terming that twitch a strike. Anyway, it's over. And Saint Joan will recant, and retire to the library to write a miserable messy little paper.

DEAN: She's a bright girl. She did brilliantly in high school.

HOLDER: Which says all that needs to be said about American high schools.

DEAN: I'm not going to argue that, Gus.

HOLDER: I wouldn't.

DEAN: No, actually, I am the bearer of glad tidings.

HOLDER: Ah. A raise in salary.

DEAN: No, Gus. Better. I think I can swing your sabbatical now.

HOLDER: My sabbatical!

DEAN: We found the money, Gus. I told the treasurer how long you had taught without a break.

HOLDER: I am tired…

DEAN: So we found the dough, Gus. You can have the second semester off. Full pay.

HOLDER: Second semester! Why I could be in Greece this spring!

DEAN: Exactly, Gus. And I think we could even cough up a little extra for transportation.

HOLDER: I could see Delphi again! We could walk among the ruins!

DEAN: Right, Gus. So shall I put you down for it, then?

HOLDER: You may put me down immediately! *(Pause.)* But what will happen here?

DEAN: Oh, well…

HOLDER: Who will teach The Old One-Two?

DEAN: We'll work it out.

HOLDER: Will you bring someone in? I'd want to interview him. Do you have a man in mind from my field?

DEAN: Oh we'll dig up someone.

HOLDER: Who? Name names. What have they written? It's my course.

DEAN: Well, I'm thinking of opening it up a little, Gus.

HOLDER: Opening it up?

DEAN: Letting various people take a crack at various versions…

HOLDER: Various people, various versions! Who and what?

DEAN: We're talking about the future, Gus…

HOLDER: We're talking about Birnbaum, and that Russell woman, and that black man, and all those other barbarians whom you have brought into this department!

DEAN: They are fine, bright people…

HOLDER: You are trying to bribe me out of this place, so that those alien hordes can teach my Greeks!

DEAN: Oh Christ, Gus!

HOLDER: You *gave* them Christ! You gave them the Bible, and Dante, and Shakespeare, and they threw it all away! Very well! Now let them divide the whole modern world between them! They'll never get their hands on my Greeks!

DEAN: They are not your Greeks, Gus…

HOLDER: They are mine, and I'll stand and protect them like a Spartan at Thermopylae! I will not allow these people, with their beards, and their cheap careerism, and their peasant sensibilities, to get their foul, unwashed hands on my Greeks!

DEAN: Oh can it, Gus.

HOLDER: The Greeks are mine. And they stay mine. And I stay here. And I will not be lured onto the rocks by the siren song of a sabbatical spring in Greece!

DEAN: At least think of your wife!

HOLDER: My wife?

DEAN: At least discuss it with her.

HOLDER: My wife stays out of this.

DEAN: That's just it. You keep her out there in the woods. You never bring her in. I never see her at the functions.

HOLDER: Don't you dare mention my wife!

DEAN: Oh Gus...

HOLDER: And don't call me Gus. I'm Professor Holder to you. And I am in charge of the Greeks!

DEAN: The course is doomed.

HOLDER: Not while I'm alive. And no Dean can prevent me from teaching it.

DEAN: I'm going to try.

HOLDER: Fine. Try. Take away my classroom. I'll teach it in the halls. Take away my schedule. I'll teach it at night. Take away my students, and I'll teach it to the janitor who comes in to erase from the blackboard the presumptuous scrawls of Birnbaum, Russell, and Johnson. Now please go. I have work to do. Unlike them, I read. I study. I prepare.

(He picks up a book. The Dean looks at him, then storms out angrily. After the Dean has gone, Holder puts down his book and dials the telephone.)

Darling, I'll be late tonight...No, I've got to work...I want to be exceptional this term...I have the feeling it's crucial...No, I'll get a sandwich from the machines, and be home very late. I'll walk from the bus...Goodbye, darling. I'll miss you, as always.

(The lights fade up on the Dean's office. The Dean storms in, goes to his telephone, pushes a button.)

DEAN: Get me Professor Holder's home, will you?...They live somewhere out in Arcadia... *(He waits, shuffling angrily through papers. The telephone buzzes. He answers.)* Hello?...Is this Mrs. Holder?...We've never met, Mrs. Holder, but I'm your husband's Dean, and I think he's making a serious mistake, and I'd like to come out and talk to you about it some time...Now?...Right now? *(Consults watch, memo calendar.)* But I've got— *(Decides.)* All right. Now. *(Grabs a pencil and pad.)* Yes...Beyond the church...Beyond the graveyard...Turn right at a grove of trees. Yes. Fine. Got it. I'll be there...Goodbye, Mrs. Holder. *(Hangs up; pushes a button; speaks into other telephone.)* Cancel all appointments for the rest of the day. *(Hangs up; gets up and grabs his coat and leaves as the light fades on his office.)*

(The lights come up on Susan Green's dormitory room. Her telephone is ringing. She comes in carrying a stack of books which she throws angrily down on her bed. She answers the telephone.)

SUSAN: Hello?...No, I'm sorry, Tommy. I can't go out after all. I'm going to write the paper. I said I'm going to write it. Everyone else has chickened out, and is writing one, and I'm going to do it too...Oh yes I am…I took every book on Homer out of the library, and I'm cutting all my other classes, and I'm going to write me the best god-damn paper he ever saw…Oh yes, footnotes, references, maps, the works!…And I'm going to have it typed professionally at a buck a page.…And I'm going to show up in class every day. And sit there with my eager little eyes on him. And nod at his sappy points. And smile at his crumby jokes. And take huge stacks of notes…Oh yes. And after I've handed in the paper, and he's corrected it, I'm going to put on my best little dress from Pick and Puke. And comb my hair neat as a pin. And wear lipstick. And I'm going to show up in his office, and sit there with my knees together, and listen politely while he gasses on about my good work…No, no, wait. And then…And then…when he hands me the paper, when he hands it back, I'm going to stand up and say, very quietly and very clearly: "This is all you want, you chickenshit bastard. A lot of old words from a lot of old books. Anyone dumb enough to take the time can write this crap. So you can take this paper, and you can shove it up your classical ass!" …I am, Tommy. I'm going to do it. And I'm going to tear it up and throw it in his face. He'll flunk me, but it'll be worth it. He'll learn something. So goodbye. I want to get going on this thing. *(She hangs up; gets ready to read and take notes; looks around; runs off angrily.)* Oh God! Does anybody have a pencil?

(The lights come up on the lectern. Holder is finishing a lecture.)

HOLDER: *(To audience.)* …and let me conclude the class by asking you to realize how much it means when Odysseus decides to leave his home and fight for the Greeks. Consider this line: *(He reads, translating.)* "He yearned to see the smoke from his own hearth, rising." *(He looks out, reflectively.)* Consider that. That natural yearning of the man, the natural rising of the smoke. Both are the same. Men yearn for their hearth just as naturally, just as inevitably, as smoke rises from it. And so when Odysseus leaves Penelope at her loom in order to do battle for the Greeks, he is willfully turning his back on the very ground of his being. And that is very difficult to do. *(The bell rings.)* Ah. The bell. *(Holds up his hands.)* One moment please. I have corrected your papers. You may retrieve them, graded and with appropriate comments, outside my office at any time this afternoon. Those papers which are unusually good, or unusually bad, I will retain and return personally during office hours. Therefore, if your paper is not in the batch outside my door, see me personally at your convenience, and at mine. *(The lights dim on the lectern as he gathers up his things and exits.)*

(The lights come up on the Dean dictating, in his office, as he paces.)

DEAN: Dear Mrs. Holder. *(Pause.)* Just a short quick note to thank you for a most pleasant afternoon. While we barely touched on the purpose of my visit, I enjoyed immensely our stroll through the misty orchard, our chat by the fire, the cheese, the wine, the music in the background... *(He forgets he is dictating, continues dreamily.)* the highlights in your hair...your deep dark eyes...your throaty voice with its mysterious accent...*(Pause. He dreams. Then he snaps out of it. He adjusts his dictaphone and starts again.)* Dear Mrs. Holder. I have always been especially fond of Simone Signoret...*(Stops; starts again.)* Dear Mrs. Holder. You might think that we administrators lead shallow, rootless, abstract lives. *(Pause.)* We do. *(Pause.)* Which is why we need occasionally to drink at the well...lean on the breast...touch the source...*(Pause; starts again.)* Dear Mrs. Holder. Just a quick note. Just a quick...Just a quickie...*(Pause; puts down his dictaphone; looks up a number in his rotary memorandum file, and dials impulsively.)* Hi. This is—*(Pause.)* How did you know I'd call. *(Pause; laughs.)* Yes, well, listen, I feel we barely touched—on the purpose of my visit, and I'd like to come out again. *(Pause.)* Tonight? Dinner? But I'd prefer it if he wasn't—? *(Pause.)* Dinner it is, then. I'll be there. Goodbye, Simone Signoret—I mean, Mrs. Holder. *(Hands up dreamily, then pushes a button on his intercom.)* Call my wife. Tell her to take the kids to MacDonald's. I've got to go out of town for the evening. *(The lights dim on the Dean.)*

(The lights come up on Holder's office, where Susan now sits demurely gotten up, jaw set, hair neat and tied back, hands clasped in her lap. After a moment Holder comes in. He sees her.)

HOLDER: Ah. Miss Susan Green.

SUSAN: The door was open. So I came in.

HOLDER: How well you look.

SUSAN: *(Coldly.)* Thank you.

HOLDER: You've changed a great deal.

SUSAN: I've changed my clothes.

HOLDER: They're very becoming. I am reminded of a line from the Electra: "I now wear different robes." *(He sits behind his desk; stares intently at her.)*

SUSAN: What about my paper?

HOLDER: Ah. Your paper.

SUSAN: It wasn't in the pile. Do you have it?

HOLDER: Of course I have it. By all means I have it. *(He continues to stare at her.)*

SUSAN: May I see it?

HOLDER: *(Snapping out of it.)* Oh of course. *(He rummages through his briefcase.)* I have it right here. *(He gets it out, holds it.)* I've read it three times. Once last night, once this morning, and once about an hour ago. *(Pause. He looks at it.)*

SUSAN: May I have it back?

HOLDER: Certainly. Here you are. *(He hands it across his desk to her.)*

SUSAN: *(Looking at the title page.)* There's no grade on this paper.

HOLDER: I know.

SUSAN: *(Flipping through it.)* No comments either…Nothing in the margins. *(Flips through to the end.)* Nothing at the end. Nothing. You didn't write anything.

HOLDER: I know

SUSAN: But why? Was it that—bad?

HOLDER: No, no. It wasn't that bad. No, no.

SUSAN: That good, then? You refuse to give A's? You refuse to—

HOLDER: No, no, no. It was neither. Neither good nor bad. Those categories don't apply. May I have it again? *(Holds out his hand for it; she gives it to him; he peruses it.)* Miss Green, I have never read a paper like this in all the years I have been teaching. I couldn't grade it. I couldn't comment on it. I simply read it, and was amazed.

SUSAN: I don't understand.

HOLDER: Ah, Miss Green, now I see why you protested so violently against writing a paper. And I don't blame you! The Herculean labor that this must have entailed! Your footnotes, your references, the way you move in and out of thousands of years of scholarship! It's a staggering job, Miss Green, and frankly I'm stunned by it!

SUSAN: But then why didn't you give me an A?

HOLDER: Oh, Miss Green: because this paper is dead.

SUSAN: Dead?

HOLDER: Dead. It is finally and simply a compilation of what other people have written. You don't trust yourself. You don't trust Homer. You lean on others. And that's ultimately dull. And dead. *(Long pause.)*

SUSAN: Oh.

HOLDER: And that's why I couldn't grade your paper. I could give you an

A for the most dogged kind of effort. I could give you an F for an appalling lack of insight. But what, really, is the grade between zero and infinity? *(Pause.)* So I gave you nothing at all.

(Pause. They sit looking at each other. Then she gets up and holds out her hand.)

SUSAN: Could I have it, please?

HOLDER: I have more to say, Miss Green.

SUSAN: Could I have my paper, please.

HOLDER: Miss Green…

SUSAN: I want my paper. I want it back.

HOLDER: Sit down, Miss Green. I said sit DOWN.

(She does.)

Now. *(Pause.)* Do you know why I came to America?

SUSAN: The war?

HOLDER: Wrong. I came after the war. Why did I come?

SUSAN: To be free?

HOLDER: Here? Free? No, no. A scholar has more freedom over there.

SUSAN: I don't know, then.

HOLDER: I came to America, Miss Green, because I am convinced that this country will be the new Byzantium.

SUSAN: Oh, please…

HOLDER: The custodian of classical culture during the Dark Ages to come.

SUSAN: Oh now, come *on*…

HOLDER: I believe that, Miss Green. I believe that long after Rome and Paris and Florence have smothered in their own traffic, when Venice has sunk into the sea, and the Mediterranean is a sewer, and all of Europe lies poisoned in its own garbage, I believe that America will live on to tell the tale. You will keep alive what Europe kept alive for two millenia. It's your turn now. *(He quotes.)* "Some God has led me over the wine-dark seas to build his altar on these dew-washed shores." *(Pause.)*

SUSAN: Why tell me?

HOLDER: Because you're it, Miss Green.

SUSAN: I'm what?

HOLDER: You're America! You're the future! Young, bright, energetic, and underneath it all, like your founding fathers, abiding love for the great traditions of Greece and Rome!

SUSAN: I *don't* have an abiding love…

HOLDER: You do, Miss Green. This paper did not spring full-armed from the head of Zeus! You wrote it!

SUSAN: I wrote it because I was mad—

HOLDER: You wrote it because you're an American. And I am telling you this because you are everything I came to this country for. And now I want to pass on the gauntlet. Now I want to turn you into a first-rate classical scholar.

SUSAN: I'm not going to be a classical scholar.

HOLDER: You are going to be the *best*, Miss Green. I am going to teach you. I intend to plant the seeds of Greece in you, and water and train and prune you till you produce nothing but Golden Apples! And I intend to start now, Miss Green. I want you to write another paper. I'm assigning a topic: Book Six of *The Odyssey*. Write on that.

SUSAN: I won't.

HOLDER: You will *(He hands her a book.)* Use my copy. Write something good! Turn it in soon. Come by for conferences. As for this paper, this…dry run…*(He tears it up.)* It's not worthy of you.

SUSAN: Professor Holder…

HOLDER: *(Grabbing his briefcase and umbrella.)* Don't talk. Stay here. Work. Use my books. Use my notes. Goodbye. I've got to leave. I'm overjoyed. I've got to jog.
   (He rushes out. She rushes after him.)

SUSAN: *(Calling.)* Professor Holder…Professor Holder…*(The lights dim on his office.)*
   (The lights come up on the Dean's office. The Dean is dictating a letter.)

DEAN: Letter to Professor Birnbaum, Miss Russell, and Mr. Johnson. Private and confidential. Dear first name. While I cannot officially promise you a renewal of contract at this time, I do feel certain that a position for you will open up in the near future. I simply don't believe that the Old One-Two will continue to monopolize our attention much longer. I fear it is an obsolete endeavor. We should no longer be tied to that tradition, or indeed any tradition. Our task today is to cultivate new life styles and new modes of behavior beyond marriage, beyond the family…*(Dreamily.)* beyond the church, beyond the graveyard…*(Pause; he snaps out of it.)* Strike that. Go back to tradition. Your course, comma first name comma, is much more appropriate for contemporary student concerns. So bear with me please. The Old One-Two is irrelevant, and I will do what I can to see that it dies a quiet, easy death. Sincerely etcetera. *(He signs off the dictaphone. Pause; then he dials his telephone.)* Hi…It's me again…*(The lights fade on the Dean's office.)*

(The lights come up on Holder at the lectern.)

HOLDER: Now at this point in Aeschylus, something very exciting is going on…*(He leaves the lectern, goes close to the edge of the stage, speaks with great excitement.)* You see, the playwright is singing a—what?— a love song, yes, a love song to the city of Athens, and to the bright new concept of human community which it represents. The Furies—those dark female forces of destruction which abide within us all—have been changed into Athenian maidens, who now carry the torches of light and understanding on into the future! And those torchbearers…*(He stops, peers out.)* These maidens who were once Furies…*(He scans the audience.)* But where is our Miss Green? *(Pause.)* I don't see Miss Green here. Is she ill? Does anyone know? *(Pause.)* I hate to continue the lecture without—*(Pause, then suddenly.)* Class dismissed. *(He gathers up his books and briefcase very quickly.)* I said, class dismissed. I was up half the night. Working this out for—*(Pause.)* Class dismissed. *(He hurries offstage.)*

(Lights come upon Holder's office. Susan sits in a chair, waiting grimly. After a moment he dashes in.)

HOLDER: Where have you been?

SUSAN: Waiting right here.

HOLDER: Why weren't you in class?

SUSAN: Because I wanted to think.

HOLDER: That's something, at least. And have you been reading?

SUSAN: Yes.

HOLDER: Have you read Aeschylus?

SUSAN: No.

HOLDER: You should have read Aeschylus.

SUSAN: *(Patting the book.)* I read this. Book Six of *The Odyssey*. I read it many times.

HOLDER: We will talk about Aeschylus. That's where I am.

SUSAN: No. I want to talk about this. *(She indicates the book.)* That's where *I* am. And that's where you are, too, really, I think.

HOLDER: What do you mean?

SUSAN: Professor Holder, I wonder if you realize what Book Six of *The Odyssey* is about.

HOLDER: Of course I realize. It's about—

SUSAN: It's about an older man falling in love with a younger girl, that's what it's about.

HOLDER: It's about—

SUSAN: It's about the aging Odysseus, naked and alone, exhausted from his battles for the Greeks, finding himself on a strange island, and falling in love with the young princess of that island.

HOLDER: It is not about—

SUSAN: It is about how he loves her, and forgets his home because of her.

HOLDER: It happens to be about—

SUSAN: It's about *that*, Professor Holder. I've read it very recently, and very carefully, and that's what it's about. And I think when you assigned it to me, you knew that.

HOLDER: I did not—

SUSAN: *Unconsciously.* You knew that. *(Pause.)*

HOLDER: *(Very quietly.)* I think you're wrong.

SUSAN: I know I'm right. I've been working very hard. And now I know a lot of things. I know, for example, that the teaching relationship is basically erotic. I know that the hostility you felt toward me at the beginning of the term was an aspect of that eroticism. I know that your remarks about my clothes were more overt signs of it. I know your desire to jog is an attempt to sublimate it. And I know that in Book Six of *The Odyssey* you were signaling to me your erotic impulses in the only way you knew how. *(Long pause.)*

HOLDER: Birnbaum! Russell! Johnson! You've been talking to the barbarians!

SUSAN: I haven't talked to anyone. These are my own conclusions.

HOLDER: They are *stupid* conclusions! They are insulting conclusions. They are ghastly example of cheap, high school, assembly-line, American-made Freud! And I refuse to discuss them.

SUSAN: *(Calmly, getting up.)* I knew you'd say that. *(She puts the book down on his desk.)* And so I'm dropping this course.

HOLDER: Dropping it?

SUSAN: Because it's a lie. I think I sensed it even in September. You refuse to deal with these things. You refuse to consider the entire world of the unconscious. *(Indicating book.)* You avoid the heart of the matter. And therefore the Old One-Two is just one long lie! *(She goes to the door.)*

HOLDER: *(Shouting.)* We have not finished this conference!
(Pause; she turns; he controls himself.)

In private conferences, I believe in giving students ample time to make their case. *(Pause.)* No matter how absurd the case may be. *(Pause.)* So we will discuss Book Six of *The Odyssey* in more detail. *(Pause.)*

SUSAN: O.K. *(She moves toward the chair.)*

HOLDER: Perhaps you'd better close the door.

(She looks at him.)

The noise from the corridor can be distracting.

SUSAN: All right. *(She closes the door, sits down, watches him.)*

HOLDER: *(Holding out the book to her.)* Would you like to refresh your memory?

SUSAN: No thanks. I know it cold.

HOLDER: All right. *(He shuffles through the papers.)*

SUSAN: Page 76.

HOLDER: Yes. Here it is. Odysseus is cast up on the shore of a strange island.

SUSAN: America.

HOLDER: America is not a strange island.

SUSAN: It is to you. *(Pause.)*

HOLDER: He is exhausted. He falls asleep.

SUSAN: As you did.

HOLDER: I did not.

SUSAN: Teaching the Old One-Two. Year after year. You fell asleep. *(Pause.)*

HOLDER: He awakens to the sound of young girls playing ball.

SUSAN: Playing games.

HOLDER: Who is playing games?

SUSAN: You called my strike a silly game! *(Pause.)*

HOLDER: *(With increasing energy.)* He watches these girls from his hiding-place.

SUSAN: Hiding behind his lectern.

HOLDER: And finally, hungry and forlorn...

SUSAN: Eager for life...

HOLDER: He approaches the lovely princess...

SUSAN: As you did me...

HOLDER: Covering his naked loins with a thick branch...

SUSAN: Covering your sexual desires with Book Six of *The Odyssey*...

HOLDER: And he introduces himself to her...

SUSAN: How do you do? *(Long pause.)*

HOLDER: *(Passionately.)* He never touches her!

SUSAN: Homer doesn't say.

HOLDER: Never does he touch her!

SUSAN: It's implied in every line!

HOLDER: He respects her innocence!

SUSAN: Oh she's not innocent!

HOLDER: She's a maiden!

SUSAN: Oh, Professor Holder. Don't be naive! *(Another long pause. He looks at her very carefully.)*

HOLDER: *(Slowly.)* Then you think...that this young princess...herself...feels...attracted to...this tired, naked, foreign old man? *(Pause.)*

SUSAN: I think she is fascinated by him. *(He closes the book. They look at each other for a long time. Finally:)*

HOLDER: Euripides.

SUSAN: What?

HOLDER: I said Euripides. It is time to teach Euripides. Not Aeschylus. He's too optimistic. Not Sophocles. He's too profound. No, it is time to teach the tragedies of Euripides!

SUSAN: Does Euripides write about—this?

HOLDER: In every word! Come to class. Please. Every day.

SUSAN: All right. I will. And I'll listen very carefully. *(She starts for the door, then stops.)* But what's his solution?

HOLDER: Solution? Euripides? Oh Susan Green, you should know: people die in Euripides.

(They look at each other as the lights dim on them.)

(The lights come up on the Dean's office. All his telephones are ringing. The Dean comes in hurriedly, looking harassed. He speaks to his intercom.)

DEAN: No calls, please! Not one! Tell them I'm getting out a memorandum...*(He sinks into his chair, loosens his tie, then takes his dictaphone and begins to dictate.)* Memo. From the Dean. To the University Community. Subject: The Old One-Two. *(Pause.)* One. In order to accommodate the increased attendance, Professor Holder's lectures on Euripides will henceforth take place in Gardner Auditorium. Two. Inasmuch as the Euripides lectures are now being taped for Educational Television, students are asked to restrain their cheers and applause until the end of the class period. Three. Because copies are no longer available in either the library or the local bookstores, students are requested to share Euripides with classmates and friends. Four...*(The telephone rings; he answers angrily.)* I said no calls, please...Oh...Put her on...*(Pause.)* Hi...I know, I'm sorry. I've been tied up night and day because of these goddam Euripides lectures ...Dinner? No, I can't. The Ford Foundation is coming in. They want to *endow* him, for Chrissake...Oh look, lady, I don't know why I hang around out there anyway. All I get is a good meal, and a good-night kiss and then you send me home like a good little boy...I don't understand you, I don't understand him, I don't understand the students, and I don't understand Euripides. *(Susan comes in; he sees her.)* Call back when I can stay a little longer, O.K.? *(He hangs up.)* Ah. Miss Susan Green. I take it you now want to major in the Greeks like everyone else around here.

SUSAN: No.

DEAN: Then I suppose you are part of that Drama group which wants to put on a Euripides festival this spring.

SUSAN: No.

DEAN: Then what?

SUSAN: I want to transfer to another college, and I need your recommendation.

DEAN: Ah. I get it. To some place with a stronger Classics department.

SUSAN: No. To Saint Mary's in the Mountains. A small college for women. Which has no classics at all.

DEAN: But why?

SUSAN: Personal reasons.

DEAN: But Susan, I can't write a recommendation without knowing—

SUSAN: I didn't think so. Which means I'll just drop out. *(She turns to go.)*

DEAN: *(Coming to her; confidentially.)* Hey. He's a fake, isn't he? The course is a put-on. The Euripides lectures are phoney. That's why you're leaving, isn't it?

SUSAN: *(Turning at door.)* Professor Holder is a heroic man. The Old One-Two is a work of art. And I'll remember the Euripides lectures the rest of my life! *(She walks out.)*

DEAN: *(Calling after her.)* Susan— *(His telephone rings. He answers.)*
(The lights come up on Holder's office, who is also on the telephone.)

HOLDER: Holder here. Have you got a pencil?

DEAN: Yes.

HOLDER: Then write these things down. Are you ready?

DEAN: Yes.

HOLDER: One, notify the Ford Foundation that the topic of my lecture tomorrow will be *The Bacchae*, by Euripides. I intend to connect it with Nixon, poverty, and the Viet Nam war.

Dean. *(With a sigh.)* All right.

HOLDER: Two. I would like to meet him for lunch. There I will ask them to endow also a sequel to the Old One-Two. It will be called the New Three-Four. It will deal with the Judeo-Christian tradition. All undergraduates will be required to take it.

DEAN: Now wait a—

HOLDER: Three. I want Birnbaum, Russell, and Johnson fired. Immediately. To make room for three more Classicists.

DEAN: Gus—

HOLDER: Sorry, but I've got to go. The TV people want to work on my make-up. They say I'll be the Julia Child of the '70s.

DEAN: *(Frantically.)* Goddam it, Gus! I'm not just a flunky! Tell me what's going on! What is it with her?

HOLDER: Her?

DEAN: Susan Green. Why is she leaving, for Chrissake?

(Holder slams down the phone, dashes out of his office, as the lights fade on it.)

Gus?…Gus?…Oh Lord, now they hang up on me! I'm totally irrelevant. *(He puts down the receiver, holds his head in his hands as the lights dim on him.)*

(The lights fade up on Susan's room. Her bag is packed, her overcoat lies across it. She is sitting on the floor making a hitchiking sign: "Ride Wanted Anywhere." After a moment, Holder bursts in.)

HOLDER: Why are you leaving me?

SUSAN: Because I can't stand it another day.

HOLDER: What? What can't you stand?

SUSAN: The course!

HOLDER: It's all for you!

SUSAN: That's why I can't stand it. Please: let me go! *(She grabs her bag and sign and tries to push past him.)*

HOLDER: If you go, everything goes!

SUSAN: I'm not up to it, Professor Holder. I'm not a tragic person.

HOLDER: Nor am I.

SUSAN: Oh you are. Those lectures were glorious!

HOLDER: They were lies.

SUSAN: Oh no.

HOLDER: Lies! I used Euripides to pander to you. I took one of the world's great playwrights, and I laid him out on the proscrustean bed of my own private longings. I stretched him until he screamed anything I wanted. I turned the Old One-Two into a lie.

SUSAN: You said beautiful things.

HOLDER: Beautiful lies.

SUSAN: You believed them when you said them.

HOLDER: I did not. Do you know what I do after class? Do you know what I do after all that magnificent talk about fate and struggle and self-control?

SUSAN: You jog.

HOLDER: *(Shaking his head.)* I've given that up.

SUSAN: Then—what?

HOLDER: I read.

SUSAN: Read? What's wrong with that?

HOLDER: It's what I read that's wrong.

SUSAN: You mean…you read Book Six of *The Odyssey?*

HOLDER: No! I don't even read Greek anymore. *(Pause.)* I read Latin.

SUSAN: Latin?

HOLDER: And what Latin I read! I read Ovid's *The Art of Love.* I read scatalogical passages in Tacitus and Juvenal. I go to the rare book room in the library and sit there for hours, pouring over full-color reproductions of the pornographic paintings on the walls of Pompeii!

SUSAN: Gosh.

HOLDER: I hardly stop reading, except to eat. I hardly go home. Except to sleep. And when I sleep, I dream.

SUSAN: Do you dream in Latin?

HOLDER: I dream in bad Latin. The Latin I dream in is corrupt. The nouns decline lecherously. The verbs conjugate repulsively. And I dream of doing depraved things—with *you.* I dream of sloshing about with you, naked, in the baths of Caracalla. I dream of copulating with you in the crowded Colosseum while even the lions look on. I dream of taking you deep into the early catacombs, and there inventing with you a unique and fantastic coital position on top of a primitive altar, while Saint Paul and Saint Peter lead frantic prayers for our mutual damnation!

SUSAN: Oh wow.

HOLDER: *(Pacing; wringing his hands.)* Oh Susan, Susan, Susan Green! You have lured me out of Classical Greece into the most degenerate period of all time. I stand before you, the true Roman, all buckled neatly into my armor, yet slavering and festering within!

(Pause; then she takes off her coat, puts down her bag and sign.)

SUSAN: Take off your armor.

HOLDER: *(Backing away.)* I can't! I'd *explode!* Like an overripe pomegranate!

SUSAN: Stop talking.

HOLDER: I can't. If I did, I'd probably ravage you, like a Sabine!

SUSAN: *(Reaching out to him.)* Come here.

HOLDER: Don't touch me! *(Pause.)*

SUSAN: Oh look. You and I, we've got to get ourselves together, Professor Holder. I know someone who has a pad. We'll go there. We'll play records, and drink wine, and smoke grass, and relax. O.K.! I'll rub your back, you rub mine, and we'll loosen up. I mean, together, Professor Holder. O.K.? *(Pause.)*

HOLDER: *(Very quietly.)* Very well. I'll call my wife, and tell her I'm working on my lecture for tomorrow. I will say I'll be here all night.

SUSAN: Yes. I'll arrange for the pad.

(He starts for the door, then stops.)

HOLDER: It won't be Euripides. It will never be Euripides again.

SUSAN: Let's just go.

(He opens the door, then stops, turns once more.)

HOLDER: I'm in your power now. The entire Western Tradition is in your hands.

SUSAN: *(Putting a finger on his lips.)* Sssshh. No more talk. Let's. Just. Go.

(He looks at her, then exits. She follows after him as the lights fade on her room.)

(The lights come back up on the Dean's office. He is at his desk, now in his shirt sleeves, a bottle and a glass in front of him. He is dictating into his machine, slightly drunkenly.)

DEAN:…and so I hereby tender my resignation as Dean of this department. Furthermore, I request a sabbatical leave so that I may travel and rest and come to a better understanding of myself and my world. I feel incompetent as an administrator, incoherent as an educator, and incapable as a man. *(The telephone rings; he answers sadly.)* Yes?…Oh hello. *(He sits up.)* When? Tonight?…All night?…Where? Out there? But what about—?…Ah. Working on Euripides, eh? O.K. Fair enough…Tonight he sleeps with the Greeks, and I sleep with you, and tomorrow's another day…Bye-bye, au revoir, and ciao…(*He hangs up, grabs his coat, puts the bottle in the drawer, starts out, stops, returns to dictaphone, takes out disk, crumples it up, tosses it away, and hurries out.*)

(*The lights come up on Holder's office. There is morning light. The telephone is ringing. Finally: the door bursts open. Holder comes in, his arm around Susan, laughing uproariously.*)

HOLDER: Susan, after last night, I am convinced you will bear me a child!

SUSAN: Oh please.

HOLDER: No, I am convinced. Whenever a god has slept with a nymph, there will be a child. You will bear him in some sacred grove of olives, and he will live to redeem America!

SUSAN: Your phone! It's time for your lecture!

HOLDER: Time is for slaves, Susan Green. Eternity is for you and me.

SUSAN: You're stoned out of your mind. I'll answer it. (*She does.*) Hello? (*Hands over receiver.*) Oh God. It's the Ford Foundation.

HOLDER: (*Regally.*) I will speak to the Ford Foundation.

SUSAN: (*Into telephone.*) He's here. But—(*Holder takes the phone with great dignity.*)

HOLDER: Yes, I have just finished preparing my lecture…Euripides? Tragedy? Are you mad?…I intend to lecture on comedy. I intend to lecture on Divine Aristophanes! I intend to talk about old men becoming young again! I intend to dance primitive, phallic dances! I intend to give you the Old One-Two! (*Pause; he jiggles the receiver.*) The Ford Foundation hung up on me. (*Pause; he looks at her, smiles.*) Oh well. Let's go back.

SUSAN: Back? Where?

HOLDER: (*Moving toward her.*) To that pad. To that superb Dionysiac music. To that sacred drug.

SUSAN: I don't want to go back. It's daylight now.

HOLDER: No matter. We'll drape the windows with batik. We'll eat crunchy Granola and organic raisins. We'll make bayberry candles and roll around on the waterbed, and do strange, calming Hindu exercises.

SUSAN: Enough is enough…

HOLDER: Tomorrow we'll find a pad of our own. Where we'll rap and groove and rip things off. We'll—

SUSAN: Oh stop! Why are you always trying to make things into a tradition? (*Pause.*)

HOLDER: What do you mean?

SUSAN: That was it, last night. That was all. I'm together now. And you should be, too.

HOLDER: Together? *Together? (Grabbing her arms.)* Woman, you have destroyed me!

(He kisses her passionately. The door burst open. The Dean stands there.)

DEAN: I thought so. *(Pause.)* Miss Green, you will call your parents immediately, and ask them to pick you up as soon as they can at your dormitory. *(Pause.)* Professor Holder, I will see you in my office when you are yourself.

HOLDER: *(Quietly.)* I'm myself.

DEAN: Then follow me. *(Pause; he looks at them both.)* I am appalled.

(He turns and exits. Susan looks at Holder and runs out. Holder stands for a moment, then squares his shoulders and goes out after the Dean.)

(The lights come up on the Dean's office. After a moment, the Dean comes in. He strides to his desk, pushes a button on his phone.)

DEAN: *(Into phone.)* No calls, please. None.

(Slams down the receiver. He sits behind his desk. Holder comes in stoically.)

Close the door.

(Holder does; the Dean indicates a chair near the desk.)

Sit there.

(Holder does. The Dean puts the microphone of his dictaphone on the desk, facing the chair.)

I'm recording this conversation. Any objections?

(Holder shakes his head. The Dean pushes the button on his machine.)

All right. I am asking you to resign immediately. If you do not, I will accuse you of moral turpitude in the next faculty meeting, and you will be voted out. There it is. Do you resign?

(Holder nods his head.)

Into the machine, please.

HOLDER: *(Very quietly.)* I resign.

DEAN: I have to bar you from teaching at any university in the United States. If you apply for a position, I will give you a negative recommendation. Do you contest this?

(Holder shakes his head; the Dean indicates the mike.)

HOLDER: *(Quietly.)* I don't contest it.

(The Dean switches off the machine.)

DEAN: Now. I have called a meeting of the Old One-Two for eight-thirty tonight. There I will announce your resignation, and turn the students over to Birnbaum, Russell and Johnson, whose contracts I can now renew and pay for out of your salary.

(Holder nods.)

I hope you will be there, for the sake of appearances. I hope you will plead exhaustion, and say goodbye to the students, and leave with dignity. May I count on you for that?

(Holder nods.)

HOLDER: *(Suddenly.)* Why, why, why can you Americans get away with things, and I can't? Birnbaum assaults his classes with four-letter words. Miss Russell once bared her breast to make a point. Johnson teaches his students to riot regularly!

DEAN: It's not the same.

HOLDER: I'm different?

DEAN: You claim to be.

(Holder nods, starts for the door.)

Where will you go, Gus?

HOLDER: *(Stopping; pensively.)* Hmmmmmmmm?

DEAN: Will you go home? To your—wife?

HOLDER: How can I go home?

DEAN: Go back to Europe, Gus. Go back there.

HOLDER: "I cannot stay in Thebes, nor return to Corinth." Sophocles. *Oedipus Rex.*

(He goes out majestically. The Dean looks after him. Then he telephones quickly.)

DEAN: *(On the telephone.)* Hi...It's me...*(He sighs.)* Well, you were right. He was with the girl last night...So that's that...No, he's not coming home. He says he can't. So there we are...Now. What I thought I'd do was move a few things out there. You know, pajamas, toothbrush, change of underwear—all very casual...Isn't that the way they do it in Europe? Isn't that the tradition?...Well when will you let me know?...Tonight? All right, let me know tonight...Wow, you are a mysterious woman, Simone Signoret...

(The lights fade on the Dean's office, and come up on Holder's. He enters, goes to his bookcase, looks at his books for a moment, shakes his head. Susan comes in, now dressed more formally.)

SUSAN: Professor Holder...

(He turns to face her.)

HOLDER: Ah, Miss Green. Should you be here?

SUSAN: I wanted to say goodbye.

HOLDER: Goodbye.

SUSAN: Did he fire you?

HOLDER: Of course. He had to.

SUSAN: My parents are driving up. In their Dodge Polara. I have to live at home, and get a job as a waitress at Howard Johnson's, and go out with nice boys my own age, and get married, and have babies, and die.

HOLDER: Oh dear.

SUSAN: I deserve it. I never was up to this. That first day, I should have just walked right out of class, straight home, back into middle America. *(She starts to cry.)*

HOLDER: Now, now…

SUSAN: It was all my fault.

HOLDER: No, no. It was the fault of all these stupid old books. Beware of Greeks, Miss Green. Don't trust anything written south of the Alps or before 1900. Caesar was right to burn the library of Alexandria, and I hope after I'm gone, our intrepid Dean will do the same with all of these!

SUSAN: Oh Professor Holder! What can I do?

(She runs from his study; the lights dim on him as he sweeps a stack of books off his desk.)

(The lights come up on the Dean at the lectern. He addresses the audience.)

DEAN: I regret that I must now announce the end of the Old One-Two. Professor Holder has decided, suddenly and sadly, to resign. When you students leave this room, you will now be able to take Professor Birnbaum, Mr. Johnson, or Miss Russell. But the Old One-Two is over, as of now. *(Pause; he looks off.)* Professor Holder wants to say a word of farewell.

(A moment. Then Holder comes out to the lectern. No books, no notes this time. He looks at the audience.)

HOLDER: Goodbye. Read Beckett. He's the man to keep an eye on these days. Read Beckett. Goodbye.

(He starts off. Susan comes down the aisle, carrying an envelope.)

SUSAN: Wait!

DEAN: Stay out of this, please.

SUSAN: *(Climbing onto the stage.)* No, wait. *(Waving the envelope.)* I have something for Professor Holder.

HOLDER: *(Ironically.)* A paper on Beckett?

SUSAN: *(Handing him the envelope.)* It's from your wife.

DEAN: *(Stepping between them.)* I think that can wait.

SUSAN: *(To Holder.)* I just drove out to see her. She gave me this envelope. She had it ready. Open it.

HOLDER: *(Putting it in his pocket.)* I don't open private mail in public.

DEAN: Of course you don't. *(To audience.)* Of course he doesn't.

SUSAN: She said to open it here.

    (Holder looks at her; then opens the envelope.)

HOLDER: Why it's…the birth certificate of our child.

SUSAN: Your child?

HOLDER: We had a child. We sent it to this country to be safe from the war. It was lost in a bureaucratic jungle. We never found it.

DEAN: But why would your wife…?

HOLDER: I don't know. *(Pause.)*

SUSAN: She said to read it out loud.

    (Holder looks at her, puts on his glasses, reads.)

HOLDER: Date of birth: July 3, 1940.

DEAN: *(Ominously.)* That's when I was born.

HOLDER: Identifying marks: Large birthmark on left breast.

DEAN: *(Ripping open his shirt.)* That's *my* birthmark.

HOLDER: Sex: Male.

DEAN: *(Undoing his belt.)* That's what *I* am! Male!

HOLDER: *(Restraining him.)* Be calm, sir!

DEAN: *(Frantically.)* But I'm an adopted child! And they told me I came from foreign parents! And I've been lost in bureaucratic jungle all my life!

HOLDER: *(Embracing him.)* Ah, my son! Come out and meet your mother!

DEAN: *(Agonizedly.)* I already have!

HOLDER: You have? And what happened?

DEAN: *(Collapsing against the lectern.)* She taught me the Old One-Two.

    (Holder puts his arm around the Dean.)

HOLDER: Splendid! I, too, feel like teaching again!

DEAN: Teach Sophocles! Quickly! Before I go mad!

SUSAN: Teach Homer again! I loved Homer!

HOLDER: No. I think I'll teach Menander.

DEAN AND SUSAN: Who?

HOLDER: Menander. A second-rate playwright who lived during the decline of Athens. He wrote tricky plots, which ended with the recovery of long-lost children and marriage. *(To Susan.)* You're not getting married, are you, Miss Green?

SUSAN: No, but this boy wants to move in with me.

HOLDER: *(Putting his arm around her.)* That's good enough. How about you, son? Are you getting married?

DEAN: *(Shakily.)* I already am.

HOLDER: *(Shaking his hand.)* Fine. Then Menander it is. He's second-rate, of course, and so he'll do perfectly for these decadent times. *(Pause; scratches his head.)* But wait. Menander always ends his plays with the freeing of slaves. *(Looks at audience.)* Slaves, you are now free to choose whatever course you want. But after what has happened…*(He puts his arm around the Dean.)* I hope you will think twice before you try to avoid the Old One-Two. *(Holder smiles proudly at the audience, his arms around the Dean and Susan, as the lights dim.)*

END OF PLAY

Scenes from American Life

A Play in Two Acts

This work stands as my first serious attempt to write a full-length play, though some might argue that I was having difficulty saying goodbye to the one-act form. It also is my first try at exploring the idea of ethnic identity.

Original Production

SCENES FROM AMERICAN LIFE was first produced at the Boston University Playwright's Workshop in Tanglewood, Massachusetts, in the summer of 1970. Among the actors were Michael Moriarty, Steve Nelson, Patricia O'Connell, and Rue McLanahan. The director was Jered Barclay. Tha play subsequently opened on March 26, 1971, in New York City at the Forum Theatre, produced by the Repertory Theatre of Lincoln Center, under Jules Irving. the cast consisted of James Broderick, Herbert Foster, Martha Henry, Elizabeth Huddle, Lee Lawson, Priscilla Pointer, Robert Symonds, and Christopher Walken. Douglas Schmidt did the sets, James Berton Harris the costumes, and John Sheffler, the lighting. David Frishberg played the piano and Dan Sullivan directed.

The Characters

The size of the cast may vary. The play is probably impossible to do with less than four men and four women. To do it with more might diminish some of the sense of virtuosity which should emerge. It is very important that the roles be evenly and variously distributed, that sons play fathers, that mothers play daughters, and so forth. This will mean that sometimes the director will have to cast against the grain. Otherwise, the play will seem to be the story of one or two families, whereas it should be the story of many. However, the same actor and actress should play the mother and father in the first and last scenes of the play.

Setting

The set should be attractive, simple and functional, without seeming stark or cold: a few flats, a few levels, easy entrances and exits. The space should conform easily into whatever a scene requires. Centrally located is a burnished, baby grand piano, around which the action should flow. Simple wooden chairs are brought in and out as needed.

Scenes from American Life

ACT ONE

No curtain. Empty stage, but for the piano. The pianist can play a sort of prelude, composed of songs from all the periods of the play, before the houselights dim.

As the houselights dim, the pianist should modulate into songs from the early thirties. As he does so, a maid, indicated simply by her white apron and white cap, places a tray of martinis on the piano. Other guests begin to drift in, with appropriate accessories to suggest 1930: a Godfather, a Godmother. Finally, as the houselights are out and the stagelights up, the pianist begins to play a lively version of "You Must Have Been a Beautiful Baby." The Mother, Father, and Bishop enter. The Bishop has a clerical collar with a purple dickey blouse; the Mother carries a doll with a long and lacy christening dress.

FATHER: *(With an arm around the Bishop.)* He's a happy baby, Bishop. He laughed all during the christening.

BISHOP: *(Taking a cocktail from the Maid.)* So did his father.

FATHER: I'm a happy man. *(Kisses his wife.)* With a lovely wife... *(Pats the doll.)* And a fat, sleek son and heir... *(Indicating the group.)* And a fine, loyal, attractive group of friends! Let me toast you all! *(Raises his glass.)* In the name of the Father, the Son and the best gin ever smuggled across the Niagara River!

BISHOP: *(Drinking.)* Now, now. *(The Maid brings out a chair for the Mother.)*

MOTHER: We've *got* to find a nickname. We have no nickname. We've all got to *think* of something.

GODFATHER: *(Steps forward.)* While we're thinking, here's a present from his godfather. *(Hands her a small box. She sits in the chair and opens it.)*

MOTHER: Why…it's a sterling silver pusher. *(Holds it out.)*

FATHER: A sterling silver what?

MOTHER: A pusher! For manners at meals! *(Demonstrates.)* To keep his hands clean! *(Busses the Godfather.)* Oh, thank you, Bill!

GODFATHER: He can pawn it if Roosevelt is elected. *(Laughter; the pianist plays a musical comment.)*

BISHOP: He gets a Bible from me. It's being engraved in New York.

FATHER: *(Waving a piece of paper.)* And a rather sizable check from his grandmother.

(Cheers; the pianist plays a fanfare.)

MOTHER: *(Hugging the baby.)* Oh, baby: you're riding on the gravy train.

FATHER: *(Raising his glass.)* I'll drink to that.

GODMOTHER: *(Steps forward.)* I won't. *(Is a little drunk. Everyone looks at her.)* I won't drink to that.

ANOTHER GUEST: The fairy godmother wants to make a prediction! *(Laughter.)*

GODMOTHER: *(Going right on.)* I'm sorry. I just want to say one word, please, to my godson.

FATHER: *(Tolerantly.)* Fine, Grace. Say it.

GODMOTHER: *(Picking up the baby; looking at it.)* Responsibility. That's what I want to say to you. Responsibility. *(Pause.)*

A WOMAN: Well, go on, Grace.

GODMOTHER: *(Boozily.)* Well, I mean he has a respons*ibih*ty. To himself. And to, well, us. And to his country. *(The pianist starts "The Star Spangled Banner." Someone salutes. The Godmother plugs on.)* I'm *serious*. We're in difficult times. There's a depression going on. People are hungry and out of work. *(Ad-libs: "Oh God. Here we go again.")* Well, it's true. And I want to propose a toast. To responsibility! *(Waves her glass; her drink spills on the baby.)* Oh dear. Did I—Oh, I'm terribly sorry.

MOTHER: *(Taking the baby, wiping it off.)* It's nothing…Look: He's asleep. He's having a little snooze. Oh, now I know what we'll call him. Snoozer! We'll call him Snoozer!

FATHER: *(Arm around the Godmother, who is crying.)* A second christening, Grace.

MOTHER: Exactly. Snoozer. Because he sleeps through everything.
(The pianist plays "Rockabye Baby." Everyone gathers around the chair and sings.)
EVERYONE: *(Singing.)* "...When the bough breaks the cradle will fall, and down will come Snooooooozer, cra—*(The Maid takes a picture with a box Brownie. They all hold still.)*—dle and all..."
(The piano modulates into a contemporary rock version of "Low Bridge, Everybody Down." The Maid takes the baby off, and the others follow, with the exception of one of the male guests, who begins to address the audience with great earnestness.)
SPEAKER: I just want to make one point, please. The real issue, it seems to me, is whether Buffalo can survive as a major city in the nineteen seventies! I say we can! And I say it's our responsibility as businessmen to see that we do! Listen: Snoozer and I did a little research in the Erie County Library. We found out about our name, Buffalo. We weren't named after that damned bison! No, sir! Buffalo comes from the French. Beau Fleuve. Beautiful river. The Niagara! The bison is almost extinct, but that beautiful river is still rolling along! And we had the Erie Canal! We were the Queen City of the Great Lakes! We were the largest fresh water port in the world! So now let's float a big new bond issue right out onto that beautiful river! Let's build a new stadium we can be proud of! Let's keep our hockey team and our football team right here in Beau Fleuve, and cheer this city on into the future! Come on, fellas! It's high time we realized who we are!
(The piano shifts to another thirties song. As the Speaker goes off, he winks at a Nurse, who comes on wheeling an elaborate English baby carriage. The Nurse [Nelly] is indicated simply by her white hat and collar. She bends over the carriage, fussing with the baby within. A Mother enters, wearing hat and gloves as if she were going out. She carries a telephone from the thirties.)
MOTHER: Now, Nelly: you and I both have lots of things to do this morning, but I'm afraid there's something we've got to discuss.
NELLY: *(Irish accent; still tucking the child.)* Yes, ma'am?
MOTHER: Nelly, I'm going to ask you point-blank: Did you have a man in your room last night? *(Nelly stops tucking.)* Nelly, I'm asking you a question.
NELLY: No, ma'am?
MOTHER: Now, Nelly, are you sure? When Mr. Pratt and I got home last night, we heard some very strange footsteps sneaking down the backstairs.

NELLY: Just to listen to my victrola, ma'am.

MOTHER: Ah hah.

NELLY: Just to listen to my records from Ireland, ma'am.

MOTHER: I won't have it, Nelly.

NELLY: Just to—

MOTHER: I simply won't have it. What if the baby had needed you?

NELLY: I could hear the baby.

MOTHER: Oh, Nelly, honestly! This is a big *house*. With lots of closed *doors*. *(Pause.)*

NELLY: I get lonely, ma'am.

MOTHER: That's not the point. We all get lonely. But we don't have strange men in our rooms. That we don't do.

NELLY: He wasn't strange, ma'am.

MOTHER: Nelly, I'm not going to argue. I do not want men in this house, nor do I want you meeting them when you walk the baby.

NELLY: I don't—

MOTHER: Nelly, you *do*. The Wheelers' Bertha said you were talking to a man in the park. Nelly, haven't you heard of the Lindbergh *kid*napping?

NELLY: He wouldn't—

MOTHER: I'm just terribly disappointed, that's all. I liked you so much during your interview. You were clean, and neat, and sweet. You were right off the boat, and I've trained you from scratch. And you're very good, Nelly, in so many way. *(Nelly begins to sniffle.)* You're marvelous with the baby's clothes. And the bathrooms are immaculate, and the baby adores you. *(Nelly starts to whimper.)* So we've decided not to let you go, Nelly. We're going to see this thing through, all of us. I've called your priest, and he's going to arrange it so you can meet some other Irish girls…*(Nelly begins to blubber. Mother takes a neat hanky out of her purse, hands it to Nelly.)* Here. Use this. Keep it. Now you have a crucial responsibility, Nelly. That child. He is absolutely in your hands. And if you get tied up with men, he will no longer get your undivided attention. And then we're *all* in trouble. *(Begins to dial the telephone.)* So we'll say no more about it. Give him plenty of fresh air. Cod-liver oil at lunch. Long nap. I'll be back at four to read him "Pat the Bunny." *(Nelly returns to the carriage. Mother begins to talk, a little furtively, on the telephone.)* Hi.

NELLY: *(To child in carriage, bitterly.)* Ah, ye've kicked yer covers off, have ye? and yer soakin wet.

MOTHER: Everything's all right in the Nelly department. I can meet you for lunch after all.

NELLY: Now I'll have to change ye.

MOTHER: Good God, no! People will see us there.

NELLY: No, no. Nelly said no-no. Don't touch that. Touch that again and Nelly will cut it off.

MOTHER: *(Still on the telephone.)* That's better.

NELLY: Dirty, dirty, dirty...

MOTHER: I'll see you there...Mmmmm. Goodbye...*(Hangs up.)*

(They go out separate ways, as the piano shifts to a dissonant version of "Auld Lang Syne." A Man in a ski parka enters carrying a very modern telephone. He is finishing dialing.)

MAN: Hello, Judge? This is Tyler Moffat...Happy New Year, and all that...Listen, Judge, could you do me a favor? I was caught in the curfew the other night. Yes, I was driving home from the club and they stopped me cold. I shouldn't have had that last drink with Snoozer...*(Laughs.)* I know. It's not the fine I mind, but it means showing up in court, and we're taking the kids skiing over New Year's...Hold it. *(Gets the ticket out of his pocket.)* The officer's name is Pulanski. One of our more serious Polish citizens, I'm afraid. *(Laughs.)* Many thanks, Judge...I know, dammit. Seven o'clock is just plain too early for a curfew. I was just in Philadelphia, and they don't start their curfew till nine! *(Laughs.)* Ah tempora, ah Buffalo!...Well, thanks again, Judge, and I'll see you in the sauna when we get back. Good-bye. *(Hangs up and goes off.)*

(The piano plays a sprightly tune, perhaps "America the Beautiful." A woman comes on briskly, carrying a folder and a small can. She puts her finger out as if to ring a doorbell. The piano sounds door chimes. A man in his undershirt comes to the "door." He carries a beer can.)

WOMAN: Hello. I'm Mrs. Arthur Bigelow from over on Middlesex Road. And I'm collecting money to save the elms. *(Rattles her can. We hear very few coins. The man looks at her.)* The elms. The American elms. *(Looks around.)* I guess you don't have any on this particular street, but they're one of the things Buffalo used to be famous for, and now they're dying like mad. *(No response.)* If you drive down Richmond or Delaware, you can see huge bare patches where the elms once were. It's awful. And those streets used to be like great, green cathedrals. *(No response. She shows him her folder.)* You see, what happens is that a tiny beetle gets under their bark and lays its eggs in their capillaries, and that stops their sap from flowing. So they die. Unless we all chip in to save them. *(Pause.)*

MAN: You want money for trees?

WOMAN: Yes! Exactly! *(The man points. The woman follows his glance.)* Oh, is that your tree? That's a nice little tree. What is it? A scrub oak or something? But it's not an American elm. No, you see the elm is perfect for the city. Their shade gives lovely lawns. And they have shallow roots which never interfere with the sewers. And their branches arch over the telephone wires. So to save them we all have to get together. *(Pause.)*

MAN: Would you like to come in for a beer? *(Pause.)*

WOMAN: Um. No. Thank you just the same.

(They stand staring at each other a moment. The piano plays a light rhythmic beat. Then they and the other actors arrange chairs into bleachers. They put on suggestions of sporty clothes: a tennis hat, a white sweater, a tennis racquet here and there. They all sit in the bleachers, their heads going back and forth in time to the music as if they were watching a match. Meanwhile, a Referee has brought on a high stool and a large silver trophy, which he places beside him as he sits on the stool.)

REFEREE: Game. Mr. and Mrs. Curtis. They lead, five games to three.

(Applause. Uncle John comes out, leading a small boy. The boy has socks pulled up over his trousers to suggest knickers, and a sailor suit collar. Uncle John wears a blazer and straw hat.)

UNCLE JOHN: *(To boy, as people make room for them.)* Now you sit here with your Aunt Helen and watch your mummy and daddy play tennis, and your Uncle John will be in the bar.

AUNT HELEN: *(In the bleachers.)* John! stay right here! You promised.

UNCLE JOHN: *(Reluctantly sitting down, the boy between them.)* I hate the goddamn game.

AUNT HELEN: That's because you can't play it.

REFEREE: *(Calling out.)* Fifteen-love!

AUNT HELEN: *(To the boy.)* These are the finals, Timmy. If your parents win, they win that great, big, shiny cup over there...

UNCLE JOHN: That battle trophy, Timmy...

AUNT HELEN: And they get their names on it, Timmy. Permanently engraved...My name is on it, actually. I won it once.

UNCLE JOHN: Before she was married, Timmy. As I am being constantly reminded.

AUNT HELEN: Never mind, Timmy. You watch.

REFEREE: *(Calling out.)* Thirty-love!

AUNT HELEN: See, Timmy? Your parents are beating Snoozer's parents! Your parents have thirty, and Snoozer's parents have love.

UNCLE JOHN: And love means nothing. *(She glances at him. Another long point. Heads go back and forth. Applause at the end.)*

AUNT HELEN: There. Mummy won that point. And I'll tell you why. When she went to the net, Daddy stayed with her. They stayed parallel all the way. If your Uncle John would stay parallel with me…

UNCLE JOHN: We could win that cup.

AUNT HELEN: Exactly.

UNCLE JOHN: We could keep it for one year.

AUNT HELEN: Exactly.

UNCLE JOHN: I could use it to mix martinis…

AUNT HELEN: Oh God, John. *(Another point is played.)*

REFEREE: Out. Forty-fifteen.

UNCLE JOHN: That was a bad call.

AUNT HELEN: Oh, John…

UNCLE JOHN: *(To Referee, standing up.)* That was a bad call! The shot was good!

REFEREE: The shot was out, John.

AUNT HELEN: John, for heaven's sake! What are you teaching the C-H-I-L-D! *(Turns to Timmy.)* Your Uncle John is wrong, Timmy. The referee is always right. Now notice Mummy. She is not complaining. She is going right on with the game, even though she may be very unhappy inside. That's what it means to be a good sport. That's what life is all about. *(Another point is played. Lots of head movement. Then applause and everyone stands up at the end and applauds politely.)*

REFEREE: Game, set, match. To Mr. and Mrs. Curtis. *(Gets off his stool, brings the cup over to Aunt Helen.)* Would he like to give the cup to his parents?

AUNT HELEN: *(Taking it.)* Oh, yes. What a wonderful idea, Bill! *(Takes the cup.)* Here, Timmy. See? Here's my maiden name, when I won with Mr. Rogers. *(Blows on it; wipes it off with her sleeve.)*

UNCLE JOHN: What're you doing? Wiping off the blood?

AUNT HELEN: Yes. Well. Now, Timmy, give this cup to your mother. Go on. Walk right out on the court. Shake hands with everyone. Good, firm grip. See? Everyone's good friends at the end of the game. *(Under her breath, to Uncle John; bitterly.)* This is it, John. I swear… *(Then all smiles.)* Go on, Timmy. Do it. Good boy.

(Everyone claps and beams as the boy reverently walks out, holds up the cup. The piano modulates to machinelike music. The crowd shifts into a group of people standing in line. A woman now sits in the Referee's stool. A man, with great apologies, pushes his way through to the head of the line, as others ad-lib protests. He confronts the woman.)

MAN: *(Breathlessly.)* Excuse me. They said out there to give you my Identification Card. *(Holds it out to her.)*

WOMAN: Thank you, sir. I'll just put it into the computer here. *(Pantomimes inserting the card into a machine. The piano plays strange noises; then stops. She removes the card, reads the results.)* It says you're registered as an Independent. *(Hands the card back, smiling.)*

MAN: That's wrong. I'm a Republican.

WOMAN: Well, you seem to come out as an Independent. *(The crowd in line ad-libs impatience.)*

MAN: Oh, my gosh. Maybe I am. My children made me shift two years ago for a disarmament candidate, and then last year I was in Canada duck hunting, and so I never shifted back.

WOMAN: There you are.

MAN: Well. Then I'm forced to vote as an Independent.

WOMAN: Oh, you can't do that without a pre-registration certificate. Do you have your pre-registration certificate?

MAN: I don't believe I do. No.

WOMAN: Wait a minute. *(Puts his I.D. card back into the machine. More noises from the piano.)* You probably have one and don't even know it. *(More sounds. She removes the card.)* Yes! You do have one. They gave you one, anyway. *(More sounds from the machine. She reads a dial.)* But you have to bring it up to date.

MAN: Well, how do I do that?

WOMAN: You apply through the District Registry after the first of the year.

MAN: Good Lord. When was this decided?

WOMAN: Oh, it wasn't *decided*, sir. It just happened.

MAN: Just happened?

WOMAN: Well, with all these young people voting now, we have to keep track of who's who.

MAN: But I want to vote *today!*

WOMAN: So do we all, sir!

MAN: But this is an important election. I have a responsibility. *(Impatient ad-libs from the people in line.)*

WOMAN: Sir, you are keeping other people waiting.

MAN: Oh. I'm sorry. This is quite disturbing. I'm not going to let this happen again!

WOMAN: *(As he leaves; calling to him.)* Next time, stay a Republican. And don't go to Canada!

(The crowd goes off as the piano plays a hymn: "Praise God From Whom All Blessings Flow." A Minister, indicated by a clerical collar, comes on, carrying a Bible. He nods to the pianist, who ends the hymn.)

MINISTER: *(To audience.)* The Gospel for today is taken from Saint Matthew, Chapter Nineteen, beginning at the sixteenth verse: "And behold, one came unto Jesus and said unto him, 'What good thing shall I do that I may have eternal life?' And He said unto him, 'Keep the Commandments.' And the young man saith, 'All these have I kept from my youth. What lack I yet?' And Jesus said, 'Go and sell what thou hast, and give to the poor, and thou shalt have treasure in heaven.' But when the young man heard that saying, he went away sorrowful, for he had great possessions. Then Jesus said to his disciples: 'It is easier for a camel to go through the eye of a needle than for a rich man to enter the Kingdom of God!'" *(Closes the Bible; a pause.)* Of course, recent scholarship tells us that there actually was a place in Jerusalem called "The Eye of the Needle." And presumably camels *could* go through it. So Jesus simply meant we must be generous, we must be charitable with our money... *(Smiles; the piano provides a coda as he goes slowly out. The piano plays children's music.)* *(A boy, indicated by his sailor collar, throws a big rubber ball high in the air. A Grandfather comes out, wearing a stiff collar, carrying a cane. He stands on a platform, to give the suggestion of height. He clasps his hands behind his back.)*

GRANDFATHER: You there! Andy! I say, Andy! Come here and see your grandfather! *(The boy keeps his distance, frightened.)* Come here, boy. Come closer. *(The boy comes closer.)* I left the bank early especially to see you, Andy. Your father tells me you have a stammer. Is that true? *(The boy nods.)* Your father also tells me you like money. Is *that* true? *(The boy nods.)* All right. I will give you five dollars if you will tell me a story. *(Takes a wad of money out of his pocket, removes a five dollar bill from it, and holds up the bill temptingly. Pause.)* Begin, lad.

BOY: *(Stammering.)* Once...once...once...

GRANDFATHER: Don't stammer.

BOY: Once upon a...upon...upon a

GRANDFATHER: Don't stammer!

BOY: Once...once...once...once...

GRANDFATHER: *(Shouting; shaking him.)* I said Don't Stammer! *(Long pause; they eye each other.)*

BOY: *(Very slowly and carefully.)* Once...upon...a...time...there... was...a big, mean...*(Pause.)*...ugly Giant!

GRANDFATHER: Good. That will do. Here's your five dollars. I'm putting it in the bank for you. *(Puts it in another pocket.)* When you're twenty-one, it will be worth seventeen dollars and sixty cents. Now run along. Play with your chums. And don't stammer again. *(Exits.)* *(The boy, exits slowly and perplexedly in the opposite way, as the piano plays a bossa nova. Mrs. Bidwell comes out, carrying a glass of liquor, holding a sixties telephone.)*

MRS. BIDWELL: *(Coldly.)* Good morning. This is Mrs. Bidwell...Let me speak to Doctor Taubman, please...Yes, I'd say this was important. Not crucial, but important...Thank you. *(Pause; then very brightly.)* Hi!...Listen I'm sorry I missed yesterday's appointment. It completely slipped my mind. What with one thing and another. *(Pause.)* No, no. Listen. What I'm calling about is...What I want to say is...No, Doctor Taubman, I really do think this psychotherapy business is not for me. We're simply not getting anywhere, you and I. You keep wanting me to talk about the most personal things. I can't. No, I just plain can't. It seems so—so whiney. No, I mean it. I'll just have to call on the old willpower to solve the drinking thing. I'll just have to pull myself together, that's all...No, I mean it...No, now send me a bill, please. I assume I don't have to pay for the session I missed...I do? I do have to pay? Now that doesn't seem quite sporty, does it?...All right, all right. Just send the bill. Good-bye. *(Hangs up. A moment. She looks at her glass; then goes off as the pianist modulates to hard rock music.)*

(A husband and wife bring out two chairs, set them up as the front seat of a "car." The husband pantomimes driving; after a moment, the wife turns off the "radio." The music stops; a moment of silence as they drive along.)

WIFE: *(suddenly.)* I want another baby.

HUSBAND: A baby!

WIFE: No, I do. I really do.

HUSBAND: What did you drink tonight?

WIFE: Freeze-dried coffee in Styrofoam cups. Oh, I hate, hate, HATE, these community action meetings! Everyone just sits around and *interrupts.*

HUSBAND: "Wake up, America! Engage in politics at the local level!"

WIFE: I didn't see you engaging. You didn't say anything.

HUSBAND: I almost fell asleep. *(Pause.)*

WIFE: I really do want another baby, Nick.

HUSBAND: We've got five babies.

WIFE: They're not babies. And they're not mine.

HUSBAND: Two of them are.

WIFE: They're not. Howard gets *at* them every weekend. They're all brainwashed. They come back waving the flag at me. Laurie wants to be a drum major*ette* now! *(Looks at him.)* And your children: they miss Ellie. They keep asking me where their *real* mother is. *(Pause.)* Well, *I* want to be a real mother just once more. Before I…dry up completely. *(A whistle from offstage.)*

HUSBAND: *(Pantomiming stopping the car.)* Now what? *(A helmeted Policeman comes on, with flashlight and nightstick. He flashes the light in their faces, speaks as if through car window.)*

POLICEMAN: Let's see the I.D. cards. *(They hand him their I.D. cards. He reads them by flashlight, checks their faces with the photographs, hands them back.)* Gotta take a detour, folks.

HUSBAND: *(Dryly.)* What seems to be the trouble, Officer?

POLICEMAN: They've blown up the water main. You can get through on Elmwood.

HUSBAND: Thanks.

POLICEMAN: And lock your doors. It's a new city ordinance.

HUSBAND: Thanks. *(They pantomime reaching back and locking the car's rear doors. The Policeman goes off. The husband pantomimes making a turn; he shakes his head.)* Still want a baby?

WIFE: Yes.

HUSBAND: On, come on.

WIFE: I'm serious.

HUSBAND: Too late for babies.

WIFE: Not for me it isn't

HUSBAND: We're too old.

WIFE: I'm not. Maybe you are. But I'm not.

HUSBAND: What's that supposed to mean?

WIFE: I'm pregnant. *(The husband pantomimes slamming on the brakes.)* Please don't stop the car, Nick. It's dangerous to stop the car here. *(He angrily starts up again.)*

HUSBAND: You're not pregnant.

WIFE: I am. I ought to know.

HUSBAND: In you go. The hospital. Tomorrow.

WIFE: Oh no.

HUSBAND: Oh yes.

WIFE: I want a baby, Nick. I've got nothing to *do* now. No one needs me. I can't get a job that means anything. And these hysterical meetings—oh, I hate it, Nick. I want to stay home and start again, with a new baby.

HUSBAND: Into the hospital.

WIFE: Says who?

HUSBAND: Says me. It's my baby too. *(Pause.)*

WIFE: *(Impulsively.)* How do you know?

HUSBAND: *(Slams on the brakes; they both jerk forward. He looks at her.)* Say that again.

WIFE: *(Doggedly.)* I said how do you know?

HUSBAND: Lookit—

WIFE: You had that thing with Katie McGowan. I had to sit that one out.

HUSBAND: There was no "thing" with Katie McGowan!

WIFE: Everybody does it these days. Why can't I have some fun if I want to? Why can't I have a baby if I want one?

HUSBAND: Who? Name the guy.

WIFE: Why should I?

HUSBAND: *(Suddenly.)* Get out of the car!

WIFE: You slept with Katie McGowan!

HUSBAND: Out! Get out!

WIFE: Oh, not *here*, Nick. Honestly.

HUSBAND: *(Starting to shove her.)* Will you get out of my car, bitch!

WIFE: All right. *(He shoves her.)* All Right! *(Gets out, stands by "door." A little plaintively:)* How will I get home, Nick?

HUSBAND: Call your lover! *(Shouts at her as if through a closed car window.)* I should have stuck with Ellie! *(She winces and moves a little away from the car. He watches her, then leans over and pantomimes rolling down the window. He shouts out to her.)* We were almost there! No kidding! I thought we were almost there! I thought we'd make it! I thought that soon both sets of kids would be out of our hair, and we'd have some time to ourselves, and you and I could…*(Softly.)* We were almost there. *(Huddles down as if leaning over the steering wheel. The wife walks slowly back to the car. She stands by the door.)*

WIFE: I was lying, Nick. It's your baby. *(Opens the door.)* I'll go to the hospital. I promise. Tomorrow. *(Gets into the car.)* I was just...I just wanted to...I was just dreaming. *(Tentatively touches his shoulder.)* Oh, Nick, I love you. Oh, sweetie, I'm so sorry. Oh, Nick, oh, sweetie, please...

(Another helmeted Policeman comes up with flashlight. He shines it on the husband who is still slumped forward over the wheel.)

POLICEMAN: *(To wife.)* Is he wounded? *(To husband.)* Buddy, are you wounded?

HUSBAND: *(Sitting up; shaking his head.)* No...Just tired.

POLICEMAN: Well, move on, folks. Get home. This is a Red Zone. *(Goes off.)*

(The husband and wife sit facing forward as the lights dim on them. The piano modulates to "Little Old Lady" as they go off. A chauffeur, in a chauffeur's hat, comes out carrying more chairs and a lap robe. He adjusts the "car" so that it becomes a limousine, as the Grandmother enters, perhaps in a fur piece and turbaned hat. The chauffeur assists the Grandmother into the car and pantomimes tucking a lap robe around her. He takes the driver's seat as a boy and girl run on. The girl wears a big bow or sash; the boy, a little boy's hat.)

CHILDREN: Hi, Granny...Hi, Granny... *(They squeeze into chairs on either side of her.)*

GRANDMOTHER: Say good morning to Edward, children. *(Pantomimes handing them a car phone.)*

CHILDREN: *(Into car phone:)* Good morning, Edward...Good morning, Edward... *(The Chauffeur tips his cap. The Grandmother takes the car phone.)*

GRANDMOTHER: Now, Edward: first we are going to the cemetery to see the swans; then downtown to the Corset Woman; and then home... *(Hangs up the car phone; turns to children.)*...where Annie is fixing us a nice luncheon with prune whip for dessert. *(The children groan.)* Prunes? Nonsense. They're good for your insides...And after luncheon we're all going to lie down for fifteen minutes, and then Edward will drive us down to the Erlanger Theatre where we will see Katherine Cornell, who comes from Buffalo, and whose father I knew very well.

BOY: Is this a Packard, Granny?

GRANDMOTHER: It is not. It's a Pierce Arrow, made right here in Buffalo. Mrs. Warren has a Packard, and her chauffeur can't get it to park.

Now bundle up under the lap robe, children. *(They snuggle up next to her.)* We don't want your mother and father to come back from Bermuda and find you with the sniffles.

GIRL: What's a Corset Woman, Granny?

GRANDMOTHER: It's a woman who makes corsets.

BOY: What are corsets?

GRANDMOTHER: They are articles of women's underclothing. *(The children giggle.)* Carleton, look at your fingernails. They're filthy. Your grandfather just fired a man at the bank for dirty fingernails.

GIRL: Do you like the Corset Woman?

GRANDMOTHER: I don't like her or dislike her. But I am always polite to her. Because she is one of the people who helps us live. Like Annie. Or Edward.

BOY: *(Looking out the window.)* Hey. Look at the nigger.

GRANDMOTHER: That's very rude, Carleton. He is a darky.

GIRL: We play Nigger Baby. Is that all right?

GRANDMOTHER: It is not. The children of darkies are called pickaninnies. *(The children repeat the word. The boy picks his nose.)* Carleton, don't do that. Whenever you have to touch your nose, go into the bathroom and lock the door. *(Looks out.)* Ah. Here's the cemetery. And there are the swans. *(Into the car phone.)* Stop the car, Edward. *(Everyone looks out.)* Aren't they beautiful? Now there is a play, children, by a Hungarian, about a princess called *The Swan*. And the Hungarian says she must never, never leave her castle. Because that would be like a swan going on dry land. Which swans don't do. No. She must stay in the middle of the lake all her life, because that is where swans belong. *(A moment. They all watch. Then she speaks into the car phone.)* All right, Edward. Drive on to the Corset Woman.

The piano plays the theme from "Swan Lake," as the lights dim on them. They go off as a man addresses the audience hastily and nervously.)

MAN: May I have the floor, please?…I hear that a number of the younger men in this club—George and Snoozer, for example—are indignant over the fact that the David Goldfarbs were blackballed from membership. Well, I want to say right now that I was the one who blackballed them. And Dave Goldfarb is probably one of my closest friends. I'll wager I've done more business with Dave than anybody else in this room. He comes to our house for dinner, and we go to his. Peggy and I and Dave and Ronna all met in Jamaica together last winter. But I blackballed the Goldfarbs because I don't want to see them hurt. I know darned well what could happen in the Grille Room at six-fifteen in the evening when a few of our anti-Stevenson people have finished their second martini. They'd start on Dave. And I won't have that. I don't want Dave and Ronna embarrassed in any way. I'd feel personally responsible for it. Some people say I should resign if that's the way I feel. But I won't. Because I think we're just going through a phase now. And I'll bet that by 1960 my friend Dave Goldfarb can play tennis here, and have a shower, and join us for a drink in the grille, and not have to worry about a damn thing.

(As he goes off, the piano plays "Good King Wenceslas." A Father, wearing a hat and overcoat, paces back and forth. After a moment, a helmeted Policeman brings in a girl [Nancy], who wears a poncho and a floppy hat.)

POLICEMAN: Here she is, sir. Take her away. Merry Christmas.

FATHER: Thank you, Officer. *(The Policeman stands aside, working on a clipboard. The father takes the girl.)* Now tell me what happened.

NANCY: I was picked *up*, Daddy. Just for hitchhiking home from college.

FATHER: We wrote you specifically not to hitchhike.

NANCY: Well, I did.

FATHER: I sent you plane fare.

NANCY: Well I hitchhiked.

FATHER: We offered you a car in September.

NANCY: I like to hitchhike.

FATHER: It's against the *law*, Nancy!

NANCY: Some law. You hitchhike home for Christmas to save on pollution, and the pigs pick you up.

FATHER: We don't call people names.

NANCY: I do. *(Pause.)*

FATHER: All right. Let's go home. Everyone's waiting. Where's your bag?

NANCY: I don't have a bag.

FATHER: You don't have a—

NANCY: I don't need a bag.

FATHER: *(With a sigh.)* Come on, then.

NANCY: *(Standing pat.)* What about Mark?

FATHER: Mark?

NANCY: He was with me. And he's still in the cell.

FATHER: Mark who, for God's sake?

NANCY: Oh, Daddy, I don't know his *last* name. I met him on the road outside of Albany.

FATHER: Where's *his* father?

NANCY: He lives in De*troit*, Daddy. I told Mark he could spend the night with us.

FATHER: Nancy, it's Christmas Eve!

NANCY: Exactly. Do you want to just leave him here, rotting in jail, on Christmas *Eve? (Pause.)*

FATHER: *(To policeman.)* Officer! I'll stand for the boy that was with her.

POLICEMAN: On recognizance?

FATHER: On recognizance.

POLICEMAN: Suit yourself. *(Exits, shaking his head.)*

NANCY: *(Hugging her father.)* Thank you, Daddy.

FATHER: We will take Mark What's-his-name home, and we will introduce him to your mother, and your grandmother, and your Uncle Snoozer, and your brothers, and Alice in the kitchen. We will have cocktails with Mark What's-his-name. We will eat roast turkey with Mark What's-his-name. We will sing carols, and hang up our stockings with Mark What's-his-name, whom you happened to meet hitchhiking on the New York State Thruway outside of Albany, and it won't be Christmas at all.

NANCY: Oh, Daddy, honestly…*(The policeman returns with a grubby, bedraggled-looking youth. Nancy goes to him.)* Daddy, this is Mark.

MARK: Hiya.

FATHER: Get in the car, both of you.

MARK: *(To Nancy, under his breath.)* Heavy… *(Nancy and Mark go out. The policeman hands the father a paper.)*

POLICEMAN: Sign here, sir. Have them back on Monday for court.

FATHER: *(Signing.)* You mean we've got him till Monday?

POLICEMAN: You're too easy on them, sir.

FATHER: *(Sighing.)* It's Christmas Eve. *(Reaches into his pocket, offers a bill to the policeman.)* Merry Christmas, Officer.

POLICEMAN: *(Coldly; refusing the tip.)* Same to you, sir.

(They exit in opposite directions, as: A Woman comes out, and begins to make strange snorting noises. Then she begins to slap herself all over. The rest of the cast comes on, doing the same: grunting, slapping, stretching. The woman is the leader for an "Encounter Group" and these are limbering-up exercises. After a brief spell of this, she claps her hands.)

GROUP LEADER: All rightee. Everyone sit on the floor, please. *(Everyone does, awkwardly. The Leader lectures them.)* Now let me explain exactly what I'm up to…I firmly believe that one of the reasons our young folks are up in arms is that we, their parents, can no longer reach them. If we can learn to communicate without relying on a dead language, and dead stereotypes of behavior, then perhaps this country can pull itself together again. Right? *(The others ad-lib agreement.)* Good. That's why we're here. To learn new techniques of relating to each other. So let's begin. Everybody on their feet. Up, up. Let's mill around the room. *(Goes to pianist.)* Play some of that milling music, please. *(Pianist plays the "Moonlight Sonata"; the group follows her orders awkwardly.)* Good. Everyone mill around the room, please...Just mill...Shhh. Shhhh. No talking!...Just move through space...That's it...Feel the ground under your feet...Feel the blood pulsing through your veins...Feel your heart beating...*(Notices a man standing aside, angrily trying to get the attention of his wife.)* You're not milling, friend. What's your name?

MAN: Wheelright. Steven Wheelwright.

LEADER: *(Loosening his tie.)* Loosen up, Steve. *(To group.)* It's first names here, people, by the by. Including me. I'm Pat.

GROUP: *(Mechanically.)* Hi, Pat.

LEADER: Good. Now mill, Steve. *(Steve mills, reluctantly.)* Good, Steve boy. You're milling now...All right, we'll have pairing: everyone select a partner—random, random, no husbands and wives, whoever's nearest—good—now: all pairs kneels down on the floor and face each other...I said, NO TALKING...Stevie, get away from your wife...*(To wife.)* What's your name?

WIFE: Marge.

LEADER: Well, Marge, you go pair off with...Who are you?

ANOTHER MAN: Gordon.

LEADER: Go with Gordon. And you, Steve. You kneel opposite me. *(All pairs kneel, facing each other.)* Now, Shhh, shhh. Everyone look into his or her partner's eyes, and just try to say something to each other without words. *(A long moment. People stare. Then a woman begins to giggle.)* Please, people...

WOMAN WHO GIGGLED: I'm sorry. Bert was being silly.

BERT: What do you mean?

WOMAN: You were wiggling your nose.

BERT: I was not wiggling my nose.

WOMAN: Well, you were doing peculiar things with your face.

BERT: I was not doing peculiar...

LEADER: Try again, please. I know it's hard. But it's worth it. *(They all kneel again. A longer moment. Then:)*

ANOTHER MAN: That's no fair, Marge.

MARGE: *(Who is opposite him.)* What? What? What's not fair?

OTHER MAN: *(To leader.)* She was looking down.

MARGE: Well, I felt embarrassed. *(Everyone ad-libs agreement.)*

A WOMAN: Perhaps if we all had a couple of good stiff drinks. *(The group ad-libs agreement.)*

LEADER: No alcohol! Please! That never works! Everyone on their feet...Up, up. *(Group gets up.)* Form a circle...*(They do.)* You...Marge...in the center.

MARGE: Why me?

LEADER: Because you're the embarrassed one, Marge, and we've got to get over that hurdle...Everyone in a circle?...Marge, please...In the center...Good...Now. Everyone do to Marge what he or she feels like doing. *(Nervous reaction from group.)*

A MAN: *(Laughing.)* Within reason.

LEADER: No, Chuck. *Not* within reason. We are trying to get around reason. Everyone do to Marge what he or she feels like doing. Clockwise. You start, Steve. After all, she's your wife. *(Steve steps into the circle, looks angrily at Marge for bringing him here, and then steps back.)* Next. *(A woman steps into the circle. She can't decide what to do. Finally, she tickles Marge. Marge jumps, shrieks. Group laughs. Leader gestures for the next. A man steps into the circle, looks at March, reaches out for her hair. She cowers back.)*

STEVE: Hey!

LEADER: Relax, Steve. Relax, Marge. *(Marge braces herself. The man takes the hairpins out of Marge's hair; her hair falls loose. Group goes "Ahh-hhh." She quickly starts to pin it up.)* Leave it, Marge. *(Marge leaves it. A woman steps in and gives Marge a sweet little hug. Group smiles "ohh-hhh.")* Exactly! Next. *(A man steps in and gives Marge a more sexual hug. Steve controls himself.)* Good Marge. Good, Steve.

(Another man steps in and kisses Marge's neck. The atmosphere gets tense. Now it is the leader's turn. She steps into the circle, faces Marge. Then she carefully touches Marge's face. Then her hands move down over Marge's breasts. A long moment. Steve then moves in angrily and grabs the leader's rear. She wheels around and slaps him frantically, and then gasps as she realizes that she has broken the rules. General consternation and confusion as the piano starts playing "Brahms' Lullaby." The group modulates into a party, saying good night to two children, a boy and a girl, indicated by the fact they wear bathrobes or carry blankets or teddy

bears or a doll. The adults are ushered off by the mother, with lots of ad-libs about the children. The mother then turns back to the children, who remain on a platform as if it were a staircase.)

MOTHER: Now, kiddie cars, as a special treat, you can listen to "I Love a Mystery," and then lights out. That's an ultimatum. *(She hugs them.)* Good night, lovebugs.

GIRL: You look so beautiful, Mummy.

BOY: And you smell so sweet.

MOTHER: *(Releasing them.)* Off you go. Upstairs. *(They separate. The children get on the platform. The mother starts toward the party, then turns again to the children.)* Oh, children! *(They look at her. A moment.)* I just want to say…I just think you should know…that you both behaved beautifully just now. You went up to people, and shook hands, and called them by name, and you spoke right up when you were spoken to. *(Glances off toward the party.)* They're all talking about you now. And…and, well, Daddy and I are just very, very proud, that's all. Now good night. *(Whooshes off. The boy and girl wait till she's gone, and then quickly sit on the stairs.)*

BOY: Didn't Mummy smell sweet?

GIRL: *(Listening to the talk offstage.)* Sssshhh…They're saying I'm going to be beautiful. Mr. Irwin is saying I've got a beautiful nose. I'm going to be as beautiful as Mummy. *(More listening.)*

BOY: But I'm the cutest. Hear that? And I'm going to be a great hockey player. *(Yawns.)* Now let's hear "I Love a Mystery."

GIRL: *(Still listening.)* Wait! Hey, I'm getting a doll house, from Schwartz, for Christmas. Oh, I knew it!

BOY: That's because you heard it at the last party.

GIRL: *(Standing up; stretching.)* I used to hate being polite to them. I used to feel so shy and awful. But now I think it's worth it.

BOY: *(As they go off.)* Gosh, didn't Mummy smell sweet!

GIRL: And I'm going to be just like her!

(They exit as: The piano plays a sturdy World War II marching song. A father comes out carrying one old wooden ski. He props in on a chair and begins to wax it meticulously. A son watches his father. The music subsides.)

SON: Please, Dad…

FATHER: *(Patiently waxing.)* Did you, or did you not, promise Miss Watson you would walk her cocker spaniel this afternoon?

SON: But I didn't know there'd be snow.

FATHER: That makes absolutely no difference. You made a promise.

SON: But I want to go skiing with you.

FATHER: I don't give a tinker's damn what you want or what you don't want. When we make a promise in this family, we keep it. That's the trouble with Hitler. He doesn't keep his promises.

SON: I can get Snoozer to walk the dog.

FATHER: *(Always waxing.)* I don't believe Snoozer was part of the understanding with Miss Watson. I don't believe Miss Watson knows Snoozer. I don't believe Miss Watson's dog knows Snoozer.

SON: The dog does know Snoozer.

FATHER: Don't get fresh.

SON: You made me get these jobs with Miss Watson.

FATHER: That's right.

SON: To pay for my new ski boots.

FATHER: That's right. To learn what money means.

SON: And now there's skiing, I can't even go. I can't even use them.

FATHER: That's right. Not this weekend anyway.

SON: *(Quietly; walking away.)* Shit.

FATHER: *(Stopping waxing; looking up.)* What did you say?

SON: I didn't say—

FATHER: *(Walking directly to him.)* What did you say?

SON: *(Defiantly.)* I said "shit."

FATHER: *(Gives him a tremendous cuff, sending him reeling.)* I NEVER want to hear that word again! Ever! Your mother is right in the next ROOM! I am thoroughly disGUSTed with you! *(The boy stands with his back to the audience, obviously crying. The father looks at him and then returns to waxing his skis.)* Now. There is nothing—nothing in this world—more valuable to me than my family. I mean that. Hitler could attack us tomorrow and I wouldn't care—just as long as Mummy and you Tinkie and Bobby were safe. These are precious years for all of us. Times moves so fast. In two years you'll be away at school. And so there is nothing I'd like more than to ski with all my family. The singing in the car, the fresh air, the exercise, the listening to "The Shadow" and Jack Benny on the way home—Oh, there is nothing I like more in this world. *(Stops waxing, turns to him.)* And so when my son, my eldest son, isn't there with us, then half the fun goes out of the day. *(Goes to son.)* But you made a deal. And you've got to stick to it. If we don't stand by our word, then the world falls apart and people start using foul language to get what they want.

(Looks at him.) O.K.? *(The son nods.)* Good. Now go help your sister with the ski-rack.

(They exit either way as a woman comes out to address the audience. She carries note cards, which she refers to continually.)

WOMAN: *(Nervously.)* Um. I want to make three quick points about this whole business of the fence. *(Glances at first card.)* Point one. Appearance. I don't like the looks of it. I know we've been having a lot of fires and robberies and terrorism, but I still don't like putting one of those ugly chain fences around the entire neighborhood. Even in the brochure, it looks terribly unattractive. That awful barbed wire. Those ghastly gates. I don't care how much planting or landscaping we do, we are still going to look like a concentration camp. And that's point one. *(Next card.)* Point two. Inconvenient. The whole thing is going to be terribly inconvenient. I hate the idea of having to get out of the car, to put my I.D. card into those gates just so they'll open and I can get home. And what about deliveries? How do the cleaners, and the milkman, and the eggman get in? The brochure simply doesn't say. *(Next card.)* Point three, and then I'll sit down. What about dogs? This fence is electrified, remember. We can train our children to stay away from it, but what about dogs? Or do we have to tie them up? I refuse to do that, frankly. You know our Rosie, our old Lab. It would kill her to be tied up. I won't do it. And yet if Rosie should run up against this fence, she should be electrocuted. So what I suggest we do is, I suggest we call our friends in Shaker Heights, and Concord, and Palo Alto, and all the other places which have put in these fences, and we find out a few more details. I mean, I'm just not sure a fence is the best solution.

(The lights shift as her husband joins her, hands her a brandy snifter; he has another for himself. We are now at another party, the sounds of which we hear off stage. Their host, Howard, guides them.)

HOWARD: Now come into the library, you two, where we can talk seriously for two minutes.

WOMAN: *(Gesturing off.)* What about your other guests, Howard?

HOWARD: They'll survive…Now, Ted, I think you're sound asleep! And Missy, so are you! And as an old friend, I'm going to try to wake you up!

TED: *(Patiently.)* Why am I asleep, Howard?

HOWARD: Because you are sitting on all those old-fashioned stocks your father left you! He's *sitting* on them, Missy, and he's sitting on *yours.*

He hasn't done a goddamn thing to his portfolio in twenty years, and I'm giving him a chance to bring things up to date!

MISSY: What is it? Some new company?

HOWARD: It is not a new company. It is a wholly owned subsidiary of one of the largest companies in this country. And the stock is going to go sky-high. And I'm giving him a chance to get in on the ground floor, and he won't touch it.

TED: Yeah...well...

MISSY: What do they make?

TED: Guns.

HOWARD: No, Teddy. Not guns. Machine guns. They've invented a machine gun—pocket-*size!*—a goddamn *toy,* for Chrissake—which can be carried by any foot soldier and which shoots 800 rounds a minute! The government has already signed the contract. And Ted's walking away from it.

TED: *(Shrugs.)* I'll stay with what I've got.

MISSY: Yes. I mean, machine guns, Howard...

HOWARD: That's where it's at, my love. Do you like this house? Do you like that painting? Do you like this new rug? Did you like that dinner, and that wine, and that brandy you're drinking right now? Well, I like it. And I'm going to hold onto it. So wake up, my friends. Invest in the future, or you'll be left out in the cold! *(Walks out, calling off.)* Now who out here wants a highball? *(Exits.) (Pause. Ted and Missy look at each other.)*

MISSY: Machine guns. How awful.

TED: I know.

MISSY: I should have argued with him. The children would have argued it out.

TED: I know.

MISSY: We should have said the whole thing is absolutely wrong, wrong, wrong.

TED: He's my friend. I'm drinking his liquor. He's my host. *(Suddenly.)* Oh, Why are we always so goddamn polite? *(Impulsively and deliberately spills his brandy on the floor. Then he looks at her.)*

MISSY: Oh, my gosh...Sweetie!

(She frantically begins mopping it up with his handkerchief as the pianist begins to play elaborate renditions of Richard Strauss. The Dancing Master comes out, in tails and with a black walking stick, and arranges three chairs, neatly in a row. Then he interrupts the pianist.)

DANCING MASTER: Well, Mr. Cromeier: and how do you like playing for the dancing school in Buffalo? It's not Vienna, is it? Oh no: it's not Vienna. But at least we're in a free country. *(Taps his stick.)*
(The pianist plays the Grand March from Aida. *Separate lines of boys and girls march out from either side of the stage, all doggedly trying to stay in step and in line with each other. The girls wear big bows and sashes; the boys, stiff collars and white gloves. When the music stops, the girls sit demurely in the chairs, the boys standing rigidly facing them across the stage. The Dancing Master taps his stick. The Dancing Master consults with the pianist. Two boys whisper.)*

FIRST BOY: Let's sneak out.

SECOND BOY: How?

FIRST BOY: I'll go to the john. You follow.

SECOND BOY: Then where will be go?

FIRST BOY: Downtown. To see Hedy Lamarr. In *Ecstasy*. You can see her boobs!

SECOND BOY: Hey, yes! Say when.

DANCING MASTER: *(German accent.)* The young gentlemen will ask the young ladies to dance. *(All boys dash across the stage and slide to a stop in front of the prettiest girl.)* Go back! *(The boys go back to their chairs.)* The young gentlemen will ask the young ladies to dance. *(The boys walk militarily across the stage; each stands in front of a girl.)* Bow! *(The boys bow, one hand behind their backs.)* Young ladies rise and curtsey. *(The girls do, in rigid order.)* Handkerchiefs out. *(The boys take clean white handkerchiefs out of their pockets.)* Music, Mr. Cromeier, if you please. *(The pianist begins to play "I'm Always Chasing Rainbows" slowly and methodically. The boys put their handkerchiefs behind the girls waists. Couples dance stiffly. The Dancing Master taps with his cane.)* One and two and one and two and...al-ways small steps... care—ful—...care—ful—... *(A couple dances.)*

BOY: I'm the boy. I'm supposed to lead.

GIRL: Then *lead*, please.

BOY: You've got Beeeee-ooooooooooow.

GIRL: Just *lead*, please. *(He leads her stiffly away.)*

DANCING MASTER: *(Calling out.)* Step and two and turn and two and... *(Another couple dances.)*

BOY: Are you a Jewess?

GIRL: No. *(They turn.)*

BOY: My mother says you are.

GIRL: Well, I *was*. We were. But we gave it up. We changed our name and everything.

BOY: Hey. Wow.

GIRL: I know it. *(They turn. First boy dances with his partner.)*

FIRST BOY: I'm ducking out. Say I'm in the john.

GIRL: I will not.

FIRST BOY: Come on. I'll give you a dollar.

GIRL: Oh no.

FIRST BOY: Come on... *(Starts furtively off-stage.)*

GIRL: *(Call out.)* Mr. Van Dam! Mr. Van Dam! *(Dancing Master notices her.)* I don't have a partner!
(Dancing Master pounds the floor rapidly with his cane. The music stops. Everyone stops dancing. First boy is heading off by now.)

DANCING MASTER: *(Calling out.)* Mr. Wickwire! *(First boy slides to a stop.)* Approach me! *(First boy hesitates; Everyone giggles.)* Approach me! *(First boy walks toward him.)* Bow to me! *(First boy does.)* Lower! *(First boy does. Dancing Master walks slowly around the boy, raising his cane as if to strike him. Then, facing the boy, he says very quietly.)* Dance with me. *(The boy looks up slowly, with horror.)* I said, dance with me. *(To pianist.)* A waltz, please, Mr. Cromeier. *(Holds out his arms to the boy.)* Now dance with me. *(The music begins; the boy takes out his handkerchief again. They dance, as everyone watches and giggles.)* I am a lovely young lady...Lead me carefully...I am glass...Turn, turn...I am fine Meissen china...I am a fairy princess... *(Then he pushes the boy away.)* Now go dance properly with Miss Jones. *(To others.)* Dance, everyone! Dance! *(Everyone does. First boy dances with Miss Jones.)*

FIRST BOY: *(Between his teeth.)* O.K. for you.

MISS JONES: *(Frightenedly.)* What do you mean?

FIRST BOY: I said O.K. for you, pal.

MISS JONES: What are you going to do?

FIRST BOY: Next week I'm going to get my boys together. Freddy, Snoozer, the whole bunch. And when you're walking to your music lesson, we're going to grab you. And take you behind Miss Watson's garage. And strip you. All the way. And then we're going to piss all over you. *(She looks at him in terror as they dance away.)*

DANCING MASTER: *(Calling out.)* Dance, everybody! Dance! The night is young, and you are beautiful! Dance! Dance! Dance!. *(Everyone does off.)*

END OF ACT ONE

Act Two

The piano plays rock music. The lights come up on a woman in a ski parka, side-stepping as if she were in line for a chair lift, which is indicated by two chairs to one side. She pantomimes the encumbrances of boots, skis and poles. A man "slides" onto the stage.

MAN: Are you a single?

WOMAN: Am I ever. *(The man engineers his way alongside her.)*

MAN: Then we'll ride up together.

WOMAN: Fine. *(They move slowly along, side by side, as if in a ski-tow line.)* Isn't the skiing marvelous?

MAN: Superb. It's worth it, isn't it?

WOMAN: Exactly.

MAN: I drove all the way up from Buffalo.

WOMAN: Then you had to get one of those travel permits—to cross a state line.

MAN: Oh, sure.

WOMAN: So did I. What a goddamn bore! I had to swear—even my *nine*-year-old had to swear—that we were not going to Stowe to incite riot! *(Both laugh.)*

MAN: Ah. You've got a family here.

WOMAN: Just the children. I'm divorced. And you?

MAN: I'm alone. My children are away at school. My wife's had a breakdown.

WOMAN: Oh, dear. Who wouldn't, these days. *(They reach the lift and side by side prepare for the ride up. They settle back into the chairs, adjusting their skis and poles.)*

MAN: Where're you from?

WOMAN: Connecticut…Greenwich.

MAN: Do you know Patty and George Tremaine?

WOMAN: I knew Patty quite well. She's dead, you know. *(Pause.)* She got caught in the September Insurrection. She was shot. *(Pause.)* They were rocking her car or something and she got out, and one thing led to another. You know.

MAN: *(Quietly.)* Oh, wow.

WOMAN: Thank heavens for this. I took the children out of school for it. It gives them some perspective.

MAN: My kids say I'm crazy to spend all my time and money just to slide down a hill. They say I'm acting out the death wish of the upper middle class. *(Both laugh.)*

WOMAN: Here's the top. *(They adjust their skis and poles and go through the contortions of getting off and getting ready to go down the hill.)* You tell your children, for me, that the trouble with their generation is they don't know how to have fun.

MAN: That's right. If we're doomed, let's at least do a few graceful turns on the way down.

WOMAN: *(Laughing.)* Exactly! And meet in the bar afterwards?

MAN: Why not?

(They pantomime pushing off in different directions down the hill. The pianist plays "Come, Ye Thankful People, Come." A father and mother place the two chairs opposite each other, to indicate a long table.)

FATHER: *(Pantomiming sharpening a carving knife.)* I would hope—at least on Thanksgiving—that someone around here is polite enough to push in his mother's chair.

MOTHER: *(Sits down, slides her chair in. Over her shoulder, as if to a child:)* Thank you, Billy.

FATHER: *(Pantomiming carving a turkey.)* All right now. I want everyone to listen carefully, and to remember what I say.

MOTHER: I'll have the wing, Ralph.

FATHER: *(Carving.)* Our nation is at war...Pass that down to your mother, Tootsie...We are fighting a death struggle against the Germans and Japanese. You children have no idea what war is, but you're going to learn. And very quickly.

MOTHER: Give Tootsie some dressing, Ralph.

FATHER: *(Carving.)* To begin with: I won't be around much. I'm going into the Army, and I doubt if I'll be able to get up from Washington more than once or twice a month. Which means that *some*one, without being told, has got to start pushing in his mother's chair!

MOTHER: *(Pantomiming serving vegetables.)* Who does *not* want gravy on their potatoes?

FATHER: And we are going to have no more maids. For the duration. Agnes will still come in to clean, but that's *it.* Which means everyone makes his own bed and helps with the dishes.

MOTHER: Billy likes the drumstick, Ralph.

FATHER: As far as food goes, only one butterball per person. Did you hear that, Tootsie? If you put more butter on your potato, then you can't have any more for your roll. And no more finger bowls. Finger bowls are out.

MOTHER: Begin, children. While it's hot.

FATHER: *(Sitting down.)* The boys will collect tin cans, and the girls will knit Bundles for Bri—...*(Stops, stand up.)* Who told you to pick up that drumstick, Billy?

MOTHER: It's all right, Ralph.

FATHER: It is not all right. Put it down, Billy. I said, put it down! Is this what war does to us? Are we reduced to gnawing at bones like jackals?

MOTHER: Oh, Ralph...

FATHER: We use knives and forks around here!

MOTHER: But he'll waste half the meat!

FATHER: We use knives, we use forks! *(Pause.)*

MOTHER: Use your knife and fork, Billy.

FATHER: *(Sitting down.)* More rules. *(Eats lustily.)* We're going to do very little driving. Everyone takes the bus. Even your mother. When we go skiing, we'll take the train. Let no one forget; this is *war!*

MOTHER: Sally, don't feed the dog at the table.

(Fadeout on the dinner table. The piano plays "There's No Place Like Home" in a rock style. A young man is getting into a barber's chair. Charlie, the barber, in a white jacket, is arranging a sheet around him and pumping the chair back. They eye each other for a long moment in the mirror in front of them.)

YOUNG MAN: *(Setting back.)* Remember me, Charlie?

CHARLIE: Sammy? Sam Curtis?

YOUNG MAN: Good for you, Charlie.

CHARLIE: I gave you your first haircut. I still cut your father's hair. I just cut your grandfather's hair. What there is left. Oh, I know all the Curtises. *(Begins to pantomime cutting.)* You're the one who's a painter.

YOUNG MAN: Right, Charlie! Good for you...Take some off the top, Charlie.

CHARLIE: Sure. You're the painter. You won a painting prize at Nichols School. You came in here and showed me your painting prize.

YOUNG MAN: *(Beaming.)* God, Charlie. You remember everything.

CHARLIE: Sure. I keep in touch. Your father tells me. Let's see. You went away to school, and then Princeton and then the Army, and now you're in New York, being a painter. Right?

YOUNG MAN: Well, I'm back now, Charlie.

CHARLIE: Just to visit, huh?

YOUNG MAN: No, no. I'm back. In Buffalo.

CHARLIE: You going to paint here, huh?

YOUNG MAN: Well, no. I'm going to be a stockbroker, actually, Charlie.

CHARLIE: You mean, work for your father?

YOUNG MAN: Right, Charlie. *(Pause.)* Better take a little more off the back, Charlie.

CHARLIE: I thought you was going to be our painter.

YOUNG MAN: Yeah, well, you know New York, Charlie. Nobody...cares.

CHARLIE: You used to come in here, and tell me you were going to be—

YOUNG MAN: Hey, Charlie. How about one of those shaves? Like the ones you give my father. With hot towels and all the trimmings. How about it? Oh boy. I just want to relax. *(Leans back, luxuriously. Charlie puts a towel around his face.)*

CHARLIE: I thought you was going to be my painter.

YOUNG MAN: *(Closing his eyes.)* Mmmmmm. That feels good. I might just...catch...forty winks...Charlie.

CHARLIE: *(Sadly; massaging his face; looks at him directly for the first time.)* My painter...

(The piano plays a few bars of party music. Female giggles from off stage. A woman comes on, carrying a telephone and a drink, to get away from the noise, gesturing that they be quiet.)

WOMAN: *(On telephone.)* Buzzy? It's your mother!...Listen, sweetie, I'm sorry to bother you at college, but Mrs. Rothenberg and Mrs. Kreb are here, and Daddy's out of town, and we've decided to try it, and we want to know where it is...It, Buzzy. It! I'm not going to mention it over the phone...*(Mrs. Rothenberg and Mrs. Kreb come on at this point and hover around the phone.)* No, we've decided to find out what it's like, before we continue to criticize, so where is it?...It is not in your top drawer. We looked in your top drawer—Oh, you mean that...That, Buzzy? That little bag?...All right, all right, now what do we do? Hold it, hold it...*(Frantic fumblings and gestures for pencil, paper. Problems of who is to hold whose drink.)* Do we have to strain it, or what? *(Writes things down.)* All right...Yes. We found the water pipe. *(Someone produces it.)* Can we just use regular water?...I see. And do you recommend any music? Let it what? Let it bleed? *(Someone knows it.)* All right. Let it bleed...All right, Buzzy. Yes, I'll pay you. I'll pay you, Buzzy. I'll send you a check...Good-bye, sweetie.

Work hard. And don't you dare tell Daddy! *(Hangs up; they all go off.)* It was in the top drawer. It was that ratty old bag of fish food. *(Exit.)* *(The piano plays "Now the Day is Over." A Rector, in a purple stole, marches slowly in, followed by three choirboys in a line, wearing surplices and carrying hymnals. All sing.)*

ALL: Now the day is over,
Night is drawing nigh.
Shadows of the evening,
Steal across the sky...Amen.

RECTOR: *(Comes forward.)* Let us pray silently for Saint Luke's School, remembering to thank God for our nation's victory in war and asking for His guidance in peace.

FIRST CHOIRBOY: *(Praying quietly.)* Oh God: thanks for beating the Germans and Japs...And please help us beat the shit out of Andover tomorrow.

SECOND CHOIRBOY: Oh God: please let me get over eighty in the Latin test so I can get out of study hall, and see the Saturday night movie. And please make it a good movie. For once.

THIRD CHOIRBOY: Please let there be a letter from Snoozer's sister in my mailbox tomorrow, saying she'll come to the midwinter dance. And please, if she comes, get her to put out.

FIRST CHOIRBOY: And please, God, make me a better guy, and keep me from picking on Fat-Pig Hathaway at breakfast...

SECOND CHOIRBOY: And please don't let there be a nuclear war with the Russians...

THIRD CHOIRBOY: And please, please, please, God, get rid of my hard-on before I have to stand up and march out.
(The pianist strikes up, "Oh, God, Our Help in Ages Past." The Rector leads them out, all singing, the third choirboy protecting himself with his book.)

ALL: Oh, God our help in ages past,
Our hope for years to come,
Our shelter from the story blast,
And our eternal home...
(A very distinguished, very old lady is escorted to the edge of the stage by her Granddaughter.)

OLD LADY: *(Addressing the audience.)* On behalf of the Lockwood family, I wish to make the following announcement to the newspapers. I am hereby donating my house and grounds in East Aurora to be a permanently endowed summer camp for Negro children from the Eighth Detention Area. These children will now have the opportunity to swim in the pool, play in the gardens, learn tennis and croquet, and do all the things my children and grandchildren once did. It is my firm belief that if colored children can spend their summers in the country, they will cease throwing fire bombs from their cars, and detention areas will no longer be necessary. *(Her granddaughter escorts her out.)*

(The pianist plays cocktail-y music as a waiter carries in a small table and two chairs. A headwaiter leads on a mother and daughter. They sit down at the table. There is the usual business of taking off gloves, powdering of noses, and so forth.)

DAUGHTER: Oh, Mummy! Thank you, thank you, thank you for the tennis dress, and the bathing suit, and the Bermuda shorts. They're just yummy, Mummy.

MOTHER: Well, they fit. Which is why we come to New York. *(To the waiter.)* We'll have Eggs Benedict, green salad, fresh strawberries and coffee. And two Daiquiris. Now.

WAITER: Is the young lady eighteen?

MOTHER: Yes, she is, thank you. *(The waiter goes off.)*

DAUGHTER: Oh, Mummy, you lied.

MOTHER: I did not lie, Pookins. And I don't like that expression. I fibbed. And I *fibbed* for a very good reason. *(Leans forward.)* You have got to learn to drink.

DAUGHTER: I don't really like it.

MOTHER: That's not the point. You've got to *learn* to like it. The way you learned to like riding. The way you learned to like Westover. Most of life is learning to like things. *(Waiter brings drinks.)* Now drink it slowly. *(Daughter sips.)* For heaven's sake, don't stick your pinkie out. You look like a dental hygienist. *(Daughter sips again.)* Good. Now. If you get tipsy, make the most of it. Tell people you're tipsy. And then you can say and do almost anything you want. *(Mother takes out cigarette.)* And when you smoke—

DAUGHTER: I don't like smoking, Mother.

MOTHER: Good for you. It's a vile habit. It's messy, and unhealthy, and expensive. And I love it. *(The waiter lights her cigarette.)* And so will you. And now, sweetie pie, you've got to make a decision, and you've got to make it in the next hour, because *Kiss Me, Kate* starts promptly at two.

DAUGHTER: What decision?

MOTHER: Probably *the* most crucial decision of your entire life. *(Leans forward.)* I talked to your father long distance, and for the first time since the divorce, we *agreed* on something. We agreed to leave the decision up to you.

DAUGHTER: *What* decision, Mummy?

MOTHER: About next *year*, Pookins. After you graduate from that nunnery. You've got to decide whether you want to go to college, or have a coming-out party. Your father will pay for one or the other, but not both. (Pause.)

DAUGHTER: Oh, I'll take college then. *(Long pause.)*

MOTHER: I see.

DAUGHTER: I mean, what's the point of coming out, anyway? I already know everybody. I'm already out.

MOTHER: Now don't get smart, Barbara. That's just smarty-pants stuff.

DAUGHTER: Well, then *explain* it to me, Mother. *(Pause.)*

MOTHER: All your friends are coming out. All. And if you don't you'll miss all the parties over Christmas and in June.

DAUGHTER: Oh, I'll be invited.

MOTHER: But you can't *Go!* Unless you give a party. It's just not fair. And I will not try to squeeze you onto the list with a cheap little tea, either. You will have a good party of your own, with Lester Lanin or Harry Marchard, or you will not go to anyone else's. And that's final. *(Pause.)*

DAUGHTER: I'll go skiing over Christmas then.

MOTHER: With whom?

DAUGHTER: I don't know. I want to go to college, Mummy. *(Pause.)*

MOTHER: Why?

DAUGHTER: Why?

MOTHER: *Why?* I said, why?

DAUGHTER: I want to...further my education. I want to have something to *do.*

MOTHER: Oh, Barbara, you sound like some immigrant. *(To waiter.)* Martini on the rocks, please. *(To daughter.)* I didn't go to college.

DAUGHTER: I know that, Mother.

MOTHER: I came *out.* And so did all my friends.

DAUGHTER: I know that, Mother.

MOTHER: None of us went to college. We never even considered it. We were having too much fun.

DAUGHTER: I know, Mother.

MOTHER: And I've done all right in the world. Without college.

DAUGHTER: Yes, Mother.

MOTHER: Or do you think I haven't? Do you think I'm stupid?

DAUGHTER: No, Mother.

MOTHER: I *read* more than you do.

DAUGHTER: I know.

MOTHER: I read all the time. I don't go to the movies twice a week like some people I know. I like to think I can carry on a decent conversation. I don't keep saying uh-huh and uh-uh like some people I know around here.

DAUGHTER: Oh, come on, Mummy.

MOTHER: Who's going to college from Westover, answer me that.

DAUGHTER: Lots of people.

MOTHER: Who? Who? Name names. *That I know.*

DAUGHTER: Betsy Wettlauffer wants to go to Wellesley.

MOTHER: She's a babe.

DAUGHTER: She's not a—

MOTHER: She's a *babe,* Pookins. She's a pew. Look at her hair sometime. *(Pause.)*

DAUGHTER: I still want to go to college. *(Pause.)*

MOTHER: I'll tell you what: we'll give a smallish party. Local orchestra. Close the bar at one. And you can go to Bennett or Briarcliffe for two years.

DAUGHTER: They're not—

MOTHER: They're very good. Wendy Pratt is going to one of them.

DAUGHTER: I want to go to—

MOTHER: No, no. Bennett. And a small coming-out party. And then listen—oh, here's the solution. We'll pass the hat and you can go to Europe for a year. You can go to Florence. *There's* your education. Pookins. And you'll learn more in the next three years, I promise, than you'll ever learn with Betsy Wettlauffer at Wellesley. Right? Right. *(Waiter brings in plates.)* Good. Here's food. *(Waiter sets plates down.)* Now. One other thing. *(Waits until the waiter goes; then speaks softly.)* Have you got a diaphragm?

DAUGHTER: A what?

MOTHER: A diaphragm. Now you're coming out, you should be fitted for a—

DAUGHTER: Oh, *Mo*ther!

MOTHER: Just asking. Skip it. Now eat up or we'll be late for *Kiss Me, Kate.*

(The waiters take off the table, as a father and son take the two chairs, placing them so as to indicate a sailboat, and then executing a sailing maneuver. The piano plays a wry arrangement of "Sailing, Sailing." The father pantomimes working the tiller, adjusting the mainsheet. The son looks off dreamily.)

FATHER: *(After a moment.)* This old boat is always at her best running with the wind. (Pause.) Look under your seat. I brought a thermos of gin-and-tonics.

SON: No, thanks, Dad.

FATHER: Oh, come on. You always used to love gin-and-tonic. Even when you were tiny, you always wanted a taste of my gin-and-tonic.

SON: *(With a shrug.)* All right. *(Pantomimes taking a sip, then hands it to his father.)*

FATHER: *(Taking a slug.)* Now admit it. Doesn't this bring back happy memories?

SON: I guess...

FATHER: This boat, poor, sad, dying old Lake Erie. They still work. You can still sail. Life's not so bad now, is it?

SON: Dad...

FATHER: I mean, can't we *talk?* Can't we even do *that?* Why did you come sailing with me? I didn't pay your bail just so we could sit here and stare at each other. Your mother can't talk to you, but I thought maybe I could.

SON: O.K. Talk, talk, talk.

FATHER: I want to know where you're going to go.

SON: I can't tell you.

FATHER: Oh look, Skipper. We're in the middle of Lake Erie. Or do you think they've bugged this *boat?* I want to know where you're going to *be.*

SON: I don't know.

FATHER: Will you telephone us? When you know?

SON: You know I can't.

FATHER: Well, write then. They don't open mail.

SON: Don't they?

FATHER: This is like some bad dream. My own son going into *hid*ing. Behaving like some criminal.

SON: Which I am.

FATHER: Which you are *not!* You haven't even come to trial yet.

SON: Some trial. Name someone who's gotten off.

FATHER: If only we had *pull.* We don't have any *pull* anymore. I called twenty lawyers in Buffalo, but they won't touch your case with a ten-foot pole.

SON: I could have told you that.

FATHER: *(Takes another slug from the thermos, then spits it overboard.)* This is awful, isn't it? Without ice. Don't drink it if you don't want to. *(Pause.)* I'm coming about. We'll tack against the wind. *(Pantomime of shifting seats, tightening lines, etc. After they're settled.)* Your mother and I strongly feel that you should show up for your trial on Monday morning.

SON: And get nailed with three years.

FATHER: How do you know?

SON: Read the new security laws, Dad. *Read* them.

FATHER: Don't shout, please. *(Pause.)* What's three years, in the long run? I spent three years in the Navy during Korea.

SON: That wasn't prison.

FATHER: Oh, what's prison these days? It's not a stigma anymore. Teddy Miller just got out. His family gave a small party for him. *(The son laughs sardonically.)* All right, all right. I know. But I talked to him at great length. He said he read a lot of good books and got very good at baseball.

SON: I'm not Teddy Miller.

FATHER: At least talk to him.

SON: I've got better things to do.

FATHER: Such as what? Hiding in the hills? Living with that little Jewish girl? Blowing up buildings?

SON: You want to go through all the old arguments?

FATHER: No, thank you. *(Pause.)* We'll never see you again. You'll be killed. *(Reaches out to touch his son's shoulder.)* You're our oldest son.

SON: *(Pulls away, looks off. Pause.)* We're getting close to those shoals.

FATHER: *(Tightening a line.)* We are not getting close to those shoals. Don't tell me about sailing. You never won a race in your life. You never stuck to anything. You ducked out, just the way you're ducking out now.

SON: Let's go in, huh?

FATHER: We gave you the finest education in the country. We sold stock.

We rented our house here for three summers—we sweltered i
city—just so you could learn how to break laws and jump bail.

SON: I want to go in now, Dad.

FATHER: You have no idea what duty means. You have no conception of
what the word duty means. We don't just quit. We don't desert the
ship. Or scuttle it. Which is what you're doing. When your mother
got into that nonsense with Mr. Fiske, I stuck *by* her. I stuck by the
rules. And so should you. Now stand up at that trial and take your
punishment like a man. Do it. No arguments. Just do it.

SON: Fuck you. *(The father slaps him across the face. The son hits his father.
They struggle, knocking over a chair. The boat is in trouble. The father
frantically pantomimes grabbing lines.)*

FATHER: Grab the tiller!...I said GRAB THE TILLER!...Head her off! I
said OFF!...Oh, my God, you can't even sail!

*(The lights dim on them, as the pianist plays a series of scales. Mrs. Hayes,
a woman of about fifty, comes in and speaks to the pianist. She wears a
hat and gloves. He stops playing and looks at her.)*

MRS. HAYES: *(Sweetly, shyly to the pianist.)* Before we begin, you probably
want to know, don't you, why I'm taking up singing lessons at my
age. I mean, I'm no spring chicken. *(Laughs embarrassedly.)* Well, you
see, the thing is...I've always wanted to sing. I've always had this...
music...in me, and now I've just got to let it out. Before it's too late.
I've always had this dream of standing on a stage, with other singers
all around me, and we're singing the sextet from *Lucia di Lammer-
moor.* You're the first person I've ever told. I've never even told my
husband. *(The pianist begins to play the sextet.)* Yes! Oh yes! That's it!
Oh, I *dream* of it! Everyone singing a different thing, nobody out of
tune, and everything fitting together so perfectly at the end. Oh,
what heaven, what bliss to be able to sing that! *(The pianist plays flam-
boyantly.)* Yes! And I'd be Lucia, a young girl, with long blond hair,
and I've made a terrible mistake. I've done just what my family
wanted me to do and married the wrong man and now I'm going
mad and I'm singing my heart out! *(The pianist begins the second chorus of the sextet. She tries to sing along with the piano. She almost makes
a high note. Then she stops.)* Oh dear. *(Quiet tears.)* Oh dear. *(Shakes
her head.)* I'm sorry. I'm terribly sorry. I'm terribly, terribly sorry.
*(She runs out, as a man dictates a letter to a pretty secretary, who sits on
a chair, taking shorthand.)*

MAN: *(Dictating.)* Dear Brad. *(Pause.)* Thanks for your note. *(Pause.)* I'm very sorry, but this year I don't think I'll cough up another nickel for Yale. I'm distressed that the library was burned but why should I keep Yale up when even its own students persist in dragging her down? *(Gets angrier.)* Indeed, why do people like you and me and Snoozer, Brad, have to keep things up all the time? It seems to me I spend most of my time keeping things up. I keep the symphony up. I keep the hospital up. I keep our idiotic local theatre up. I keep my lawn up because no one else will. I keep my house up so the children will want to come home someday. I keep the summer house up for grandchildren. I keep up all that furniture Mother left me because Sally won't keep it up. I even keep my morals up despite all sorts of immediate temptations. *(The secretary glances up at him.)* I keep my chin up, I keep my faith up, I keep my dander up in this grim world. And I'm sick, sick, sick of it. I'm getting tired supporting all those things that maybe ought to collapse. Sometimes all I think I am is an old jock strap, holding up the sagging balls of the whole goddamn world! *(Pause.)* Strike that, Miss Johnson. Obviously. And excuse me. *(Pause.)* Strike out the whole letter, Miss Johnson. *(Pause.)* Begin again. *(With a sigh.)* Dear Brad. Enclosed is my annual check for Yale. I wish it could be larger. Sally joins me in sending love to you and Jane. Sincerely. And so forth.

(The pianist bursts into a fast medley of Lester Lanin-type songs: "From This Moment On." Couples twirl onto the stage. The actress can wear long skirts, the actors black bow ties. A couple twirls.)

BOY: Fabulous party.

GIRL: I know it. *(They turn.)*

BOY: Fabulous music, fabulous decorations, everything's fabulous.

GIRL: I know it. *(They turn.)*

BOY: Who's giving it, do you know?

GIRL: I am. *(They turn. An older couple dance by—doing the sliding fox-trot of their generation.)*

WOMAN: It's a lovely party, Howard.

MAN: Better be. Cost me a cool ten thou.

WOMAN: What is it you do again?

MAN: We make parts for rockets.

WOMAN: You mean, for Korea?

MAN: For all over the world! *(They turn. Another boy and girl dance by.)*

GIRL: Why were you kicked out of Williams?

BOY: I refused to go to compulsory chapel on Sunday nights.

GIRL: How brave! Don't you believe in God?

BOY: Oh, sure. But I could never get back from Vassar in time.

(They dance off. Another couple dances in, followed by a boy with glasses.)

BOY WITH GLASSES: *(Calling to them.)* Hey! They've got a TV set here. You can see the McCarthy hearings!

OTHER BOY: *(Breaking away from his partner.)* No kidding!

GIRL: *(Standing pat.)* Don't tell me you're going to sit around and watch the boob tube!

OTHER BOY: *(Looking at girl.)* I guess I'll stay and dance.

BOY WITH GLASSES: *(Going off.)* Suit yourself.

GIRL: *(Looking after him.)* How shallow can you get! Watching TV! When you can be with *people! (Dances off with the other boy.)*

(Two boys stand, back to the audience, as if at urinals. The second boy makes a loud burp.)

FIRST BOY: I'll bet you say that to all the girls. *(They pantomime washing their hands, adjusting ties, combing hair, now facing audience.)*

SECOND BOY: Janie put out for me tonight.

FIRST BOY: Oh, yeah?

SECOND BOY: Sure. I took her out by the pool. And she really came across.

FIRST BOY: How much did you get?

SECOND BOY: *(Spreading his arms.)* Yay much.

FIRST BOY: Oh well. I've had that.

SECOND BOY: Janie?

FIRST BOY: Oh, sure. She drops on a dime.

SECOND BOY: Janie? My Janie?

FIRST BOY: Oh, sure. She's got round heels from the word go.

SECOND BOY: *(Sadly.)* It figures. *(Pause.)*

FIRST BOY: Well. I've got to go dance with my mother.

SECOND BOY: Ditto.

(They go off. Two girls meet in the ladies' room. One girl is wiping off the other's dress.)

FIRST GIRL: He suddenly just leaned over and barfed all over my goddamn dress.

SECOND GIRL: How awful.

FIRST GIRL: Seventy-five dollars at Peck and Peck. Down the drain.

SECOND GIRL: Send him the bill.

FIRST GIRL: It doesn't matter. I'm on the shelf, anyway. No one will invite me to a thing next year.

SECOND GIRL: What are you going to do?

FIRST GIRL: Oh, God. Go to New York. Parlay my art major into a job at some museum. Live in a grubby apartment with a bunch of gals, where everyone gets the curse at the same time. Unless...

SECOND GIRL: Unless what?

FIRST GIRL: Well...He asked me to marry him before he barfed on me.

SECOND GIRL: Oh, Susie!

(They both squeal and embrace and jump up and down and go off. Music up. A couple dances by. A grandmother marches up to them and cuts in.)

GRANDMOTHER: Drive me home, Billy.

BILLY: Aw, Gram! The night is young!

GRANDMOTHER: I have to get up early and memorize Milton.

BILLY: Memorize *Milton*?

GRANDMOTHER: Otherwise my mind will go. Drive me home. *(Starts out.)*

BILLY: *(Staring after her; to girl.)* She doesn't memorize Milton...

GRANDMOTHER: *(Reciting as she walks out.)* "Hence! Vain deluding joys, The brood of folly, without father bred!

How little you bested,

Or fill the fixed mind with all your toys!

Dwell in some idle brain..." *(She is out by now. Billy looks at his girl, and then trots after his grandmother. The piano plays a Bunny Hop. Everyone available dances it. A boy and girl break away. The boy wears a naval officer's hat.)*

GIRL: I love your uniform.

BOY: Thanks.

GIRL: Will the Navy get you to Europe this summer?

BOY: Oh, sure.

GIRL: I'll be in Paris. And so will Nancy, and Tookie, and Honey, and Muffy, and Squeakie. Can you get leave?

BOY: Oh, sure.

GIRL: I just think it's fantastic what you boys are doing about the Korean War. I just think it's superb, frankly.

BOY: Well. Somebody's got to hold the line against Communism. *(They rejoin the Bunny Hop.)*

A FATHER: *(Coming onstage, holding telephone.)* Hello...Roger?...Can you hear me?...(*The mother rushes in, stands anxiously by the father as he talks.*) We got your letter. Yes. Your mother is sick about it. She can't talk. We're here at the Gardners' coming-out party, and we can hardly face people...No, now you listen to me, Roger. If you insist on marrying that Japanese girl, I'm going to fly down to Washington and speak to an admiral and have you committed to a mental institution...That's ridiculous. You are not happy. You can't be happy... No. Now take a leave and come home and think about it. I'll pay your fare...Roger? Roger?

MOTHER: What? *What?*

FATHER: He hung up.

MOTHER: Oh Lord, oh Lord!

FATHER: Relax. I got through to him. Let's get back to the party! (*Joins two boys, beginning to harmonize around the piano. A fourth tries to make out with a girl.*)

SINGERS: "We're poor little sheep who have lost our way...Baaa, baaaa, baaaaa..."

GIRL: (*Fending off the boy.*) But why won't the Negroes sit in the back of the bus?

BOY: It's the principle of the thing.

SINGERS: "Little black sheep who have gone astray, baaaaa, baaaa, baaaa."

GIRL: (*Desperately fighting him off.*) I like the back of the bus.

BOY: (*Pantingly.*) But it's the principle of the thing...

SINGERS: "Gentleman songsters off on a spree...damned from here to eternity..."

GIRL: (*One last stab.*) Can they sit next to the window?

BOY: (*Losing control.*) Yes.

GIRL: Then what are they complaining about? (*He rolls her back onto the floor.*)

SINGERS: "Lord have mercy on such as we...baaaa, baaaa, baaaa."

(*The piano modulates to the Wedding March. A girl comes on, now wearing a bridal veil. A Groom joins her. Everyone else congratulates them. Two people bring on a table with champagne glass on a white tablecloth. The Bride and Groom pantomime cutting the cake. She feeds him a piece, then they kiss. Cheers, applause, cries of "Speech." Everyone shushes everyone else. The Groom speaks nervously, perhaps even with a stutter.*)

GROOM: I understand it's the custom among the rich for the groom to toast his bride. (*Laughter.*) Before he deflowers her. (*Laughter.*) I'm nervous. I shook like a leaf all during the ceremony. *(Laughter.)* Gosh. And here I am marrying a girl I danced with at dancing school! *(Laughter.)* Here I am, marrying a girl I've known all my life! *(Laughter; pause.)* Why? Why am I doing it?

BEST MAN: For her body! *(Laughter.)*

FATHER-IN-LAW: For her money? *(Laughter.)*

A BRIDESMAID: For her soul! *(General laughter.)*

GROOM: No, no. Really. Why am I marrying her? Why am I, from an old family, marrying a girl from another old family to live in this dying city under these dying trees on this dying lake? *(A moment of silence and sadness. He pulls out of it.)* Why, because I love her! I love her and you and this city and these trees and this lake! And so let's have one final frantic toast to all of us here today!

BEST MAN: And gone tomorrow!

(Laughter, raising of glasses. People line up. The Bride pantomimes throwing her bouquet. Then the Bride and Groom run through two lines as people pantomime throwing rice at them. The piano plays the Wedding March in fast time. People follow the Bride and Groom off, ad-libbing "Give my regards to Bermuda" and so forth. Someone removes the white tablecloth from the table, revealing a stark desk underneath. A man remains on stage, and from under the desk takes out a sheaf of papers and an Army officer's hat. The pianist plucks the bass strings of the piano to give a sharp, menacing, mechanical sound. The Army Officer sits at the desk, shuffling through his papers. An Enlisted Man comes in, followed by a Civilian.)

ENLISTED MAN: Excuse me, Colonel. This guy says he knows you. *(Colonel looks up.)*

CIVILIAN: *(Brightly.)* Hi.

COLONEL: I'm very busy.

ENLISTED MAN: He's very busy.

CIVILIAN: I'm Phil Ramsay, from Yale.

COLONEL: Phil…Ramsay?

RAMSAY: Sure. And you're Bucky Kratz. You were on the Dartmouth hockey team. Right wing, third line. I played goalie for Yale, same year. *(Pause.)* Sure! And we met again at Peggy Niles' coming-out party here in Buffalo. Oh, sure, Bucky Kratz. When I heard that you were the new District Commander, I said I know that guy. I know Colonel Kratz. I played hockey with him. *(Moving to desk: holding out his hand.)* Hi, Bucky.

COLONEL: *(Getting up, a little reluctantly; shaking hands.)* Phil…

RAMSAY: Ramsay. Don't you remember? We beat you three-to-one in overtime. I think I stopped a slap-shot of yours, Bucky. From the blue line. I think we talked about it afterwards. In the shower.

COLONEL: Maybe…

RAMSAY: Sure! And then, the day after the party, I think I beat you in tennis, Bucky. We drove over to the Tennis Club, and I think I whipped your ass. *(Laughs nervously.)*

COLONEL: Phil Ramsay… *(He nods; the Enlisted Man goes out.)*

RAMSAY: Sure. And now you're District Commander. Wow, Bucky! All this from—what? Army ROTC, at Dartmouth?

COLONEL: We can all thank God that it's only temporary.

RAMSAY: That's right. That's right, Bucky. You had to do it. The Army had to take things in hand. Things were falling apart. We all realize that. All of us here. *(Pause.)*

COLONEL: Well, what's on your mind, Phil Ramsay?

RAMSAY: Bucky, I want my job back.

COLONEL: Where do you work?

RAMSAY: At the Buffalo City Bank. I was vice-president there, Bucky.

COLONEL: I can't—

RAMSAY: No, no. Now listen. Your man, Bucky, the man you put in there, he fired me. Bucky. Point-blank. Just called me in and canned me. My grandfather started that bank, Bucky. I've been there twenty-three years!

COLONEL: We don't normally tinker with civilian jobs unless there's a good reason.

RAMSAY: Of course you don't! I mean, where are we? Nazi Germany? There's some stupid mistake.

COLONEL: *(Pantomiming pushing a buzzer.)* Let's look at your file.

RAMSAY: My…file?

COLONEL: Yes. Your file. *(Enlisted Man comes in.)* Would you bring in this gentleman's file, please? Mr.—what is it?—

RAMSAY: Philip R. Ramsay. The Third.

ENLISTED MAN: *(As he exits.)* Philip the Third. *(Colonel laughs.)*

RAMSAY: *(Nervously laughing.)* My file eh? I've got a file, huh?

COLONEL: Everyone's got a file.

RAMSAY: Wow. Modern efficiency, eh? Computers and all that stuff, eh? *(The Enlisted Man returns with the file, hands it to the Colonel, exits. The Colonel begins to look it over. Ramsay crosses behind desk, and tries to look over his shoulder. Genially.)* Can't wait to see my own file.

COLONEL: *(Closing it immediately.)* Hey, hey, hey! This is private stuff! *(Ramsay looks at him, nods and sits down. Colonel, reading, flipping pages.)* Hmmmm-mm…Hmmmmmmm. *(Looks at Ramsay, and then reads some more.)* Ummmmm-hm.

RAMSAY: What? What?

COLONEL: I see you signed a petition to stop the bombing back in sixty-six.

RAMSAY: Oh, well. Who didn't sign one of those, Bucky?

COLONEL: I also see you protested against the Security Laws in 1978.

RAMSAY: I didn't march.

COLONEL: Ramsay, you MARCHED! You carried a sign, saying "Stop Fascism in America." There's a picture here. Do you want to see your own picture? *(Pause.)*

RAMSAY: No.

COLONEL: *(Reading.)* And you've got a son in detention camp, and a daughter in Canada. *(Closing the file.)* There you are, Phil.

RAMSAY: Where am I?

COLONEL: You're not a V.P. at the bank, buddy. I can tell you that. Money's important, pal. We're devaluating. It's a tricky business.

RAMSAY: I know money, Bucky. I've worked with money all my life.

COLONEL: Yeah, well, we're talking about new money, Phil.

RAMSAY: I served in Korea, Bucky. Does my file say that? I was in the Navy during Korea. I was in the service, Bucky!

COLONEL: Sorry.

RAMSAY: I need money, Bucky.

COLONEL: Dig into Grandpa's.

RAMSAY: There's none *left*, Bucky.

COLONEL: Oh, come on. Sell some antiques.

RAMSAY: I need a job, Bucky. Really.

COLONEL: I'm not the Yale Placement Bureau, friend.

RAMSAY: No, you're NOT! *(Pause.)* No. You're not. *(Pause.)* So what do I do now?

COLONEL: You go.

RAMSAY: *(Nods mechanically, starts out, and then suddenly turns and explodes.)* We all laughed at you, you know. When you played tennis. You wore black socks and basketball shoes, and we all laughed, and I whipped your ass!

COLONEL: Get the hell out of here!

RAMSAY: I should punch you right in the nose!

COLONEL: *(Calling off.)* A little help here! *(The Enlisted Man comes in.)* Get him out of here! *(The Enlisted Man takes Ramsay's arm.)*

RAMSAY: *(Shaking his arm loose.)* And now I suppose your goons will put me in detention!

COLONEL: Hell, no. You're harmless. All of you guys. Harmless. *(To Enlisted Man.)* Go on. Get him out of here. *(Returns to his work as Ramsay is dragged out.)*
(The piano continues the metallic noise. A girl appears speaking into a modern telephone, isolated in light.)

GIRL: Daddy?...Did I wake you up?...I'm sorry, but you said to call... Anyway, we made it, Daddy. We're here, and we're safe...Dave already has a job, and I've got one lined up, and the commune helps care for the baby...We feel like pioneers...Pioneers. No, Daddy, we don't *need* money. You'll never get it out and we don't need it. We're all right. We're fine...No, I don't think we'll ever come back. Not unless things change. Really change... *(Suddenly.)* Who's that?...Is someone cutting in?...Daddy, we're being cut off!...Daddy? *(Very quickly.)* Good-bye, Daddy...Good-bye, good-bye, good-bye...
(The piano takes up once again the rhythmic, metallic beat. A man enters from the opposite side, and addresses the audience.)

MAN: *(To audience.)* I'll be very brief because we've gotten word that they've revoked the club's license, and so we are technically illegal. *(Glances at notes.)* Bill Satterfield has sent out Christmas cards with a resistance message. Apparently they can be used as evidence, so when your card arrives, burn it. *(Glances again at notes.)* Pug Washburn's boat is available for people who want to get across the river to Canada. As far as I know, they haven't touched it because of Pug's connections with the military. So if you want to emigrate, see Pug. Before they confiscate the boat. *(Another glance.)* Chuck Spaulding has a few extra guns. He's broken up his father's gun collection, and says there are some excellent firearms in it. Chuck needs the money, so check with him if you want a gun. *(A loud knocking off stage. He remains calm.)* There they are. *(Glances at notes.)* Snoozer's funeral services will be at Trinity Church next Thursday at four. *(More knocking; then the sound of someone running.)* Poor Esther has yet to receive an adequate explanation of how he died... *(Speaks as if to Soldiers directly off stage.)* We are have a meeting here. This is a private club, founded in 1893, and we are having a meeting, and you have no right to break in on us...

(Lights change on him. He sits on the edge of a platform, we hear singing off stage: "In the Evening by the Moonlight." The piano is now silent. A mother, played by the same actress who played the mother in the first scene, comes out, as if onto a terrace.)

MOTHER: *(Quietly.)* Oh, look at the lake! *(Calling back in.)* Bring your coffee out here, everybody, and look at the lake! *(The rest of the cast begins to come out, some carrying coffee cups. The boys are still singing: "...You can hear their banjos ringing." The mother speaks to the man sitting on the edge of the porch.)* Have you ever seen it so calm? And there's the harvest moon....*(Turns to the others, now on the terrace.)* Listen, everybody. I'm issuing an ultimatum: no more talk about the moon landing tonight. Not a word!

DAUGHTER: *(Mary.)* It was a lovely dinner, Mother.

MOTHER: It was fair. That creature in the kitchen can't cook corn.

DAUGHTER-IN-LAW: *(Esther.)* The leaves are going. You can see the lights from the city.

MOTHER: Well. Tomorrow's Labor Day. And then we'll be gone. *(Pause.)* Where's your father?

DAUGHTER: *(Sibby.)* Getting the tennis balls.

MOTHER: Oh. Right.

SON-IN-LAW: *(Tom.)* *(Looking out, with his wife.)* This was the time the fish used to jump. Remember?

MOTHER: Don't remind me. It's so sad. Oh, while we're all here, I don't think the children should swim in the lake next year. It's just not healthy. I think we should build a pool. Down by the tennis court. You can all chip in, and your father and I will cough up a thousand apiece. *(Father comes in carrying a large old wicker basket. He is played by the same actor who played the father in the first scene.)* Ah. Here's the master of the hounds.

FATHER: Who's first.

MOTHER: Wait, wait. We have to explain things to Ray here. *(Turns to Ray who has been standing silently.)* Now, Ray, if you're going to marry Sibby, you've got to learn our annual family ritual. Just as Sibby is going to learn about grace before meals, and saluting the flag, and all those things *your* family does.

SIBBY: Oh, Mo-thurrrrr.

MOTHER: Aaaaaaaaanyway. Ray, on the Sunday night before Labor Day, we take all the old tennis balls of the entire summer, and the children take turns throwing them into that canoe. And the first one to get a tennis ball in the canoe...

MARY: ...which *stays* in the canoe. And doesn't bounce out...

MOTHER: ...gets first choice of when he or she can have the house next summer.

RAY: You throw away all those tennis balls?

SIBBY: They're useless, Ray. They've lost their weight.

FATHER: And this is a burning year. We burn the canoe. I've doused her with kerosene, and, after the tennis balls, I'll give the signal to Chipper down there on the dock, and he'll light her up, and push her out, and we'll watch her burn.

MOTHER: And it looks perfectly lovely.

RAY: You burn that boat?

FATHER: It leaks like a sieve. Its ribs have all rotted. I can't repair it anymore.

A SON: *(Snoozer.) (Laughing.)* Well, we sort of let it go, Dad.

FATHER: Not true. There's a certain point in the life of a boat when it's better to burn it.

RAY: *(Scratching his head.)* I'll bet I could fix it.

SIBBY: Oh, Ray, *relax.*

MOTHER: All right. Ladies first. One at a time. Sibby, you're the youngest. *(Sibby pantomimes throwing. Everyone laughs. Ad-libs: "Sibby, you're hopeless." Sibby: "I never could hit it and I never will.")*

Next, Mary. *(Ad-lib from Tom, her husband: "You're throwing for two this year, baby." Mary bends down awkwardly to get the tennis ball, throws clumsily. Mary: "And both of us missed." Laughter.)*

Now, Esther. *(Esther throws with great vigor. Everyone groans. Ad-libs: "You aiming for Canada, Esther?" etc.)*

Now the guest. Your turn, Ray. *(Ad-lib from Snoozer: "Let's see a good old Amurrican throw." Ray gets set carefully and throws the ball. Cheers and congratulations. The mother intervenes, shouting them down.)*

No, no, no. That doesn't count. You stepped over the line, Ray. *(Groans from group.)*

RAY: What line?

MOTHER: That line. That old line. Can't you see that line? Snoozer carved it twenty years ago with his jackknife. Sorry. Who's next? You, Snoozer. The eldest son. *(Ad-lib from Esther: "Don't you want to sober up first?" Snoozer throws neatly, with a backspin, obviously using an old* system. *Cheers. He gets it in.)* Snoozer wins! Snoozer and Esther get their choice!

FATHER: *(Calling out.)* O.K., Chipper! Light her up and push her out!

SNOOZER AND ESTHER: *(Confer briefly.)* We'll take the first two weeks in July! *(Groans, ad-libs: "You luckies." "You get the Fourth of July Tournament.")*

MOTHER: *(To Ray.)* Better luck next year, Ray. Learn where the line is.

ESTHER: *(Pointing off and out.)* Look, look. The canoe. It's burning.

EVERYONE: Ahhhh...*(They all look. A reddish glow begins to light their faces.) (Snoozer and Tom begin to sing very quietly. Others join in, except for Ray, who stands apart, watching the canoe.)*

THE FAMILY: *(Singing.)*"It was sad,
It was sad,
It was sad when the good ship went down, to the bottom of the,
Husbands and wives,
Little children lost their lives,
It was sad when the great ship went down..."
(They repeat the song. One by one they stop. Everyone watches, transfixed, as the red glow slowly fades and leaves them in darkness.)

END OF PLAY

(The piano should play a lively version of "The Good Ship," both during the curtain calls and as the audience is leaving.)

ADDENDUM

Possible replacement for tennis scene...

(...the piano plays a hectic rhythm as the actors arrange a few chairs into bleachers. They put on suggestions of sporty clothes, and one or two squash racquets are in evidence. They look out and down, as if they were in a balcony, watching a squash match down in front of them. A referee sits to one side, calling the game.)

REFEREE: Game! Dudley Dunbar! He leads two games to one.

(Applause from the crowd. Uncle John comes on, leading a small boy, Tim.)

UNCLE JOHN: *(Making room in the stands.)* All right now, Tim, you sit here, and look down into that white box, and watch your daddy play squash. (A *woman, Helen, slides over to sit next to John.)*

HELEN: *(Furtively.)* I was hoping you'd be here.

JOHN: Thought I'd show my god-son the game.

HELEN: That's what I was hoping.

REFEREE: Let!

JOHN: "Let" means "take it over," Timmy. Mr. McKay got in your father's way, so the referee is asking them to replay the point.

HELEN: *(Low to John.)* I know a point or two I'd like to play over.

JOHN: Ssshh. *(They watch.)*

HELEN: I didn't see you at the Watson's the other night.

JOHN: *(Watching the game.)* I wasn't there.

HELEN: You said you'd be there.

JOHN: I couldn't make it.

REFEREE: Eight-five.

JOHN: Do you see, Timmy? The purpose of the game is to hit that little black ball just as hard as you possibly can, and then to step smartly out of the way.

HELEN: Are you mad at me, or what? Have I done something wrong?

JOHN: Not at all.

HELEN: You seem mad at me.

JOHN: Not mad. Why should I be mad?

HELEN: You seem so…distant. *(Crowd gasps.)*

REFEREE: Let again?

JOHN: Now there! You see, Tim? Your father called another let, rather than hit his opponent and hurt him. *(To Helen.)* I think you should go.

HELEN: But you and I…I mean, I thought you and I…

REFEREE: *(Standing up.)* Point, game, and match! *(Crowd applauds, stands, begins to disperse.)*

JOHN: And there it is, Tim. See? The man lost, but he's still shaking hands with your father. Your father may have beaten him, your father may even have hurt him, but now they're putting their arms around each other and going off to take a shower.

HELEN: So it's just good-bye, then?

JOHN: Not good-bye, really…

HELEN: I mean we won't be seeing each other.

JOHN: We'll be seeing each other.

HELEN: Where? Where will we be seeing each other?

JOHN: Around…

HELEN: Around? *Around?* Oh God John, I could *kill* you! You know that? I could really *kill* you! *(She leaves, rudely pushing someone out of the way.) (Pause.)*

JOHN: *(Quietly, to Tim.)* Women don't play squash, Tim. They don't like it, they don't understand it. Men learn it when they're young. Tell your father you want lessons. Snoozer's already taking them. He's learning you can have a tough, aggressive match, and still be friends at the end. That's what you learn in squash. *(They go off together.)*

Possible addition after the Dave Goldfarb scene…

(The pianist plays "American the Beautiful." A young boy, James, about eight, comes out and begins to recite, as if to a class.)

JAMES: Maine, Augusta, on the Kennebec…New Hampshire, Concord, on the Merrimac…Vermont, Montpelier, on the Winooski…Massachusetts, Boston, on Boston Bay…Rhode Island—
(The teacher, Miss Emerson, comes on.)

MISS EMERSON: That's very good, James. You can do the rest for your parents this evening. I imagine they'll be delighted to see Geography back in the curriculum.

JAMES: Yes, Miss Emerson. *(He stand by.)*

MISS EMERSON: And now for spelling. Betsy Babcock, let's hear you spell the word "fascism."
(Betsy comes on, stands stiffly.)

BETSY: Fascism. F-A-S *(Pause; then proudly.)* C-I-S-M. Fascism.

MISS EMERSON: Good, Betsy. And did you look it up in your dictionary?

BETSY: *(Again, by rote.)* "Fascism was a system of government popular earlier in this century that advocated the merging of state and business leadership, with an ideology of belligerent nationalism."

MISS EMERSON: Excellent, Betsy. And was fascism good or bad, Betsy?

BETSY: Fascism was bad. Fascism caused World War Two.

MISS EMERSON: Well done! All right now, class we will all assemble in the gymnasium for the Memorial Day March against communism in

Costa Rica. And don't forget to pick up your uniforms, which have been specially donated by General Electric and I.B.M.
(*The pianist strikes up the Marine Hymn as they march off.*)

Possible addition after the choirboy scene...

(*As the choirboys go off, a girl, Alice, comes on. She is about sixteen. The last choirboy peels off from his group and stays to watch her. His name is George.*)

ALICE: (*Reading from a paper.*) Resolved: that every great democracy has maintained itself through the responsible public service of an elite class.

GEORGE: That's the topic?

ALICE: That's it. We've got the affirmative. Exeter's taking the negative...Want to do it?

GEORGE: That's a tough topic.

ALICE: It's not so bad. We'll talk about the Roman Republic, and Nineteenth century Great Britain, and then us.

GEORGE: Us?

ALICE: We're a great democracy.

GEORGE: I know, Alice. But we don't have an elite class. I mean, we do, but it's constantly changing. I mean, your grandfather was a shoe salesman and you've got early admission to Harvard next year, and mine was Secretary of the Navy, and they won't let me even apply.

ALICE: Maybe they would if you were on the Debating Team.

GEORGE: I don't have time, I keep telling you.

ALICE: You've got all Christmas vacation.

GEORGE: That's taken. I'm playing in the Philadelphia Invitational Squash Tournament, and then I have to visit my grandmother in Palm Beach.

ALICE: Well, wave to Washington as you fly over. (She goes off.)

GEORGE: (*Following her.*) What's that supposed to mean, huh, Alice? Was that supposed to mean anything? (*He exits.*)

Possibly to follow immediately after debating scene, in place of Old Lady monologue.

(A woman—Jane—comes on briskly, carrying her purse. She is stopped by a man carrying an elaborate clipboard.)

MAN: May I help you, ma'am?

JANE: Yes. I'm here to pick up the lady who cleans for us...Belinda Jackson.

MAN: *(Working his clipboard.)* Jackson...

JANE: Belinda...Would you hurry, please? I'm double parked.

MAN: Jackson, Belinda...Here we are...No go. She's restricted.

JANE: Restricted? On what grounds?

MAN: Says here four three four.

JANE: Four three four? That's ridiculous! Belinda never threw a firebomb in her life!

MAN: Then some member of her family did.

JANE: Well then I'll just have to post bond. I know my rights. I'm invoking a seven six seven. *(She opens her purse, takes out her credit card.)*

MAN: *(Putting her credit card into his clipboard mechanism.)* That'll cost you, lady. They've added a handling charge.

JANE: I know all that. I wasn't born yesterday.

MAN: *(Handing back the credit card.)* O.K. Go in and get her.

JANE: *(Coldly.)* Thank you. *(She starts off.)*

MAN: Hold it!

(Jane stops.)

JANE: Now what?

MAN: Are you armed?

JANE: Of course I'm armed.

MAN: Then display it!

JANE: Oh God. *(She takes a pistol out of her purse.)* I find it slightly embarrassing having to wave this thing around.

MAN: You know the rules, lady.

JANE: Yes well sometimes I think we're all being a little too fussy around here.

(They go off either way, Jane with her pistol very much at the ready.)

A.R. GURNEY

A. R. Gurney was born in Buffalo, NY in 1930 and attended St. Paul's School in Concord, NH. He graduated Magna Cum Laude and Phi Beta Kappa from Williams College, and, after serving as an Officer in the United States Navy, he graduated from the Yale School of Drama in 1958. He was a Professor of Literature at M. I. T. for over twenty years. Mr. Gurney also has received honorary degrees from both Williams College and the State University of New York at Buffalo.

Mr. Gurney's plays include: *The Golden Fleece, Scenes from American Life, Children, The Dining Room, Richard Cory, The Middle Ages, The Golden Age, What I Did Last Summer, The Wayside Motor Inn, Sweet Sue, The Perfect Party, Another Antigone, The Cocktail Hour, Love Letters, The Old Boy, The Fourth Wall, Later Life, A Cheever Evening, Sylvia,* and *Overtime.* He has also written several novels: *The Gospel According to Joe, Entertaining Strangers,* and *The Snow Ball,* later adapted to a play of the same name.

Mr. Gurney has been the recipient of numerous awards, including: a Drama Desk Award; a National Endowment for the Arts Playwrighting Award; the Rockefeller Playwrighting Award; the Lucille Lortel Playwrighting Award; a New England Theatre Conference Award; and an Award of Merit from the American Academy and Institute of Arts and Letters.

Mr. Gurney currently resides in Roxbury, CT with his wife, Mary; they have four children.

GAYLORD S